DEATH AND AFTERLIFE

DEATH AND AFTERLIFE

A Theological Introduction

TERENCE NICHOLS

BrazosPress

a division of Baker Publishing Group
Grand Rapids, Michigan

Published by Brazos Press
a division of Baker Publishing Group
P.O. Box 6287, Grand Rapids, MI 49516–6287
www.brazospress.com

Printed in the United States of America

Library of Congress Cataloging-in-Publication Data
Nichols, Terence L., 1941–
    Death and afterlife : a theological introduction / Terence Nichols.
        p.   cm.
    Includes bibliographical references and index.
    ISBN 978-1-58743-183-8 (pbk.)
    1. Death—Religious aspects—Christianity. 2. Future life—Christianity. I. Title.
BT825.N49 2010
236'.2—dc22
                                                                2009042263

10   11   12   13   14   15   16   7   6   5   4   3   2   1

For my family. May they
abide in God's love in this
life and the next.

CONTENTS

INTRODUCTION

The last enemy to be destroyed is death.

1 Corinthians 15:26

A Good Death?

Diane died about twenty years ago. A member of our charismatic prayer group at church, she was in her mid-forties and left behind a husband and two teenage boys. We prayed for months that her leukemia would be cured, but in the end our prayers were not answered in the way we had hoped. Diane died young, but she died gracefully. She was convinced that she was going to a better life with God and that her family would be taken care of. She planned her own funeral, chose the readings, and asked that it be a joyful occasion. Before dying, she said good-bye to all those she loved and asked them not to be bitter about her death. Her funeral was more like a celebration than a lament. Even her family felt this. After her death, her family and friends also felt an inexplicable sense of peace and joy about her passing. About six months later her husband took a job in another city and eventually remarried, as Diane had hoped he would.

Did Diane die a good death? Many would say no. What could be worse than dying in the prime of one's life and leaving behind a young family? This kind of event often leaves bitterness and lasting scars. But none of this happened in Diane's case. Contrary to usual expectations, her passing was joyful. She was sure that her family would be taken care of and that she was going home to God. If one is going to die in the prime of life and leave behind a beloved family, one could hardly manage it more gracefully than did Diane. What made her death different was her and her family's certainty that she would continue to live on with God. All the prayers helped too. The months before her death were a time of letting go, acceptance, and preparation for death. When Diane died, she was ready to move on, confident that her journey into God would continue. This changed the whole quality of her death for her and for those around her.

Three things made Diane's death joyful: she was confident about an afterlife with God, she was prepared emotionally and spiritually for death, and she died close to her loved ones and to God in an atmosphere of prayer.

Questions about Afterlife

Not many people die like Diane. Many people die unsure about God or any future life with God, unprepared to meet death, depressed, uncertain, afraid, and often alone. For example, a recent article in *America* magazine discusses the state of Christian belief in Sweden. About 9 percent of the population there is Christian; 3 percent actually go to church. The rest are described as agnostic. "They're convinced you cannot speak about God. Is there a God? Is there not a God? I don't know, they will say."[1] It is true that Christian belief is more widespread in the United States than in Sweden, but the same secularizing trends are at work here as well. For years I have been teaching a course titled "Death and Afterlife" at the University of St. Thomas. It is a popular course among students. Yet to my surprise, I often find in my students a deep uncertainty about afterlife and a fear of death. These are connected. People fear death because they have no positive vision of afterlife. Christian martyrs, who often died terribly painful deaths, did not fear death because they were convinced that they would be sustained by Christ and would be with him in heaven. But a cliché among students is: "No one has died and come back to tell us about it." The typical opinion is that the best death is quick and painless, contrary to centuries of Christian teaching, which stresses the need to prepare for death. Even some practicing Christians are uncertain and troubled about death. Increasingly, pastors do not talk about afterlife. Often they simply offer brief slogans, such as "He is with God now." I once asked a pastor in my athletic club what he told his flock about the soul after death. His response was, "Our theologians tell us not to talk about it." This seems to be the case in mainline Protestant churches and is becoming true in some Catholic churches. It's even more true in popular culture. I ask people if anyone ever brings up the topic of death and afterlife at a party. Of course not, they laugh; people don't talk about it.

A consequence of the uncertainty about afterlife is that people don't think about death and therefore don't prepare for it. It's easier to deny it—why dwell on what you can't change? So people typically don't think about death until it's too late. They don't prepare to meet death; rather, it runs into them like a truck.

So the question is, Why is there such uncertainty about life after death? After all, Christianity has taught for centuries that persons' souls survive death and that in the end times their souls will be united with their resurrected bodies. In fact, throughout almost all of Christian history, people didn't worry about whether they would survive death. Instead, they worried about their state *after* death, their ultimate salvation: would they make it into heaven or would they fall into hell? In medieval cathedrals like Chartres, the scene of the last judgment (Matt. 25:31–46) was sculpted over the entrance doors so that people would see in frightening detail the damned falling into the clutches of demons and the bodies of the saints rising from their tombs to be with Jesus and the angels in heaven. Augustine, Luther, and Calvin were greatly concerned about salvation and did not think that most people would be saved.

Furthermore, almost all world religions teach that one's personal spirit or soul survives bodily death. One finds this belief in tribal and animistic religions around the world, such as those of American Indians and African peoples; in ancient Egyptian religion; in Hinduism; in most forms of Buddhism (e.g., Mahayana and Tibetan Buddhism); in Chinese religions; in traditional Judaism; in all of Islam; and in traditional Christianity. So why are contemporary Americans and Europeans so unsure about afterlife?

Challenges to Afterlife

There are several reasons for the uncertainty about an afterlife. Foremost is the challenge of philosophical naturalism or materialism. This is the (philosophical) belief that nature, or matter, is all that really exists. As the late Cornell astronomer Carl Sagan expressed it in his television series *Cosmos*, "The universe is all that is, all there ever was, and all that will ever be."[2] Sagan promoted this as the scientific worldview, and in fact naturalism is often associated with science but is not necessarily entailed by it. One can do good science while being a devout believer in God. Most of the great founders of modern science—Galileo, Newton, Robert Boyle, Christian Huygens, Michael Faraday, James Clerk Maxwell, Max Planck—believed in God.[3] Conversely, many people who are naturalists or materialists are not scientists and know little of science. Thus naturalism is a *philosophical* belief, which may or may not be associated with science. Nonetheless, naturalism as a worldview has subtly pervaded the media, books, universities, and school classrooms so that it is now the atmosphere in which we live. As John Hick says, "Naturalism has created the 'consensus reality' of our culture. It has become so ingrained that we no longer see it, but see everything else through it."[4] Naturalism has gradually displaced the older Christian worldview, with its confidence in God and in a sacramental universe that exists in and expresses God. Instead, according to Sagan, we now live in a naturalistic, self-sufficient universe that is all that is and in which God is otiose—a vestigial memory.[5]

Second, bodily resurrection, which is the central hope of Christianity (as well as of traditional Judaism and Islam) is hard to believe in today's world. If the body is resurrected, where does it go? Into outer space? We all know that heaven is not "up there" and that hell is not "down there," that is, in the center of the earth. Modern cosmology has taught us that the heavens are not the abode of God, gods, or angels, as people used to believe. It was easier to make a case for resurrection when everyone believed that heaven was up amid the stars and that hell was in the fiery interior of the earth. But now we know that the stars are fiery bodies that exist in empty space and cannot support life. There is no physical space for heaven (or hell) in today's universe. This makes it hard to believe in the resurrection of the body and in traditional teachings about heaven and hell.

Nonetheless, many religious persons—Christians, Muslims, Jews, Hindus, and others—continue to believe that the souls of their loved ones go to be with God. But it is also becoming more difficult to believe in a soul. There is no support in science for the existence of a soul, or even for a mind, that survives bodily death. Neuroscience demonstrates that our thoughts and emotions are tightly correlated with states of the brain. CAT scans, for example, reveal that particular regions of the brain are active when people think, visualize, meditate, and so on. Strokes and head injuries that damage particular areas of the brain result in the loss of highly specific mental faculties, such as the ability to recognize familiar faces. Brain damage, including Alzheimer's disease, can result in pronounced changes to one's personality. So it is much more difficult to make the case that our personal consciousness is carried by an immaterial soul. Rather, our personality and reason seem to be a result of and depend on the development of our brains. The corollary of this is that when the brain dies, the person dies; there is no survival of the mind or soul after death. This is the message from neuroscience.

Finally, there are philosophical and theological challenges to traditional teachings on heaven and hell. For many people, heaven seems static and boring. What would we do in heaven? And hell as a place or state of eternal punishment seems hard to believe. What kind of a God would consign people to a place or condition of eternal torment? Interestingly, though many world religions, such as Hinduism and Mahayana Buddhism, do teach the existence of hell and portray it dramatically in their art, they also teach that persons only reside in hell for a period of time until their karma or sin has been repaid; then they move on. Today the major religions that teach an eternal hell are Orthodox Judaism (but not Reformed or Conservative Judaism), parts of Islam, and traditional Christianity. But even many Christians have begun to doubt the eternality of hell. For example, Hans Urs von Balthasar, an extremely conservative Catholic theologian, wrote a book titled *Dare We Hope That All Men Be Saved?*"[6]

For all these reasons, and many others, people question the traditional pictures of afterlife and therefore many do not prepare spiritually for death.

Three Themes

In this book I will attempt to meet these questions and challenges. The book presents three main themes. First, I will argue that while scientific and philosophical challenges force us to rethink our conceptions of the soul, resurrection, and heaven and hell, we can still make a credible case for life after death with God, for a soul that survives bodily death, for bodily resurrection, and for heaven and hell. I will lay out this case in chapters 1 through 9. One of my principal concerns will be to respond to scientific and naturalistic challenges to the soul, the resurrection, and to heaven and hell.

My second main theme concerns the need to prepare for death (chap. 10). If we want to die well, to die into God, so to speak, we need to start working on our relationship with God (and with others) while we are young and healthy, rather than waiting until death is knocking at the door. Developing a relationship with God takes time and sacrifice, conversion and repentance, discipline and prayer—just as it takes time, discipline, practice, and self-sacrifice to reach proficiency in a sport, in music, or in a profession. Of course, God is always present, closer to us than our own jugular vein, as the Qur'an says. But the problem is that usually we are not tuned into God. To use an analogy: we are surrounded by radio and television waves, but if we do not tune in a receiver we can't hear the message. So also with God. God is always present, but without a tuned receiver we can't communicate with God. Tuning in the receiver means tuning ourselves into God. And this means eliminating self-centeredness and moving toward God-centeredness. Jesus calls this move repentance or conversion, a total change of mind and heart. Usually this takes years of prayer and discipline, not just weeks or months. I tell my students that dying is like graduation: if we have prepared well, it is the gateway into a brighter future. But if we have not prepared or have prepared poorly, it can be a terrible failure. So the second theme concerns the need to develop a relationship with God that will carry us through death. The earliest name for Christianity, "the Way" (Acts 22:4), captures this idea that the Christian life is a preparation and a journey into God that begins in this life but continues after death. For any journey, it is important to know where one is going to spend the first night, the second night, and so on. But it is also important to know the ultimate destination of the journey. Where are we going in the end? The end of the journey affects which way we turn even in the first stages of the journey. As with a journey, so with life; it is important to know the ultimate end and destination. The surprising thing is that many people do *not* know what is the ultimate destination of their lives. Like some of my students, they are uncertain about life after death, and so do not know how to prepare for death.

The third theme of this book is hope. For Christians (as well as Jews, Muslims, and others), afterlife with God is the ultimate hope. Even the most successful earthly life cannot escape disappointments, mistakes, failures, losses, and estrangements. Thus this earthly life cannot serve as the basis for our ultimate hope. As we read in the book of Ecclesiastes: "I saw all the deeds that are done under the sun; and see, all is vanity and a chasing after wind" (Eccles. 1:14). Paul writes: "If for this life only we have hoped in Christ, we are of all people the most to be pitied" (1 Cor. 15:19). Reconciliation with God and the Blessed in heaven has sustained the hopes of Christians from the beginning. It is the great hope of heaven that carried Diane joyfully through death and can carry us as well. These three themes form the core of this book. It is intended as a kind of theological guidebook for dying well, which is to say, dying in the presence of God.

Outline of the Book

This book is comprised of ten chapters and this introduction. Chapter 1, "Underworld, Soul, and Resurrection in Ancient Judiasm," deals with the view of death and afterlife in the Old Testament and in the intertestamental writings. In early-Hebrew belief, the shades of the dead sink into the underworld. The belief in bodily resurrection begins to appear in later writings, especially in Daniel. And Jewish writings influenced by Greek thought (e.g., the book of Wisdom) state that after death the souls of the just are in the hands of God.

We shall also consider Jewish apocalyptic writings concerning the judgment and the end of the world.

Chapter 2, "Death and Afterlife in the New Testament," looks at the range of views in the New Testament. What did Jesus teach about the soul, bodily resurrection, and the end times? What was Paul's idea of the resurrected body? What was the view of the end times and of judgment in the book of Revelation? This chapter considers all these questions and more.

Chapter 3, "Death and Afterlife in the Christian Tradition," briefly surveys the ideas on death and afterlife in the Christian tradition from the early church to modern times. There is a much wider range of opinion among Christian thinkers across the ages on these topics than most people realize.

Chapter 4, "Scientific Challenges to Afterlife," takes up challenges to the existence of a soul that survives brain death and challenges to bodily resurrection.

Chapter 5, "Near Death Experiences," responds to some of the challenges in chapter 4 by considering some striking examples of recent near death experiences and what we can learn from them about afterlife.

Chapter 6, "On the Soul," discusses the nature of the soul and whether it can survive bodily death (I argue it can). I hold that in this life persons are psychophysical unities (hence the brain influences the mind and vice versa) but that because of God's personal relationship with each person, one's soul—the subject of one's consciousness, freedom, and intentions—will survive death.

Chapter 7, "Resurrection," deals with the equally difficult question of bodily resurrection. How is such a thing possible? According to Christians, Jesus himself has been resurrected. Where is his body now? Is it physical like our bodies? Building on the biblical witness, but also considering scientific objections, I shall make a case that the resurrected body must exist in a spiritualized yet physical condition—a higher state of matter—or what N. T. Wright calls a "transphysical" state.

Chapter 8, "Justification and Judgment," asks, How can we be righteous before God and therefore worthy of salvation in the judgment? In other words, How do we get to heaven? Through faith? Through works? Both? This has been a contested question since the Reformation. This chapter will lay out the basic arguments and offer some conclusions.

Chapter 9, "Heaven, Purgatory, and Hell," considers how we can understand heaven, purgatory, and hell. Theologically, heaven is the state of being in perfect union of love with God: "In your presence there is fullness of joy" (Ps. 16:11). But is heaven a place? Is it a parallel universe? Is there time in heaven? Or is it a state of timeless eternity? My view is that heaven, if it is the fullness of joy, will be not simply the sanctification of desire but also a dynamic, endless growth into the infinite love and understanding of God. Heaven will also include a resurrected creation (Rom. 8:18–23) and hence probably animals, for there is no point to a resurrected body if there is no environment for the body. Hell, by contrast, is simply the state of being cut off from God and others. God is still present even to those in hell, but those in hell have cut themselves off (or tuned themselves out) from God. Traditional Christianity has taught that hell is eternal, but this has been widely challenged in recent times.

Chapter 10, "Dying Well," deals with death as the fulfillment of our journey into God and how we can prepare for death.

This is a short book and cannot present a comprehensive scholarly treatment of all the relevant material. Such a treatment of even a single topic, for example, Jesus's resurrection, would be many times the length of this book, as N. T. Wright's recent 817-page book on Jesus's resurrection demonstrates.[7] I shall therefore summarize much of the scholarly writing on various topics and refer the reader to more-extensive treatments in the notes. As much as possible, I will base my arguments directly on primary sources, especially the Bible, rather than appealing to a putative consensus of scholars, whose consensus may be wrong and, in any case, changes every decade or so.

I am writing from a Christian perspective and will appeal primarily to a Christian audience. But almost all the arguments in this book could apply equally well to Judaism, Islam, and other forms of theism. Although I believe that ultimately all who are saved are saved through the work of the incarnate Logos, Jesus the Christ, I emphatically do *not* believe that only professed Christians can be saved. As Peter says in his speech to Cornelius, "I truly understand that God shows no partiality, but in every nation anyone who fears him and does what is right is acceptable to him" (Acts 10:34–35).

Finally, I hope it is clear that in making a case for afterlife I am *not* saying that we should discount this present life. Our world, with all its beauty and blessings, is given to us as the creation of God, and we are obligated before God to care for it as stewards. To say that we can ignore our responsibilities for God's good creation because the afterlife is coming soon (which we cannot know, see Mark 13:32) is to insult God. How can we expect reward in the afterlife if we abuse God's gifts in this life? The same goes for our obligation to care for the poor and unfortunate: if we ignore them and their urgent calls for justice, how can we expect to share in the blessings of the world to come (Matt. 25:31–46)?

Many people have helped make this book possible. I want to thank my colleagues at the University of St. Thomas who reviewed individual chapters or extended parts of the manuscript, in particular Corrine Carvalho, Paul

Niskanen, Catherine Cory, Peter Feldmeier, Philippe Gagnon, Michael Hollerich, and Philip Rolnick. My wife, Mabel, and my sister, Gaydon Peck, read the entire manuscript and made valuable suggestions. My daughter, Michele Cella, helped me with the endnotes. Finally, I wish to thank Rodney Clapp and Jeffery Wittung, editors of Brazos Press, for their careful and critical reading of the manuscript and their many suggestions for improvement.

1

UNDERWORLD, SOUL, AND RESURRECTION IN ANCIENT JUDAISM

I called to the Lord out of my distress, and he answered me;
out of the belly of Sheol I cried, and you heard my voice.

Jonah 2:2

The writings of ancient Judaism—the Hebrew Bible and the so-called intertestamental writings—span a period of about a thousand years.[1] Not surprisingly, there is a development in the understanding of death and afterlife during the course of these writings. In the earliest Hebrew texts, there is no notion of heaven or hell; rather, the souls of the dead are believed to sink into an underworld (usually called Sheol) where souls dwell as weak, dim shades with no consolation from God. The only real hope after death was to be remembered by one's descendants. Thus Abraham was blessed by God in the promise of many descendants (Gen. 22:17–18).

Over time, however, the Jewish prophets developed the idea that God would reward or punish each person for his or her own sins, not for the sins of his or her ancestors ("A child shall not suffer for the iniquity of a parent," Ezek. 18:20). In later Jewish Scriptures, the belief developed that God would not abandon the righteous to the netherworld. Rather, the righteous individuals would be rewarded and the wicked punished by God in a resurrected life after death, as seen in the book of Daniel (ca. 150 BCE). In the book of Wisdom, about a century later, we find a vision of the souls of the righteous living on with God (Wis. 3:1–9). Both these views of afterlife continued and influenced the thought of Jews and Christians in the time of Jesus.

There was, therefore, a wide range of beliefs about death and life after death in ancient Israel. We will consider specific texts that express these views of afterlife and then summarize our findings in a conclusion.

The Underworld

In earliest writings, the dead were thought to sink into the underworld, which was associated with the grave or a place of darkness.[2] There the shades (*rephaim*) of the dead survive but with no strength, vitality, hope, or worship of God.

> For my soul is full of troubles, and my life draws near to Sheol. I am counted among those who go down to the Pit; I am like those who have no help, like those forsaken among the dead, like the slain that lie in the grave, like those whom you remember no more, for they are cut off from your hand. . . . Do you work wonders for the dead? Do the shades rise up to praise you? (Ps. 88:3–5, 10)

Another text describing the underworld is given in Isaiah, in which the prophet issues a taunt against the king of Babylon:

> Sheol beneath is stirred up
> to meet you when you come [i.e., die];
> it rouses the shades [*rephaim*] to greet you,
> all who were leaders of the earth;
> it raises from their thrones
> all who were kings of the nations.
> All of them will speak
> and say to you:
> "You too have become as weak as we!
> You have become like us!" (Isa. 14:9–10)

The most natural reading of this passage is that the shades retain personal identity in the underworld. They are portrayed in physical terms (as speaking, for example), and this might cause some interpretative problems with the passage, but they certainly are not resurrected. I agree with Robert Gundry that the shades are portrayed in physical terms by way of analogy—how else could the writer portray them?[3]

There are many other passages in the Old Testament that indicate personal identity continues after the death of the body: "But God will ransom my soul from the power of Sheol" (Ps. 49:15); "You will save his life from Sheol" (Prov. 23:14 RSV). Isaiah 38 gives a moving piece attributed to King Hezekiah, composed after he recovered from an apparently lethal illness. Hezekiah writes:

> In the noontide of my days
>   I must depart;
> I am consigned to the gates of Sheol
>   for the rest of my years. . . .
> But thou hast held back my life[4]
>   from the pit of destruction, . . .
> For Sheol cannot thank thee,
>   death cannot praise thee;
> those who go down to the pit cannot hope
>   for thy faithfulness. (Isa. 38:10–18 RSV)

The most striking account of contact with a dead spirit from the underworld[5] is given in the story of Saul visiting a medium at Endor (1 Sam. 28). Though Saul had previously expelled mediums and wizards from the country, he was fearful of an impending battle with the Philistines and sought the advice of the dead prophet Samuel. Saul disguised himself and went to consult a medium, asking her to summon the spirit of Samuel. She did so and said: "'I see a divine being [elohim] coming up out of the ground.' He [Saul] said to her, 'What is his appearance?' She said, 'An old man is coming up; he is wrapped in a robe.' So Saul knew it was Samuel, and he bowed with his face to the ground, and did obeisance. Then Samuel said to Saul, 'Why have you disturbed me by bringing me up?'" (1 Sam. 28:13–15). Saul told him that the Philistines were warring against him and that God did not answer him by dreams or prophets, so he summoned Samuel to tell him what he should do. Samuel's reply was devastating. Tomorrow, he said, "the LORD will give Israel along with you into the hands of the Philistines; and . . . you and your sons shall be with me" (v. 19). And indeed Saul and his sons were killed on Mount Gilboa the next day.[6]

The underworld, then, is like the grave where the dead survive as shades (rephaim) of their former selves.[7] True, Psalm 139:8 declares that God is even in the underworld (Sheol): "If I ascend to heaven, you are there; if I make my bed in Sheol, you are there." But even if God is present in the underworld, there is no indication that this provides any comfort for the dead, who dwell in darkness, not in the light of God. All who die go to the underworld and do not return; there is no indication of reward for virtue or punishment for misdeeds there. Even the great prophet Samuel dwells in the underworld with the rest of the dead. The underworld, then, is not the fulfillment of human hope.

The identity of the dead apparently survives (as can be seen in the episode in 1 Samuel), but their spirits are not comforted by the presence of God nor are the righteous rewarded and the wicked punished. All go to the same place: "the same fate comes to all, to the righteous and the wicked, to the good and the evil" (Eccles. 9:2).

The ancient Hebrew concept of the underworld is very similar to the conception of the dead found in the writings of Homer (ca. 850 BCE). Homer portrays the lot of the dead as dwelling in the underworld—Hades—as insubstantial "shades" who have lost their strength and life force. In a striking chapter of Homer's *Odyssey*, Odysseus sails to the land of Persephone, goddess of the dead (see chap. 11). There he is directed to dig a small pit, sacrifice a black ewe and ram, and let their blood fall into the pit so the shades of the dead can lap it up and thereby have strength to speak. Odysseus performs the rites and addresses the "blurred and breathless dead." Then the souls of the dead gather: "From every side they came and sought the pit / with rustling cries, and I grew sick with fear." The lot of the dead is not enviable. The shade of the seer Teiresias tells Odysseus: "Any dead man whom you allow to enter where the blood is / will speak to you, and speak the truth; but those / deprived will grow remote again and fade." Odysseus sees his own mother among the dead, speaks with her, and tries to embrace her: "I bit my lip, / rising perplexed, with longing to embrace her, / and tried three times, putting my arms around her, / but she went sifting through my hands, impalpable / as shadows are, and wavering like a dream." The shade of the great soldier Achilles also appears to Odysseus, saying: "How did you find your way down to the dark / where these dimwitted dead are camped forever, / the after images of used-up men." Odysseus replies to Achilles: "We ranked you with immortals in your lifetime, / . . . and here your power is royal / among the dead men's shades. Think, then, Akhilleus: / you need not be so pained by death." But Achilles replies: "Let me hear no smooth talk / of death from you, Odysseus, light of councils. / Better, I say, to break sod as a farm hand / for some poor country man, on iron rations / than lord it over all the exhausted dead."[8]

In both early Hebrew and early Greek thought, the shades of the dead, and something of their personalities, survive in the underworld. Odysseus speaks with his mother and she with him; he tries to embrace her, but her shade has no substance. He recognizes Achilles and talks with him. But the shades in the underworld have no life force or strength; they must imbibe blood to have the strength to speak. This seems strikingly similar to the condition of the dead in the Hebrew Scriptures.

Note that the shades of the dead are not immaterial souls. They retain their physiognomies and physical appearances and so are recognizable. Samuel, for example, is described by the medium and Saul recognizes him from the description. What survives is not an immaterial soul but a shade or ghost that lacks the vitality and solidity of the fleshly person but retains personal identity.[9]

For this reason, the hope of afterlife expressed in the early Hebrew Scriptures was not one of individual survival in the underworld but of the continuance of the people Israel, the land, and one's descendants.[10] Abraham, for example, was blessed by God in his descendants, not by the promise of a happy afterlife: "I will indeed bless you, and make your offspring as numerous as the stars of heaven and the sand that is on the seashore. And your offspring shall possess the gate of their enemies, and by your offspring shall all the nations of the earth gain blessing for themselves, because you have obeyed my voice" (Gen. 22:17–18). Anglican biblical scholar N. T. Wright summarizes:

> For the vast majority in ancient Israel, the great and solid hope, built upon the character of the creator and covenant God, was for YHWH's blessings of justice, prosperity, and peace upon the nation and the land, and eventually upon the whole earth. Patriarchs, prophets, kings, and ordinary Israelites would indeed lie down to sleep with their ancestors. YHWH's purposes, however, would go forward, and would be fulfilled in their time.[11]

Belief in Bodily Resurrection

Over time in Israel, the hope developed that God will not let his righteous ones languish forever in the underworld but will raise them from the dead. One of the earliest of these visions is found in the prophet Isaiah:

> Your dead shall live, their corpses shall rise.
>   O dwellers in the dust, awake and sing for joy!
> For your dew is a radiant dew,
>   and the earth will give birth to those long dead. (Isa. 26:19)

Notice that the vision of afterlife here is not that of individual, disembodied souls dwelling with God in heaven; it is a vision of a restored and embodied afterlife. Israelite thought developed in a different direction than Greek thought. Greek thought after ca. 500 BCE came to hope in the survival of the individual soul, not the body.[12] This is fully expressed in the writings of Plato. In his great dialogue *Phaedo*, which recounts the death of Socrates, Socrates is confident that his soul will go to a better state, comparing the body to a prison. Hebrew thought, however, conceived of afterlife primarily, but not exclusively, in terms of a reanimated and resurrected body living with others in a world of justice and peace that was governed by YHWH.

Another famous text that conveys this idea of an embodied afterlife (or renewed life) in company with the people Israel is found in the book of Ezekiel:

> The hand of the LORD came upon me . . . and set me down in the middle of a valley; it was full of bones. . . . He said to me, "Mortal, can these bones live?" I answered, "O Lord GOD, you know." Then he said to me, "Prophesy to these bones, and say to them: O dry bones, hear the word of the LORD. Thus says the Lord GOD to these bones: I will cause breath to enter you, and you shall live. I will lay sinews on you, and will cause flesh to come upon you, and cover you with skin, and put breath in you, and you shall live; and you shall know that I am the LORD."
>
> So I prophesied as I had been commanded; and as I prophesied, suddenly there was a noise, a rattling, and the bones came together, bone to bone. I looked, and there were sinews on them, and flesh had come upon them, and skin had covered them; but there was no breath in them. . . . I prophesied as he commanded me, and the breath came into them, and they lived, and stood on their feet, a vast multitude.
>
> Then he said to me, "Mortal, these bones are the whole house of Israel. They say, 'Our bones are dried up, and our hope is lost; we are cut off completely.' Thus says the Lord GOD: I am going to open your graves, and bring you up from your graves, O my people; and I will bring you back to the land of Israel." (Ezek. 37:1–12)

This was written when the people of Israel were in Exile (in Babylon, ca. 550 BCE). It anticipates teachings concerning the resurrection of the body but is actually an allegory of the restoration of the people of Israel to their own land. It prophesies the end of their exile, but it closely connects the language of bodily resurrection with the restoration of the Israelites. This theme will be echoed in the New Testament in Jesus's teaching on the kingdom of God.

At the end of the Old Testament period, we find the clearest statement of the future bodily resurrection of the dead in the book of Daniel.

> At that time, [the angel] Michael, the great prince, the protector of your people, shall arise. There shall be a time of anguish, such as has never occurred since nations first came into existence. But at that time your people shall be delivered, everyone who is found written in the book. Many of those who sleep in the dust of the earth shall awake, some to everlasting life, and some to shame and everlasting contempt. Those who are wise shall shine like the brightness of the

sky, and those who lead many to righteousness, like the stars forever and ever. (Dan. 12:1–3)

This was written when Israel was under Greek control and Greek practices were being forced on the Jews. Antiochus IV Epiphanes forbade the Jewish practice of circumcision; replaced Jewish sacrifices with Greek sacrifices, which included sacrificing pigs; and even set up an altar to Zeus in the temple area. This led to the Maccabean revolt (167–164 BCE). The book of Daniel was written to encourage those Jews who were resisting Antiochus and suffering martyrdom for their faith. They would not simply sink into Sheol. Daniel envisages a great time of trial and a cosmic battle at the end of history. At that time the angel Michael will arise and fight for his people, the Jews. Then many of those who "sleep in the dust," that is, the dead, will be raised from the dead. There will be a cosmic judgment; the righteous will be vindicated and the wicked punished.

The nature of the punishment of the wicked is not clear except that it will entail everlasting shame and contempt. Similarly, the nature of the risen state of the righteous is not entirely clear but rather is given in symbols. N. T. Wright thinks this means the righteous will be raised to a state of rulers in God's new creation. "They will be raised to a state of glory in the world for which the best parallel or comparison is the status of stars, moon, and sun within the created order."[13] In ancient cosmology, though, stars were not believed to be composed of the same type of matter as the earth, so being raised to a status similar to that of stars probably connoted being raised to a different kind of materiality. Bodily resurrection, then, is *not* the same as simple resuscitation. Resuscitated persons will eventually die again and their bodies decompose. Resurrected persons, by contrast, will not die again. This alone indicates that the status of resurrected bodies must be different from our bodies here on earth, which age and finally perish. We will encounter this same idea again in the New Testament accounts of bodily resurrection.

Note also that the resurrection in Daniel's vision is set in a context of judgment and vindication for all Jews who have been righteous. It is not simply an individual matter. Like Ezekiel's vision of the dry bones being revived (Ezek. 37:1–12), Daniel's vision involves the vindication of an entire people.

Where did the idea of bodily resurrection, so different from Greek thought, come from? A common explanation is that it was imported from the Zoroastrians in Persia when many Jews were exiled in Babylon (587–539 BCE). N. T. Wright, however, has a different interpretation. He thinks it developed out of the earlier belief in Sheol. Israel's faith in a God of justice, who was committed to the goodness of the creation and to the covenant with Israel, eventually led to the belief that God would not allow the righteous dead to languish forever in Sheol separated from God's presence. Rather, God would restore the dead in fully embodied form. "The belief [was] . . . not that humans are innately immortal, but that YHWH's love and creative power are so strong that even death cannot break them. . . . It grew directly from the emphasis on the goodness of creation, on YHWH as the god who both kills and makes alive, and on the future of nation and land."[14]

The Intermediate State

The belief in the resurrection of the dead both assumed and entailed the belief that the dead who were resurrected continued their existence in an intermediate state between their death and resurrection in the end times. As Wright explains:

> Likewise, any Jew who believed in resurrection, from Daniel to the Pharisees and beyond, naturally also believed in an intermediate state in which some kind of personal identity was guaranteed between physical death and the physical re-embodiment of resurrection. . . . Unless we are to suppose that "resurrection" denoted some kind of newly embodied existence into which one went immediately upon death—and there is no evidence that any Jews of this period believed in such a thing—it is clear that some kind of ongoing existence is assumed.[15]

It is important to stress this point, because recently many biblical scholars argue that the Bible—particularly the Old Testament—teaches the resurrection of the body, not the immortality of the soul.[16] These two have been seen as opposing each other: resurrection was the Hebrew belief while an immortal soul was the Greek belief.[17] Wright's comment on this is as follows:

> Jews, it used to be said, believed in resurrection, while Greeks believed in immortality. Like most half truths, this one is as misleading as it is informative, if not more so. If the Bible offers a spectrum of belief about life after death, the second-Temple period provides something more like an artist's palette: dozens of options, with different ways of describing similar positions and similar ways of describing different ones.[18]

Old Testament scholar James Barr offers a survey of this trend of thought, as well as a trenchant criticism of it, in his book *The Garden of Eden and the Hope of Immortality*. Barr makes the same point, that there is a wide variety of beliefs about afterlife in the Old Testament. To insist that there is only one, or only one authentic one, is to let ideology triumph over evidence. Barr claims that "much in the turn against the immortality of the soul was not a return to the fountainhead of biblical evidence but a climbing on the bandwagon of modern progress. . . . Nevertheless, the turn against the soul and its immortality continued, and to this day continues, to be represented as a move back towards the Bible."[19]

Another indication of belief in an intermediate state in the Old Testament period was the practice of necromancy, that is, of consulting the dead. Several passages in the Old Testament warn against this. For example Isaiah says: "Now if people say to you, 'Consult the ghosts and familiar spirits that chirp and mutter; should not a people consult their gods, the dead on behalf of the living, for teaching and instruction?' Surely, those who speak like this will have no dawn!" (Isa. 8:19–20). Several passages in the Israelite law forbid consulting the dead (see, e.g., Lev. 19:31; 20:6; Deut. 18:11). Obviously, there is no need to pass laws forbidding something unless people are actually doing it. Old Testament scholar Helmer Ringgren therefore concludes: "Belief in afterlife is also indicated by the practice of necromancy."[20]

John Cooper, after a long and careful analysis of the Old Testament conception of afterlife, concludes that the Hebrew idea of the dead is both holistic and dualistic. It is holistic because they did not think of the person as divided between body and soul but thought of the person as a psychophysical unity. But it is dualistic because "they believed that human persons continue to exist after death, though in a state far less desirable than earthly life."[21] He calls this belief "holistic dualism" and considers that it is similar in the Christian tradition to the belief of Thomas Aquinas (see chap. 3).

Hellenistic Judaism and the Immortality of the Soul

Near the end of the Old Testament period, in the latter part of the first century BCE, we find another belief concerning afterlife, namely, a fully developed belief that the souls of the righteous survive death not in Sheol but in the presence of God. This is expressed in the Wisdom of Solomon, a book written in Greek, probably in Alexandria, where there was a large community of Greek-speaking Jews. This book was included in the Septuagint, the translation of the Hebrew Scriptures into Greek, and was part of the Bible of the early church.[22] The relevant passage from this book is worth quoting in full:

> But the souls of the righteous are in the hand of God,
> and no torment will ever touch them.

> In the eyes of the foolish they seemed to have died,
> and their departure was thought to be a disaster,
> and their going from us to be their destruction;
> but they are at peace.
> For though in the sight of others they were punished,
> their hope is full of immortality.
> Having been disciplined a little, they will receive great good,
> because God tested them and found them worthy of himself;
> like gold in the furnace he tried them,
> and like a sacrificial burnt offering he accepted them.
> In the time of their visitation they will shine forth,
> and will run like sparks through the stubble.
> They will govern nations and rule over peoples,
> and the Lord will rule over them forever.
> Those who trust in him will understand truth,
> and the faithful will abide with him in love,
> because grace and mercy are upon his holy ones,
> and he watches over his elect. (Wis. 3:1–9)

This striking passage, which is regularly read at Catholic funerals, reflects Hellenistic (Greek) influence, specifically the influence of Plato and Middle Platonism. Plato taught that the essence of the person was the soul, that the soul was naturally immortal, and that the body was like a prison.[23] Wisdom echoes this view of the body when it says: "for a perishable body weighs down the soul, and this earthly tent burdens the thoughtful mind" (Wis. 9:15).

The book of Wisdom does differ from Platonism, however, at some points that mark it as distinctly Jewish. First, the souls of the righteous are in the presence of God because of God's "grace and mercy" (Wis. 3:9) and because "God tested them and found them worthy of himself" (Wis. 3:5), not because they are naturally immortal. As always, in Jewish thinking God is the source of all life and blessing, and a blessed afterlife can come only from God. Second, the text says the righteous will "govern nations and rule over peoples" (v. 8). This sounds like the text from Daniel and may refer to the resurrected state, not to a state of discarnate immortality. The curious phrase "in the time of their visitation they will shine forth, and will run like sparks through stubble" (v. 7) also requires interpretation. N. T. Wright argues that this phrase refers to judgment—the wicked are the "stubble" that will be burned in the judgment. On this reading, the passage does not refer to a permanent abode of disembodied souls resting in heaven but instead refers to the temporary state of the souls of the righteous resting in heaven ("in the hand of God," v. 1) that will be followed by the resurrection and the judgment, in which the righteous are vindicated and in the resurrected state given governance of peoples.[24]

Wisdom, then, combines the Greek belief that the souls of the righteous are in the hand of God with the belief in an eventual bodily resurrection. This would become the central belief of Christianity as well.

Jewish Apocalyptic, Eschatological, and Intertestamental Literature

The Greek word *apokalypsis* ("apocalypse") means "revelation." Apocalyptic literature is concerned with the revelation of divine secrets or mysteries about heaven, the supernatural world, and the future typically given through visions to the seer by an angelic messenger.[25] The language of apocalyptic literature is highly symbolic, and the authorship is usually attributed to a famous figure in the past (e.g., Enoch, Baruch, Ezra). Apocalyptic literature is radically pessimistic about the present, seeing evil powers in control of the world. It foresees a final cosmic battle between good and evil and a radical intervention by God in which he will destroy the present evil age. Then will come bodily resurrection and a cosmic judgment of all the dead and the living in which the wicked are punished and the righteous rewarded in a glorious new kingdom either in heaven or on earth. The Old Testament book of Daniel is an apocalyptic book, as is the book of Revelation in the New Testament. Individual sections of the New Testament that deal with the end times (e.g., Mark 13) and the last judgment (e.g., Matt. 25:31–46) are often classed as apocalyptic as well.

Apocalyptic literature is usually connected with eschatological visions, that is, visions of the end of history, when God will intervene to establish a kingdom of the righteous. But apocalyptic is not just concerned about the end times. C. K. Barrett writes:

> The secrets in which apocalyptic deals are not simply secrets of the future—of the Age to Come; they include secrets of the present state of the heavenly world. Indeed, these two mysteries, of heaven and the future, are very closely allied, since in apocalyptic the significant future is the breaking into this world of the heavenly world, and to know what is now in heaven is in consequence almost the same as knowing what will be on earth.[26]

Christopher Rowland argues that apocalyptic, therefore, must be understood as revealing a "vertical dimension," that is, the secrets of heaven now, as well as a horizontal, future dimension.[27]

Apocalyptic is important to our study of death and afterlife because much of it is concerned with life after death. Indeed, an apocalyptic outlook per-

meates the New Testament, including the teachings of Jesus—especially his
teaching of the kingdom of God—and of Paul (see chap. 2). Intertestamental
apocalyptic literature is therefore a bridge between the last books of the Old
Testament (Daniel, ca. 165 BCE) and the New Testament. And in this literature we find a development of the ideas of the abode of the dead, of bodily
resurrection, and of the last judgment. Here I will follow D. S. Russell's account of this subject.[28]

We saw above that the underworld (Sheol) in the Old Testament writings
was the abode of the dead, who survived only as shades with no life force.
Everyone, the righteous and the wicked, sank into the underworld, where they
had no rewards and no comfort from the presence of God. This changed in
the intertestamental apocalyptic literature. Russell writes:

> One change is that . . . the dead are no longer described as "shades" but as
> "souls" or "spirits" and survive as individual conscious beings. . . . There is
> seen to be a continuity between life on earth and life in Sheol in which the de-
> parted . . . can yet maintain a life of fellowship with God whose jurisdiction is
> acknowledged beyond the grave. . . . According to their . . . lot in the afterlife
> they experience restlessness or repose, remorse or gratitude, fear or calm as-
> surance (II Esdras 7.80ff.).[29]

A second change is that moral distinctions become part of the afterlife in
Sheol:

> As in life, so in death, men [sic] are separated into two distinct categories, the
> wicked and the righteous, on the basis of moral judgments. . . . Men determine
> their destiny in Sheol by the choice they make in this life: "For though Adam
> first sinned and brought untimely death upon all, yet of those who were born
> from him each one of them has prepared for his own soul torment to come,
> and again each one of them has chosen for himself glories to come" (II Baruch
> 54.15, cf. 51.16).[30]

A third difference is that "now Sheol is regarded . . . as an intermediate state
where the souls of men await the resurrection and the final judgment and in
which they are treated according to their deserts, i.e., Sheol becomes a place
of preliminary rewards and punishments."[31]

In some of these books, there is the possibility of the dead being helped
by intercessory prayer, especially by the prayers of prophets like Abraham
and Moses. In the majority of the books, however, the fate of the dead is
fixed at death: "Man's destiny, both in Sheol and at the last judgment, is
determined by the life he has lived on earth. Once inside the gates of Sheol

no progress is possible for the departed soul either upwards or downwards (cf. *1 En*. 22)."[32]

Finally, in these intertestamental apocalyptic books, Sheol is divided into compartments so that it is described as both the abode of the wicked and the abode of the righteous. For example, *1 Enoch* 22 views the place of the dead as divided into four compartments: one for the righteous, where there is a spring of water; one for sinners who have not been punished for their sins in life and who therefore experience great pain; one for the righteous martyrs; and one for sinners who had already received punishment for their sins in their earthly life. Russell notes that "in this passage we have the first reference in the apocalyptic writings to the idea of Hell as a place of torment, although the actual word is not used here."[33]

In Jewish apocalyptic literature, a wide range of visions of the resurrection and the resurrection body can be found. In some texts a resurrection is imagined that occurs on earth with a physical, earthly resurrected body while in other texts a heavenly resurrection is envisioned with a spiritual resurrected body that corresponds to its heavenly environment. Russell writes:

> These "spiritual" bodies are described in several apocalyptic books under the figure of "garments of light" (cf. II Esd. 2.39, 45, etc.) or "garments of glory" (cf. *1 En*. 62.15, etc.). . . . Thus in the Similitudes of Enoch when the kingdom is set up in a new heaven (45.4; 51.4) and a new earth (41.2; 45.5) the righteous dead are clothed in "garments of glory" and dwell with the holy angels (39.4–5).[34]

In a number of places, the resurrection body is described as a transformed physical body. This prefigures the idea of the resurrected body that is found in the New Testament (see chap. 2).

Finally, Jewish apocalyptic literature emphasizes the last judgment. Russell writes: "The doctrine of the last judgment is the most characteristic doctrine of Jewish apocalyptic. It is the great event towards which the whole universe is moving and which will vindicate once and for all God's righteous purpose for men and all creation."[35] Typically the judgment is based on one's deeds:

> Every man [sic] is judged according to what he has done of righteousness or of wickedness. . . . In the Testament of Abraham . . . two angels record the sins and righteous deeds of the departed (chap. 13) whose souls undergo two tests, one of fire (chap. 13) and one by judgment of the balance in which a man's good deeds are weighed over against the bad (chap. 12, cf. *1 En*. 41.1; 61.8).[36]

Again, this prefigures the strong New Testament emphasis on the last judgment, though in the New Testament it is Christ who will be the judge (Matt. 25:31–46; 2 Cor. 5:10).

Conclusion

There is, then, a spectrum of beliefs concerning death and afterlife in ancient Judaism: the underworld; the eventual bodily resurrection of the dead, associated with judgment; the souls of the righteous resting in the hand of God; and apocalyptic eschatological visions of the end times. All these options are carried forward in the Jewish Scriptures and in the intertestamental writings. Furthermore, different sects in Judaism espoused one or another of these various beliefs concerning the afterlife. Evidence for this is found both in the New Testament and in the writing of the Jewish historian Josephus. The Sadducees, aristocratic Jews who controlled the temple and collaborated with the Romans in governing Judea, denied the resurrection and (apparently) any form of afterlife and, according to the ancient Jewish historian Josephus, held "that souls die with the bodies."[37] The Pharisees, a party or sect concerned with the fine points of the law, taught the resurrection of the body and also the survival of the soul after death. Concerning the Pharisees, Josephus writes:

> They also believe that souls have an immortal vigor in them, and that under the earth there will be rewards and punishments, according as they have lived virtuously or viciously in this life; and the latter are to be detained in an everlasting prison, but that the former shall have the power to revive and live again; on account of which doctrines, they are able greatly to persuade the body of the people.[38]

The Essenes, a group not mentioned in the New Testament but associated with the monastery at Qumran, the Dead Sea Scrolls, and an apocalyptic eschatological outlook, apparently believed that the soul survived the death of the body and expected an eschatological war and judgment in the near future. N. T. Wright argues that they may also have believed in the resurrection, but this is uncertain.[39] Finally, the mass of ordinary Jews, the "people of the land," probably did not belong to any of these sects. They likely hoped for the deliverance of Israel and for the resurrection in the last days.[40] Wright surmises in summary:

> The evidence suggests that by the time of Jesus . . . most Jews either believed in some form of resurrection or at least knew it was standard teaching. Com-

paratively few remained skeptical. Some held to a kind of middle position . . . in which a blessed, albeit disembodied, immortality awaited the righteous after their death. But there is widespread evidence that the belief which burst into full flower in Daniel 12 had become standard.[41]

There was, then, a long development and refinement of belief concerning death and afterlife in ancient Israel, from the oblivion of the underworld to the survival of the souls of the blessed and the resurrection of the dead in the last days. Resurrection meant judgment; it was not only a vindication of the righteous and punishment of the wicked but also a restoration of the righteous people of Israel.[42] It was therefore both individual and communal, a feature we shall also find in the New Testament.

All these beliefs flowed from Israel's basic belief that God, YHWH, was the creator and king of the world and that YHWH was faithful to his covenant with Israel. God would not abandon his faithful ones to the wicked or to the forces of death and the underworld. One day at the end of the age he would come again to restore a kingdom of justice, peace, and prosperity and would restore his (resurrected) people to their land. This would be the day of the Lord, and the beginning of the "age to come." On that day, even the Gentiles would recognize that YHWH was God of all the earth and would stream to Israel, as to a teacher who was seen as the light of the nations (see Isa. 49:6). Wright notes, "All of this was concentrated, for many Jews, in the stories of the righteous martyrs, those who had suffered and died for YHWH and Torah. Because YHWH was the creator, and because he was the god of justice, the martyrs would be raised, and Israel as a whole would be vindicated."[43]

All these ideas carry forward and, for Christians, are consummated in the life, teachings, death, and resurrection of Jesus of Nazareth. To this we now turn.

2

DEATH AND AFTERLIFE
IN THE NEW TESTAMENT

I consider that the sufferings of this present time are not worth
comparing with the glory about to be revealed to us.

Romans 8:18

The New Testament tells of the life, teachings, death, and resurrection of
Jesus of Nazareth. Jesus's teachings, miracles, and resurrection were revolutionary in the world of ancient Judaism and remain so today. Then as now, it
was the rich, the powerful, the corrupt, and the warlike who seemed to control
events. But Jesus taught that all this would be transformed and that in the long
run it was the kingdom (or reign) of God that would matter. He died an apparent
failure, but he and his hope in God's reign were vindicated by his resurrection.

His story is profoundly relevant to our quest for the truth about death and
afterlife, for the kingdom of God, which Jesus preached, was and is the whole
goal of Christian life *and* afterlife. *Heaven* is nothing more than the full presence of the kingdom of God, which begins here on earth and is completed
and consummated in the afterlife.

Jesus's Teaching and Preaching

The core of Jesus's teaching and preaching was his proclamation of the kingdom of God. This is expressed especially in the Beatitudes (Matt. 5; Luke

6), the Sermon on the Mount (Matt. 5–7), and the parables of the kingdom (Matt. 13, 25; Mark 4). "Kingdom," in this usage, refers to the reign of God or the kingship of God. It is an apocalyptic idea (see chap. 1): the heavenly world of God is breaking into this world; God's power of justice, mercy, and love is coming into the world of oppression, fear, sickness, and sin, the world ruled by Satan (in the New Testament's view). The agent for the in-breaking of God's kingdom is Jesus, who both proclaims the kingdom and enacts it through miracles and exorcisms.

The kingdom therefore entails a reversal of social status: the rich and powerful will be put down and the lowly exalted. We can see this expressed in the Beatitudes and the woes of the "Sermon on the Plain" in Luke 6:20–25:

> Blessed are you who are poor,
>   for yours is the kingdom of God.
> Blessed are you who are hungry now,
>   for you will be filled.
> Blessed are you who weep now,
>   for you will laugh. . . .
> But woe to you who are rich,
>   for you have received your consolation.
> Woe to you who are full now,
>   for you will be hungry.
> Woe to you who are laughing now,
>   for you will mourn and weep.

Here, it is the poor, the hungry, and those who weep—that is, the poor and oppressed—who will be blessed by God in the kingdom, while the wealthy will reap sorrow. New Testament scholar John Meier comments: "In the background of these beatitudes stands the whole OT picture of God as the truly just king of the covenant community of Israel, the king who does what Israel's human kings often failed to do: defend widows and orphans, secure the rights of the oppressed, and in general see justice done (so, e.g., Ps. 146:5–10)."[1]

Matthew's version of the Beatitudes (Matt. 5:3–11) is better known than Luke's version and brings out the interior dimension of the kingdom as well as the dimension of social justice. Thus to enter the kingdom one must become "poor in spirit" (humble), merciful, meek, a peacemaker, pure in heart, and righteous under the (Mosaic) law. As Jesus's discourse in Matthew 5 makes clear, purity of heart and intention means that one does not even intend sin, much less enact it. Even those who look at another lustfully are guilty of adultery in their hearts (Matt. 5:28). Even those who are angry with their brother and insult that brother are in danger of judgment (Matt. 5:22). Finally, Jesus enjoins his disciples to love not only their friends but also their enemies: "I say to you, Love your enemies and pray for those who persecute you" (Matt. 5:44).

The in-breaking of the kingdom in the person and mission of Jesus demands an attitude of acceptance or rejection. This is the core of Jesus's message, as summarized in Mark: "The time is fulfilled, and the kingdom of God has come near; repent, and believe in the good news" (Mark 1:15). The word "repent" here translates the Greek verb *metanoein*, which means a total change of heart and mind, a conversion. Repentance is also expressed in such parables as that of the prodigal son (Luke 15). Meier writes:

> Jesus proclaimed the loving forgiveness of God the Father, a prodigal father who freely bestows his forgiveness on sinners who have no strict claim on God's mercy (see, e.g., the parable of the prodigal son, the lost coin, the lost sheep, the unmerciful servant, the great supper, the two debtors, the rich man and Lazarus, and the Pharisee and the publican). It is God alone who acts in the end time to establish his kingdom of justice and love.[2]

This raises the question of when the kingdom will come. On the one hand, its fullness lies in the future. Jesus therefore instructed his disciples to pray for its coming in the "Our Father" prayer: "Father, hallowed be your name. Your kingdom come" (Luke 11:2). On the other hand, the power of God's kingship is already present and active through Jesus in his preaching, miracles, and exorcisms. Jesus's saying in Luke confirms this: "But if it is by the finger of God that I cast out the demons, then the kingdom of God has come to you" (Luke 11:20). So the kingdom is already inaugurated in the work of Jesus but will not be fulfilled until the end of history. Until it is fulfilled, the kingdom of God and the kingdom of Satan remain in conflict.

The kingdom also entails judgment, in which the wicked will be punished and the good rewarded. This can be seen in some of the parables, for example, the parable of the dragnet, in which Jesus likens the kingdom to a net full of fish from which the fishermen keep the good fish and throw out the bad. In the same way, at the close of the age the angels will separate the good from the wicked (Matt. 13:47–50).

The great parable that expresses the judgment at the end of history, when Jesus will come again enthroned in glory to judge the living and the dead, is found in Matthew 25:31–36. This is one of the most explicit statements in the New Testament concerning the kingdom, judgment, the end times, heaven, and hell. It has been enormously influential in Christian theology and history and is worth quoting in full.

When the Son of Man comes in his glory, and all the angels with him, then he
will sit on the throne of his glory. All the nations [*panta ta ethnē*, "all peoples"]
will be gathered before him, and he will separate people one from another as
a shepherd separates the sheep from the goats, and he will put the sheep at his
right hand and the goats at the left. Then the king will say to those at his right
hand, "Come, you that are blessed by my Father, inherit the kingdom prepared
for you from the foundation of the world; for I was hungry and you gave me
food, I was thirsty and you gave me something to drink, I was a stranger and
you welcomed me, I was naked and you gave me clothing, I was sick and you
took care of me, I was in prison and you visited me." Then the righteous will
answer him, "Lord, when was it that we saw you hungry and gave you food, or
thirsty and gave you something to drink? And when was it that we saw you a
stranger and welcomed you, or naked and gave you clothing? And when was it
that we saw you sick or in prison and visited you?" And the king will answer
them, "Truly, I tell you, just as you did it to one of the least of these who are
members of my family, you did it to me." Then he will say to those at his left
hand, "You that are accursed, depart from me into the eternal fire prepared for
the devil and his angels; for I was hungry and you gave me no food, I was thirsty
and you gave me nothing to drink. . . . Then they also will answer, "Lord, when
was it that we saw you hungry or thirsty or a stranger or naked or sick or in
prison, and did not take care of you?" Then he will answer them, "Truly I tell
you, just as you did not do it to one of the least of these, you did not do it to
me." And these will go away into eternal punishment, but the righteous into
eternal life. (Matt. 25:31–46)[3]

The criterion here for entrance into the kingdom is not what we might
expect. Jesus, the returning king, does not ask whether people believed in
him. Rather this passage is consistent with his saying in Matthew 7:21: "Not
everyone who says to me 'Lord, Lord,' will enter the kingdom of heaven, but
only the one who does the will of my Father in heaven." Thus deeds of mercy
and love to the poor and outcast count in the last judgment. Love is the master
key to the kingdom. And in this vision, the full coming of the kingdom is at
the end of time. Only then will Jesus return in all his glory.

The kingdom, then, has been inaugurated in the life, teachings, death,
and resurrection of Jesus, but in this life it is challenged by radical evil (both
human and satanic), according to the New Testament.[4] The kingdom is therefore already present in this world but will be consummated only in the next
world, when radical evil will finally be defeated.[5] This is important for our
understanding of death and afterlife and for a Christian way of dying well.
The kingdom is already present to us now, and we need to respond now. The
kingdom, after all, requires a radical conversion to love of God and neighbor.
A radical conversion may happen quickly (the dying thief on the cross in Luke,

for example), but usually it takes time—years, decades, even a lifetime. After all, we do not know how long we will live, thus it is important to be ready. Jesus emphasizes the importance of being ready in many of his parables. For example, in the parable of the wise and foolish bridesmaids Jesus says: "Keep awake therefore, for you know neither the day nor the hour" (Matt. 25:13).

The Death of Jesus

After Mel Gibson's 2004 film *The Passion of the Christ*, it is probably not necessary to remind readers of the horror of crucifixion. It was a mode of death reserved for the worst criminals and insurgents, calculated to inflict maximum pain, disgrace, and humiliation. To most of the onlookers, it would have meant that Jesus was a failed messiah. Yet Christians interpret the death of Jesus—in the light of his subsequent resurrection—not as a terrible, shameful death but as a victorious one. How did Christians manage to reverse the interpretation and meaning of the cross?

In the early church, Jesus's death was interpreted primarily as a sacrifice that replaced the sacrifices offered in the Jewish temple, which by 70 CE had been destroyed by the Romans. This is stated explicitly in the Letter to the Hebrews. Christ, the author argues, is the true high priest, whose offering of himself was the definitive and final sacrifice that obtains redemption from sin:

> But when Christ came as a high priest of the good things that have come . . . he entered once for all into the Holy Place, not with the blood of goats and calves, but with his own blood, thus obtaining eternal redemption. . . . For this reason he is the mediator of the new covenant, so that those who are called may receive the promised eternal inheritance, because a death has occurred that redeems them from the transgressions under the first covenant. (Heb. 9:11–15)

The Gospel of John also emphasizes the sacrificial nature of Jesus's death. When he sees Jesus, John the Baptist exclaims: "Here is the lamb of God who takes away the sin of the world!" (John 1:29). Here John refers to the Passover lamb, which was sacrificed on the feast of Passover. In John's Gospel, Jesus is described as dying at exactly the time—three in the afternoon on the Day of Preparation for Passover—that the priests in the temple were slaughtering the lambs in preparation for Passover. Jesus, then, is the Passover lamb. And in the view of the writer of the Gospel of John, Jesus's death replaces the sacrifices of animals under the old (Jewish) covenant. After the death of Jesus, no animal sacrifices were required, at least in Christianity.[6]

If Jesus's death was a sacrifice, its effect was to reconcile believers with God. This is the basis for what in theology is called the "atonement" (literally, at-one-ment), which makes the believer one with God. Atonement has been a major theme in the teaching and theology of the Christian church through the centuries. However, there are a number of different theories as to exactly how Jesus's death atones for sin.[7] There is also disagreement among Christians as to the role of faith in the process of atonement. (We will consider these points in chapter 8.)

Recent theology has emphasized that on the cross Jesus gave himself entirely to the Father and to humanity out of love. He reserved nothing for himself. It is in his act of dying that we see most clearly what the New Testament means when it says, "For God so loved the world that he gave his only Son, so that everyone who believes in him may not perish but may have eternal life" (John 3:16). The Greek word for this kind of love is *agape*, which is self-sacrificing love, like that of siblings. It is the love of God the Father and of the Son that is revealed on the cross.

Was Jesus's death a good death? And is it a model for our own deaths? Certainly it was a terrible death if we consider the suffering involved. But if Jesus accomplished the work of salvation on the cross, if he did indeed reconcile sinful humanity with God, then we would have to say it was a good death—in fact, the best death ever. His death was good, then, in the sense that we think a heroic death on the battlefield is good. Christians have traditionally seen in his death, coupled with the resurrection, the ultimate victory of life over death, of love and good over evil, and of God over Satan. It was not painless or without agony, but it was a triumph nonetheless.

Jesus's death has been a model for Christians since the beginning of the church. Those who died as Jesus did—witnessing to their faith—have been acclaimed "martyrs," a word that in Greek means "witness." According to tradition, Peter, Paul, and many of the apostles died as martyrs. Most of those honored as saints in the first few hundred years of the church were martyrs.

Eternal Life and Resurrection

Jesus's promise to his followers was the gift of eternal life. "Truly I tell you, there is no one who has left house or brothers or sisters or mother or father or children or lands, for my sake . . . who will not receive a hundredfold now in this age . . . and in the age to come eternal life" (Mark 10:29–30). Eternal life differs from our present life because it is imperishable. But it is also life of a different quality: it is life raised to a higher power, so to speak, that is without suffering, fear, boredom, grief, loneliness, and so on. It is life in the full presence of God, Jesus, and community. Jesus's own entrance into eternal life was through the door of death and into the resurrection.

Jesus's resurrection is one of the most startling, unexpected, and difficult-to-explain events in history. For many people, it is simply an impossibility: dead people do not rise again; it is scientifically impossible; the canons of normal history do not apply to it, because if it occurred it was a unique event unlike any other we know of. Not only do we not see resurrections happening today, but it seems to fly in the face of the scientifically demonstrated regularity of the laws of nature. Consequently, many theories have been put forward to explain away the resurrection. It is said that Jesus's body was stolen from the tomb by his disciples, who then circulated the story of the resurrection. Or, Jesus survived the crucifixion and revived in the cool of the tomb. Or, the empty tomb, and indeed the whole resurrection story, was an invention of the early church, and so on.

I will deal with the modern problems of belief in the resurrection in chapter 7. Here I simply want to lay out the New Testament position. I note, however, that Jesus's resurrection was not easy to believe in ancient times either, and that only extremely powerful evidence could have convinced the disciples that Jesus had been raised from the dead.

Let us recall that in the first century CE Pharisees' belief in the resurrection was the belief that the dead would be raised in the end times. This would precede the vindication of the righteous, the punishment of the wicked, and the newly embodied life of God's people in the kingdom of God, free from oppression, injustice, suffering, and death. But no one expected a resurrection before the end times. N. T. Wright explains: "There are no traditions about a Messiah being raised to life: most Jews of this period hoped for resurrection, many Jews of this period hoped for a Messiah, but nobody put these two hopes together until the early Christians did so."[8] Christians did so because they saw Jesus as the Messiah, and he had been resurrected, contrary to all expectations.

The earliest written statements concerning Jesus's resurrection are found in the letters of Paul, which are also the earliest writings in the New Testament.[9] We will therefore consider Paul's account of the resurrection first.

The longest treatment of the resurrection in Paul's letters occurs in 1 Corinthians 15. This letter was written to the nascent church in Corinth and concerned some serious problems occurring in that church. One of the problems was that some were denying the resurrection of the body (v. 12). Paul takes this as tantamount to denying the Christian faith: "For if the dead are not raised, then Christ has not been raised. If Christ has not been raised, your faith is futile and you are still in your sins" (vv. 16–17). He therefore recites a list of witnesses who saw the risen Christ just after his resurrection:

> For I handed on to you as of first importance what I in turn had received: that Christ died for ours sins in accordance with the scriptures, and that he was buried, and that he was raised on the third day in accordance with the scriptures, and that he appeared to Cephas [Peter], then to the twelve. Then he appeared to more than five hundred brothers and sisters at one time, most of whom are still alive, though some have died. Then he appeared to James, then to all the apostles. Last of all, as to one untimely born, he appeared also to me. (vv. 3–8)

Though Paul wrote this letter ca. 56–57 CE, he is appealing to what was "handed on" (i.e., taught) to him when he was first instructed in the faith, just after his conversion around 36 CE, only three to six years after Jesus's death. Of the witnesses he cites, at least one, Paul himself, had not believed in Jesus before the resurrection appearances. Paul notes that most of these witnesses were still alive at the time he wrote the letter. This means that if what Paul was writing were not true, he could have been contradicted by the very witnesses he cites. This makes it unlikely that Jesus's resurrection was simply an invention of the early church—too many people would have had to agree to the fabrication. Further, because Paul had not known Jesus during his earthly ministry, and had persecuted the church before his conversion, his credentials as an apostle were suspect. This makes it even more unlikely that he would report what he knew to be untrue if the resurrection had not happened. Finally, many of the witnesses he cites, including himself, went on to die as martyrs. It is hard to believe that they would have done this if they knew their story of Jesus's resurrection were not true.

Next Paul turns to the question (probably raised by the Corinthian community) of how the dead are raised. What kind of body do they have? (1 Cor. 15:35). His answer is to note that there are different kinds of bodies even in the physical world: "there is one flesh for human beings, another for animals, another for birds, and another for fish. There are both heavenly bodies and earthly bodies, but the glory of the heavenly is one thing, and that of the earthly is another" (1 Cor. 15:39–40). Likewise with the resurrection: the resurrected body is a different kind of body than our mortal bodies, for it is imperishable.

> So it is with the resurrection of the dead. What is sown is perishable, what is raised is imperishable. It is sown in dishonor, it is raised in glory. It is sown in weakness, it is raised in power. It is sown a physical [*psychikon*] body, it is raised a spiritual [*pneumatikon*] body. . . . The first man [Adam] was from the

earth, a man of dust; the second man [Jesus] is from heaven. . . . Just as we have borne the image of the man of dust, we will also bear the image of the man of heaven.

What I am saying, brothers and sisters, is this: flesh and blood cannot inherit the kingdom of God, nor does the perishable inherit the imperishable. . . . We will not all die, but we will all be changed. . . . For the trumpet will sound, and the dead will be raised imperishable, and we will be changed. For this perishable body must put on imperishability, and this mortal body must put on immortality." (1 Cor. 15:42–53)

This passage has occasioned a great deal of exegetical discussion, but the general sense seems clear enough. Paul reflects ancient physics in arguing for different kinds of bodies, both among living creatures and among the earth and stars. Similarly, the body as resurrected will be in a different state of materiality—namely, an imperishable state—than are perishable earthly bodies. Both states of the body, however, are physical; that is the thrust of Paul's argument. The English translation in this respect is misleading; it might seem to indicate that our present bodies are physical, while the resurrected bodies are spiritual and thus not physical bodies at all. But that is not what Paul is saying. Our present bodies are physical and perishable and therefore cannot inherit the kingdom of God. They must be changed into imperishable physical bodies, or, as Paul says, glorious bodies. "But our commonwealth is in heaven, and from it we await a Savior, the Lord Jesus Christ, who will change our lowly body to be like his glorious body, by the power which enables him even to subject all things to himself" (Phil. 3:20–21 RSV). N. T. Wright argues that the resurrected body is "transphysical," that is, it is physical but it also transcends the limits of our space-time universe.[10] So there is a continuity between the perishable body on earth and the resurrected body, but there is also a discontinuity. The resurrected body is *not* simply a resuscitated body—like that of Lazarus, who was resuscitated but would die again. Yet the state of the resurrected body is very hard to describe. We can see Paul struggling with this problem and reaching for metaphors from the physics of his time. These metaphors don't work well today precisely because we now see all matter as made of the same constituents—quarks, gluons, electrons, atoms, and molecules. But that does not mean the resurrection is a physical impossibility, only that it is beyond the reach of present science and of our experience.

We can see the same ideas about Jesus's resurrection in the Gospel accounts: the resurrected Jesus is not a spirit or a ghost—he can be touched—yet he appears and disappears, indicating that his resurrected body is not limited by the laws of space and time. Most of the Gospels report resurrection appearances, but the Gospel accounts differ from one another. The usual explanation of this is that the Gospels incorporate a number of different oral traditions concerning Jesus's resurrection appearances.[11]

The Gospel of Luke (chap. 24) records two appearances of the risen Jesus: first to two unnamed disciples on the road to Emmaus and then to the eleven and their companions in Jerusalem. Luke's account emphasizes the physical nature of Jesus's risen body:

> "Why are you frightened, and why do doubts arise in your hearts? Look at my hands and my feet; see that it is I myself. Touch me and see; for a ghost does not have flesh and bones as you see that I have." And when he had said this, he showed them his hands and his feet. While in their joy they were disbelieving . . . he said to them, "Have you anything here to eat?" They gave him a piece of broiled fish, and he took it and ate in their presence. (vv. 38–43)

Yet Luke's account also indicates that the risen Jesus is not limited by the usual laws of time and space. The two disciples on the road to Emmaus do not recognize him until they are eating with him and he suddenly vanishes from their sight. Luke also records, at the end of his Gospel and at the beginning of Acts, that Jesus was carried up into heaven (Luke 24:51; Acts 1:9). So the resurrected Jesus is physical but not limited by space and time. This transcendent quality of the resurrection is also indicated in Jesus's own saying about the resurrection reported in Matthew and Luke: "For in the resurrection they neither marry nor are given in marriage, but are like angels in heaven" (Matt. 22:30; see also Luke 20:35).

John records four appearances of the risen Jesus to his followers: to Mary Magdalene on Easter Sunday morning; to the disciples in a locked room on Easter Sunday evening; to the disciples again a week later, with Thomas present; and finally, in chapter 21, to some of his disciples in Galilee.[12] These appearances indicate the same paradox that we saw in Luke. The risen Jesus is physical. The apostle Thomas, who had not been with the disciples when Jesus first appeared to them on Easter evening, says, "Unless I see the mark of the nails in his hands, and put my finger in the mark of the nails and my hand in his side, I will not believe" (John 20:25). But when Jesus appeared to the disciple a week later, he told Thomas: "Put your finger here and see my hands. Reach out your hand and put it in my side. Do not doubt but believe." Thomas responds by saying, "My Lord and my God!" (John 20:27–28). Yet Jesus also seems to transcend the laws of matter: Jesus twice appears among the disciples as they are meeting in a room with locked doors (John 20:19, 26).

The New Testament accounts insist that the tomb was found empty; that Jesus appeared in the flesh, was touched, ate, and spoke to the disciples; that he was not restricted by the usual laws of matter and space; and that after his appearances to the disciples he ascended into heaven.

The ascension, like the resurrection, does not fit well with our present cosmology. Where did Jesus ascend to? A planet in outer space? Obviously not. Ascension means that he ascended into a higher state of being. (The New Testament says he is "seated at the right hand of the Father"—an obvious metaphor.) Such a higher state of being is difficult to conceive in our cosmos (but see chap. 7) yet is demanded by the doctrine of the ascension. The real question is, Where is the heaven to which Jesus ascended? N. T. Wright puts it this way:

> Heaven relates to earth tangentially so that the one who is in heaven can be simultaneously present anywhere and everywhere on earth: the ascension therefore means that Jesus is available, accessible, without people having to travel to a particular spot on earth to find him. . . . When the Bible speaks of heaven and earth it is not talking about two localities related to each other within the same space-time continuum, or about a nonphysical world contrasted with a physical one but about two different kinds of what we call space, two different kinds of what we call matter, and also quite possibly . . . two different kinds of what we call time.[13]

And, we might add, two different kinds of life: biological, earthly life and eternal life, which can begin on this earth but carries forward into heaven.

Jesus's resurrection was taken by early Christians as an indication that the end times were near (or had already begun); that Jesus's faithful followers could expect the Lord to return soon, perhaps in their lifetime; and that they would then be resurrected or raised themselves. Paul deals with this issue in his earliest letter, 1 Thessalonians (ca. 50–51 CE):

> But we do not want you to be uninformed, brothers and sisters, about those who have died ["fallen asleep," in Greek], so that you may not grieve as others do who have no hope. For since we believe that Jesus died and rose again, even so, through Jesus, God will bring with him those who have died. For this we declare to you by the word of the Lord, that we who are alive, who are left until the coming of the Lord, will by no means precede those who have died. For the Lord himself, with a cry of command, with the archangel's call and with the sound of God's trumpet, will descend from heaven, and the dead in Christ will rise first. Then we who are alive, who are left, will be caught up in the clouds together with them to meet the Lord in the air; and so we will be with the Lord forever. (1 Thess. 4:13–17)

This is an important passage for several reasons. It shows that Paul's idea, and probably that of other early Christians, of the final resurrection is not one of simple physical resurrection and return to earthly life but rather one that includes an ascension into glory as well—"caught up in the clouds together," as Paul says. Just as Jesus had ascended into heaven, so would his followers, even those who were still alive when he returned. The resurrection, then, cannot be interpreted as a return to life on earth as we know it. It involves physicality—the believers will be caught up in the clouds in their very bodies—but it also involves a transformation of the body and an ascension to a transfigured state of materiality. As Paul states in 1 Corinthians 15:51 (cited above), "we will not all die, but we will all be changed." Paul seems to have believed, at least at the time he wrote 1 Thessalonians, that some of those alive would live long enough to see Jesus's triumphal return. They would be caught up into the clouds but would need to have their bodies changed in order to enter the kingdom of God.

A second point to notice is that here we have probably the first written reference to the anticipated return of the Lord. Paul expects this return to occur in the lifetime of those then living, though Paul also recognizes that "the day of the Lord will come like a thief in the night," that is, no one will know when it is coming (1 Thess. 5:2). But Paul was mistaken in thinking that the Lord would return in his lifetime. So obviously if Paul did not know when the Lord was returning and Jesus himself said neither he nor the angels know but only the Father knows (Mark 13:32), then no one should presume to know *now* when or how soon the Lord is returning. Rather, the lesson is, as Jesus is reported to have said, "Beware, keep alert; for you do not know when the time will come" (Mark 13:33). This is wise advice for our generation also: we should not presume that the Lord is coming soon, but we should be prepared. This is especially true for each of us concerning the time of our own deaths, which we cannot know.

The Intermediate State

As the passage from the first Letter to the Thessalonians indicates, the center of Christian hope in the New Testament is that believers will be raised with Jesus. But this did not mean that Jesus and his followers thought that persons who had died simply ceased to exist after their deaths. As N. T. Wright notes (chap. 1, above), belief in the resurrection at the end of time entailed also a belief in some kind of intermediate state in which the personality survived after death and awaited the resurrection of the body. We have also seen that belief in the survival of the soul in an intermediate state between death and resurrection was common in apocalyptic intertestamental literature, which formed the background of the New Testament.

For some time, however, many New Testament scholars have maintained that the New Testament belief was bodily resurrection but *not* immortality of the soul. There is some truth in this point: it would be a mistake to believe that the New Testament idea of afterlife is that the soul is *naturally* immortal, as the Platonists believed, and that therefore resurrection is unnecessary. But the idea that the New Testament position is resurrection but not immortality, as if these two ideas were opposed, is misleading. N. T. Wright comments:

> Jews, it used to be said, believed in resurrection, while Greeks believed in immortality. Like most half-truths, this one is as misleading as it is informative, if not more so. The Bible offers a spectrum of belief about life after death. . . . [Platonic immortality] is not the view of those biblical writers who, it seems, came to believe that their relationship with YHWH would continue after death. Such continuation was based solely on YHWH's character (as the loving, powerful, Creator) not on anything innate within human beings. Thus all who believed in "resurrection" believed in some sense in the continuing existence, after death, of those who would be raised. . . . Resurrection . . . meant life *after* "life-after-death": a two-stage future hope, as opposed to the single-stage expectation of those who believed in a non-bodily future life [i.e., the Platonists who believed in immortality but not resurrection].[14]

In fact, a number of New Testament passages indicate a belief in personal survival after death but before resurrection. I will mention several taken from various books and genres in the New Testament.[15]

One frequently cited passage is found in Matthew 10:28, where Jesus is reported as saying: "Do not fear those who kill the body [*sōma*] but cannot kill the soul [*psychē*]; rather fear him who can destroy both soul and body in hell." In English this seems straightforward enough; the body can be killed without killing the soul. Soul and body are therefore distinct and separable. In Greek, however, *psychē* has a wider range of meaning than does "soul" in English; it can mean "life." But even if we were to speak of one's "life" surviving the death of the body, that would seem to include personal survival.

A second passage is the well-known parable of the rich man and Lazarus, found only in Luke 16:19–31. According to this parable, the rich man ignored a poor man named Lazarus, who laid at the rich man's gate. Lazarus died "and was carried away by the angels to be with Abraham" (Luke 16:22). The rich man also died and went to Hades, where he was tormented. The rich man looked up and saw Abraham with Lazarus at his side and begged Abraham to send Lazarus to him with water to ease his torment. But Abraham refused. The rich man asked that Lazarus be sent to the rich man's brothers to warn them. But again Abraham refused: "Abraham replied, 'They have Moses and the prophets; they should listen to them.' He [the rich man] said, 'No, father Abraham; but if someone goes to them from the dead, they will repent.' He [Abraham] said to him, 'If they do not listen to Moses and the prophets, neither will they be convinced even if someone rises from the dead'" (Luke 16:29–31). Now this parable is not primarily about afterlife; it is about the duties of the rich to the poor. But it assumes that the hearers—the people of the New Testament—believe in the survival of persons after death but before resurrection. After all, the rich man has just died, he still has living brothers, he is conscious and carries on a conversation with Abraham. In the same way, the parable of the Good Samaritan is not about roads, travelers, inns, and so forth, but it assumes the existence of these things in the ambient culture. If that assumption were mistaken, the parable would make no sense. So based on this parable it is safe to assume that the idea of personal survival after death was commonly accepted by Luke's audience—and Jesus's audience. Note that in this parable the resurrection of the dead has not yet occurred—the rich man has brothers still living on the earth—and, as N. T. Wright notes, no one at that time imagined the resurrection occurring before the end of history. So the parable must refer to an intermediate state after death.

New Testament scholar Joel Green, however, observes that the characters are portrayed as existing bodily (the rich man's thirsts, they speak, etc.) and questions whether Jesus is speaking of a disembodied existence in this parable.[16] Yet given that this is a parable, it is hard to imagine how else the characters could be portrayed except as physical. Thus I think the physicality of the characters is a storytelling device employed to sharpen the impact of the story on its hearers.

Another passage that indicates many Jews in Jesus's day believed in the possibility of the personal soul or spirit existing outside the body is found in the disciples' reaction to the appearance of the risen Jesus in Luke 24: "Jesus himself stood among them. But they were startled and frightened, and supposed that they saw a spirit [*pneuma*]." Jesus then assured them that he is bodily: "See my hands and my feet, that it is I myself; handle me, and see; for a spirit has not flesh and bones as you see that I have" (Luke 24:36–39 RSV). As Joel Green comments on this passage, "It is difficult not to see in the disciples' responses a dualist anthropology; accordingly, in their imaginative categories, they were encountering a disembodied spirit, a phantasm."[17] This, then, makes the point that the disciples—and presumably other Jews of their day—thought that disembodied personal existence was possible. And this in turn supports the point above, that the presumption of Jesus's parable of the rich man and Lazarus is that the souls or spirits of the dead can continue to exist after death, even though the nature of that state after death and before resurrection was portrayed in various ways in their culture.

Another passage often interpreted as indicating personal survival in an intermediate state between death and resurrection is Jesus's words to the dying thief on the cross: "Truly, I tell you, today [sēmeron] you will be with me in Paradise" (Luke 23:43). "Today" here means the time when the thief will be in heaven, that is, that same day (even Green concedes this).[18] The issue, then, is this: does "Paradise" refer to heaven, in which the thief will exist after death but *before* the general resurrection, or does it mean that the thief goes directly to his eternal, and hence resurrected, state?[19] The former seems far more likely than the latter. We have seen that there was a widespread belief in an intermediate state after death in the Judaism of Jesus's day.[20] If, by contrast, we are to believe that Jesus meant the thief would be resurrected immediately after his death (while his dead body was still on earth), we would have to attribute to Jesus a belief in what is called "immediate resurrection." But this belief, though defended by some writers today, is not taught anywhere in the New Testament. Jesus, when he is talking about the end times (Mark 13), seems to think that the resurrection will be preceded by very hard times; Paul also thinks of the "Day of the Lord" [the time of judgment] as in the future: "Let no one deceive you in any way; for that day will not come unless the rebellion comes first and the lawless one is revealed" (2 Thess. 2:3). Thus it seems far more probable that the thief will be with Jesus "today" in heaven, but not in a resurrected state; in other words, he will be with Jesus in heaven in an intermediate state, before the resurrection of the dead. And this means that his soul will be in heaven, but not his body (which would have remained on earth).

An intermediate state also seems to be implied in the following statement from Paul:

> For we know that if the earthly tent we live in is destroyed, we have a building from God, a house not made with hands, eternal in the heavens. For in this tent we groan, longing to be clothed with our heavenly dwelling—if indeed, when we have taken it off we will not be found naked. For while we are still in this tent, we groan under our burden, because we wish not to be unclothed but to be further clothed, so that what is mortal may be swallowed up in life. He who has prepared us for this very thing is God, who has given us the Spirit as a guarantee.
>
> So we are always confident; even though we know that while we are at home in the body [sōma] we are away from the Lord—for we walk by faith, not by

sight. Yes, we do have confidence, and we would rather be away from the body [*sōma*] and at home with the Lord. (2 Cor. 5:1–8)

At first sight this passage is perplexing, and it has occasioned a good deal of exegetical comment. Yet if we recall that for Paul our body of flesh and blood—our earthly tent—must be transformed into a glorified body to enter the kingdom of God, the passage becomes clearer. The house not made with hands, which is in the heavens, is that glorified body with which we will be clothed in the resurrection. How then could we be found "naked" after we have taken off this earthly body but before we are clothed in the glorified body? This "nakedness" would seem to refer to the intermediate state. This state occurs after we have died and have been stripped of the earthly body but before we have put on the resurrected glorified body, which will occur only at the end of time—the parousia—when the Lord comes again. I agree with Ben Meyer that Paul here implies not two states of life—earthly tent and resurrected body— but three states of life: earthly body, "naked" separated soul (waiting to be clothed with the glorified body), and the transformed, resurrected, glorified body. The last state is the best of all, but the second state—being away from the [earthly] body but at home with the Lord (2 Cor. 5:8)—is better than the first state, our earthly life, in which we "groan" under the burden of this earthly tent or body.[21] The only other interpretation of this passage would be the "two-state" theory, that is, that Paul believed that there was only this earthly body and a glorified heavenly body. But that would mean immediate resurrection upon death. And that would be contradictory to the idea of this body being transformed, because Paul knew, as did everyone else, that when people die their bodies do not disappear and become immediately resurrected. Rather, they remain in the earth, from which they will be raised when the Lord returns, as Paul states in 1 Thessalonians.

Another passage that indicates Paul thought it possible to be in a state in which the soul or mind was out of the earthly body, but not yet resurrected, is 2 Corinthians 12:2–4:

I know a person [RSV: man] in Christ who fourteen years ago was caught up to the third heaven—whether in the body [*somati*] or out of the body I do not know; God knows. And I know that such a person—whether in the body or out of the body, I do not know; God knows—was caught up into Paradise and heard things that are not to be told, that no mortal is permitted to repeat.

The person referred to is universally considered to be Paul himself. Here Paul assumes that it is possible to be out of the body, to be conscious, and still be the same person as was in the body while not being resurrected ("being out of the body" could not refer to the resurrection, which is not "out of the body" but in a resurrected body). So even though Paul does not know if he was out of the body or in it, he clearly thinks it is possible that he was out of the body, thus also indicating that he thinks the mind and personal identity can exist out of the body.

The fourth passage I will consider is found in Revelation 6:9–10:

> When he opened the fifth seal, I saw under the altar the souls [*psychas*] of those who had been slaughtered for the word of God and for the testimony they had given; they cried out with a loud voice, "Sovereign Lord, holy and true, how long will it be before you judge and avenge our blood on the inhabitants of the earth?"

The meaning of this passage does not depend on how we interpret the Greek term for soul (*psyche*) because the context makes it clear that the consciousness of those who have been killed, the martyrs, survives even after death. These persons are physically dead but not resurrected. Yet they are conscious and their personalities remain. This is a vision, to be sure, but the author of Revelation 6 takes it for granted that the souls of the dead can survive the death of their bodies. Old Testament scholar James Barr also notes that there was a strong tradition that the martyrs survived (but not their bodies) and came into the presence of God.

> The particular concentration on resurrection, characteristic of Christianity, appears late and seems to be associated with martyrdom. . . . But did the martyrs simply go out of existence until, at some future date, their bodies were recreated? Hardly, and there was a strong tradition that those who passed away passed at once into the divine presence.[22]

These passages make the case that some sort of intermediate state of survival between death and resurrection was envisaged by New Testament writers, even though it was not consistently thought out and even though the usual New Testament word for soul, *psyche*, has a wider meaning than the English term "soul." The widespread influence of Jewish apocalyptic—for example, *1 Enoch*—and its belief in the existence of an intermediate state after death makes this hypothesis even more likely. Yet this does *not* mean that the New Testament teaches a modern kind of dualism, for example, that of Descartes, because it consistently looks forward to the resurrection of the whole person. It is the soul that carries the personal identity of the dying person beyond death to the resurrection of the body in the last days.[23]

New Testament Apocalyptic and Eschatology

We have seen that Jesus's vision of the kingdom of God was apocalyptic and eschatological. Like apocalyptic, the kingdom has both a vertical dimension that reveals the secrets of God and God's plan and a horizontal, future dimension that points toward a coming eschatological judgment and resurrection of the dead. We saw that Paul and many early Christians thought this judgment was imminent.

Jesus's predictions about the suffering and destruction that will precede the end times occur in Matthew 24, Mark 13, and Luke 21. As is often the case with apocalyptic literature, there is no scholarly consensus on how to interpret these New Testament passages. N. T. Wright thinks that the predictions of destruction refer to the destruction of Jerusalem and the temple by the Romans in 70 CE and do not refer to the end of the space-time cosmos, which he believes would have been unthinkable for a Jew.[24] Most scholars, however, think these predictions refer both to the destruction of Jerusalem and to the end of the world, however the latter might be interpreted. The story of the last judgment in Matthew 25:31–46 certainly refers to the end times and has nothing to do with the destruction of Jerusalem. I think certainty about the aim of these passages is unobtainable, but I agree with John Meier that Jesus's message was eschatological and that Jesus himself probably expected the end of the age in the near future.[25] But Jesus also states: "But about that day and hour no one knows, neither the angels of heaven, nor the Son, but only the Father. . . . Then two will be in the field; one will be taken and one will be left. Two women will be grinding meal together; one will be taken and one will be left. Keep awake therefore, for you do not know on what day your Lord is coming" (Matt. 24:36–42).

For each of us, the day we die will be the day the Lord comes to us in judgment. The lesson is clear: we should not be caught unprepared for death but must be ready, whenever it comes.

The most thoroughgoing book of apocalyptic and eschatology in the New Testament is the Apocalypse of John (the book of Revelation).[26] This work was written probably between 95 and 96 CE during the time of the Roman Emperor Domitian (81–96 CE), making it one of the latest books in the Bible. At this time, Christian communities were suffering from severe persecution. Like the book of Daniel, also written during a time of persecution (of the Jewish community, see chap. 1), the message of Revelation is that the righteous martyrs do not die in vain. God remains in control, and the suffering of the present will come to an end. There will be a judgment; the wicked will be terribly punished, and the good will be rewarded and live with God and the

Lamb (Jesus) in a new heaven and a new earth (Rev. 21). Thus Revelation is a book that presents hope in a time of crisis, suffering, and martyrdom.

Like other apocalyptic texts, Revelation is full of vivid and exotic visions, both heavenly and hellish, many of which have entered into Christian art. In Revelation we find visions of God's throne and the Lamb, the four horsemen of the apocalypse, a huge company of saints before the Lamb, angels, the woman clothed with the sun, the great Dragon (Satan), the destruction of the wicked, the fall of Babylon, the resurrection of the dead, the last things, and the heavenly Jerusalem. These are captivating symbols, both exalted and terrifying. But it would be a mistake to take them as literal events on earth. They are visions of realities in heaven—of spiritual warfare between Christ and the angels of God and the evil forces of Satan. Revelation is a great book of hope, with its vision of the risen Christ, who is the Alpha and the Omega; the justification of the righteous; and the heavenly Jerusalem, whose light is from God. But we cannot tell from these visions when or how they will play out on earth. And so we have to be patient and prepared, knowing that all events are in God's hands.

More than any other book in the New Testament, Revelation is concerned with God's wrath and fury. The book is full of terrible punishments and judgments. For example, God sends terrible plagues on the earth, a third of the earth dies, an angel appears with a sharp sickle and harvests the earth: "So the angel swung his sickle over the earth and gathered the vintage of the earth, and he threw it into the great wine press of the wrath of God. And the wine press was trodden outside the city, and blood flowed from the wine press, as high as a horse's bridle, for a distance of about two hundred miles" (Rev. 14:19–20).

These texts can lead to serious misunderstandings about God and human suffering. Though God is often pictured in popular imagination as wrathful and vengeful, theologically we should not think that people suffering from plagues, diseases, or calamities are suffering from God's wrath and so deserve their suffering. Jesus speaks directly against this in Luke: those who perish in a tragedy are not worse sinners than anyone else (Luke 13:1–5). Revelation views people as either saints or wicked, with no middle ground. But living people are almost never like that; almost all of us have both good and evil elements in our characters. The line between good and evil does not run between groups of people but within every human heart. If we tend to think of one group of people as wholly good and another as wholly evil, the only recourse is war. And for Christians, war is not a virtue but rather a vice; Jesus said "Blessed are the peacemakers" (Matt. 5:9). Furthermore, God does not get angry and throw people into hell. Anyone in hell is "there" because he or she has deliberately and freely rejected God. In fact, God is as present in hell as anywhere else, but those in hell have cut themselves off, or tuned themselves out, from God's presence. Their sufferings are spiritual, not physical. The flames of hell—hellfire—are metaphorical, not literal. They could be understood as hatred, for instance. We will discuss the question of heaven and hell in more detail in chapter 9.

Conclusion

We often think of a dualism between earth and heaven, between this life and the next life. But this is not really the New Testament's understanding. While there are several kinds of dualism in the New Testament, one of the most important is that of the forces of good and evil, God and Satan. In this life the forces of evil seem to be winning. But the kingdom and victory of God has been inaugurated by Jesus, who has opened the way to eternal life for those who convert and respond to God's call. For them, death is a transition to a greater and more perfect form of life, eternal life. For those who reject God's call, death is a transition to a lesser state cut off from God, a state Revelation calls the "second death" (Rev. 2:11). Afterlife, therefore, is not a series of extrinsic rewards and punishments; it is the fulfillment and consummation of choices we have made in this life, for or against God. Death is what we call the transition to afterlife. Suffering and death are an unavoidable part of this life; even Jesus, the incarnate Word of God, suffered and died. But what is primary, in the New Testament's view, is where we end up in the afterlife—with God or cut off from God—by our own choice. We may think that our life's journey is ended at death, but that is not the case according to Scripture. Our life is fleeting and short (Ps. 90); we need to take the long view.

3

Death and Afterlife
in the Christian Tradition

Thus, no limit would interrupt growth in the ascent to God,
since no limit to the Good can be found nor is the increasing of
desire for the Good brought to an end because it is satisfied.[1]

Gregory of Nyssa

This chapter will sketch the development of Christian ideas concerning
death and afterlife from the end of the New Testament period to the
beginning of modern times (the seventeenth century, the scientific revolution,
and the philosophy of Descartes). This is, of course, a vast subject, and so the
treatment given here will not be comprehensive. Instead, I will focus on major
themes and figures in the tradition: the themes of martyrdom, the soul, bodily
resurrection, heaven, hell, and purgatory. I will also examine certain pivotal
figures: Justin Martyr, Tertullian, Origen, Augustine,[2] Aquinas, Luther, Calvin,
and Descartes. I will refer the reader to more extensive studies in the notes.

Martyrdom

Martyrdom was prized as a heroic example of dying well in the early church.
The word "martyr" (*martys*) meant "witness." Christians believed that the

martyrs were the ultimate witnesses to the Christian faith. Through their heroic suffering, they gave compelling witness to Christian virtues even under torture. Christ himself was thought to be present to the martyrs, strengthening them in their trials. The martyrs were therefore revered as saints, who went directly to heaven to be with Christ. The days of their deaths were commemorated by the early church.

One of the most moving accounts of martyrdom in all of Christian literature is *The Martyrdom of Perpetua*.[3] Perpetua, a young woman about twenty years old, was martyred with other Christians in Carthage, North Africa, around 203 CE. Her story is preserved in her prison diary and in the narration of her death by Christian eyewitnesses. The account of her suffering and that of her fellow Christians emphasizes the power and grace of God to carry these martyrs through their sufferings to a victorious death and entrance into heaven. Their nearness to heaven is emphasized especially in the visions that Perpetua and the others had of their coming trials.

Perpetua's first vision, which she had while awaiting trial in prison, was of a bronze ladder reaching up to heaven, so narrow that only one person at a time could ascend. Attached to the sides of the ladder were weapons—swords, lances, daggers, and hooks—making the ascent dangerous. Under the ladder was a monstrous dragon, threatening those who tried to climb. Perpetua saw herself ascending the ladder in her vision, protected by the name of Jesus Christ. At the summit was an immense garden with thousands of people in white robes. When Perpetua awoke from this vision, she realized she was to be martyred and gave up any hope in this world. This was remarkable because she was at the time nursing an infant son, whom she later gave over to her mother's care.

Her second vision was of her blood brother, Dinocrates, who had died years before of a cancer that had disfigured his face. In her vision, he was suffering from heat and thirst, still wounded by the cancer, and was near a pool of water whose rim was too high for him to reach. After this vision, she prayed for him for several days, then had another vision. In this second vision, he was healed, clean, and refreshed and the pool of water was now lowered to his waist. There was a golden bowl he could drink from; he was no longer thirsty and was playing as children do. She awoke and realized he had been freed of his suffering. Perpetua had several other visions, one in which she was fighting a gladiator, whom she realized was Satan. But she was victorious.

On the day of her martyrdom, she entered the arena singing songs of victory. She and the other Christians were attacked and mauled by wild beasts, then stabbed to death. Their courage and joy in the face of torture were so impressive that many who saw them converted to Christianity. The ancient church handed on their story as an evident manifestation of the power of the Holy Spirit. Perpetua's vision is important evidence of Christian belief in a transitional state after death, a transitional state that can be affected by the power of the saints' intercessory prayers.

After the Roman Empire became Christian, martyrdom became more rare, until recent times when there has been an increase in martyrs, especially in Communist countries. Martyrdom was therefore reinterpreted to include not only physical sacrifice but also spiritual sacrifice. Gregory the Great insisted on the life of the Christian as a spiritual martyrdom. The daily dying to self and selfishness and the practice of charity to others were understood as a kind of martyrdom that should occur in the life of all genuine Christians.

The stories of the martyrs provide important lessons in how to die well. Almost all deaths involve suffering and therefore a kind of martyrdom. Through their sufferings, the martyrs were purified and drew closer to Christ, who, they thought, suffered with them in their trials and carried them to heaven. In their deaths, they were joined with Jesus Christ, the supreme martyr, who delivered them from the pains of this world into heaven. It is noteworthy that the martyrs believed they would be delivered into heaven immediately upon their deaths. Certainly they believed in the resurrection, but they also believed in the survival of the soul after death. In his final prayer, Polycarp, bishop of Smyrna martyred ca. 155–156 CE, spoke of the "resurrection to eternal life, of soul and body in the immortality of the Holy Spirit; among whom may I be received in thy presence *this day* as a rich and acceptable sacrifice."[4] A third-century Christian bishop in Alexandria, advocating mercy for Christians who had lapsed under the threat of persecution, appealed to the martyrs' example as merciful cojudges with Christ: "Thus even the divine martyrs among us, who now sit by Christ's side as partners in His kingdom, and share His authority, and are His fellow-judges, opened their arms to their fallen brethren who faced the charge of sacrificing."[5]

St. Justin the Martyr

Justin was born in Samaria, studied philosophy (mainly Platonism), and later converted to Christianity.[6] He taught as a Christian philosopher until he was martyred in Rome in 165 CE. He is one of the earliest of the so-called Apostolic Fathers and hence is a valuable witness to the faith of the early church.

A crucial observation that led to Justin's conversion was that Christians did not fear death. "For I myself, too, when I was delighting in the doctrines of Plato, and heard the Christians slandered, and saw them fearless of death, and of all other things which are counted fearful, perceived that it was impossible that they could be living in wickedness and pleasure."[7] Eventually he concluded that the truth taught by the philosophers was most fully expressed in Jesus Christ, the incarnate *Logos* or Word of truth. The mind, Justin thought, could know that God existed, but the soul, when it was set free from the body, could see God when it "gets possession of that which it was wont continually and wholly to love."[8] The soul, then, survived death: "The souls of the pious remain in a better place, while those of the unjust and wicked are in a worse, waiting for the time of judgment."[9] Justin believed that there would be a resurrection of the just and a thousand-year kingdom in which the just will reign with Christ in a renewed Jerusalem. Thereafter would be the final judgment and the resurrection of all the dead, good and evil. The just would live on with God in resurrected bodies that have "put on incorruption,"[10] echoing Paul, while the wicked will be cast into everlasting fire with the devil and his demons.

Thus Justin largely follows the teachings of the New Testament, including the belief in a thousand-year reign of Christ and the saints found in the book of Revelation. He clearly teaches that the soul survives bodily death and the body is resurrected, the same body that the dead carried on earth. These bodies will be fleshly but will also be transformed, rendered incorruptible and immortal by God's grace.

Certainly some Christians found the incorporeality of the soul, and therefore its immortality, an alien concept. The great Christian teacher Origen of Alexandria (see below), for example, debated publicly with fellow Christians who believed that the soul should be equated with the blood and therefore died along with the body,[11] an easy conclusion to draw from passages like the Greek version of Leviticus 17:11 ("the soul of all flesh is blood").

As more Christian authors became involved with the study of Greek philosophy and its Roman spinoffs, such views began to retreat. Depending on the philosophy, however, materialist conceptions of the soul often continued to flourish. This brings us to the thought of the Latin father Tertullian.

Tertullian

Tertullian was born in Carthage ca. 155 CE and died sometime after 220 CE. He was one of the first theologians in the early church to write in Latin rather than in Greek. Among his many writings are a treatise on the soul and an essay on the resurrection.

Tertullian's *Treatise on the Soul* is perhaps the first extended Christian writing on this subject. Tertullian challenges all the philosophical views of the soul prevalent in his own time. In his view, the soul is corporeal (here he follows the Stoics), made of a rarified matter. That is why, he says, the rich man and Lazarus in Luke 16 are portrayed as having bodies even after death. Tertullian understands the soul as the body's principle of vitality, as the seat of intelligence and free will. He also thinks it grows in its capacities along with the growth of the body. The soul of the first man, Adam, was created by God's breath, but each human soul after that derives from its male parent—it is passed on in the semen, a position known as traducianism. Finally, the souls of all survive bodily death. Tertullian thinks they remain in Hades, a vast cavity under the earth, awaiting the final judgment. Hades has two regions, one for the good and another for the wicked. Only the souls of the martyrs go directly to paradise; all others wait in Hades for the judgment and resurrection.[12]

In his treatise *On the Resurrection of the Flesh* (*De carnis resurrectione*)[13] and elsewhere, Tertullian argues that the resurrected body is the same body that dies but is radically transformed. Against pagan philosophers, he defends the goodness of the fleshly body: it was made by God and is animated by the soul so that it is the principal work in God's creation. The flesh accompanies the soul in all human conduct, and so it is appropriate that the flesh accompany the soul in eternity. St. Paul's analogy of the seed (1 Cor. 15) indicates that it is the same body that died that shall rise again. But the body that rises in the resurrection will be fully restored, even if it had been mutilated at death, like the bodies of the martyrs. Finally, Tertullian holds that resurrected saints will be "equal to the angels," as Jesus promised (Luke 20:36 RSV). "We shall then be changed in a moment into the substance of angels, even by the investiture of an incorruptible nature."[14] Thus, like earlier writers, Tertullian insists that Christians hold on to both sides of a paradox: on the one hand, the very same flesh we have in life shall be resurrected—God can reassemble it—and on the other hand, the resurrected saints will be transformed into the likeness of the angels. The damned, however, will be punished in everlasting fire.

Origen

Origen was born ca. 185 CE, probably in Alexandria, Egypt, and died ca. 253 CE in Caesarea in Palestine. A brilliant and original thinker, Origen is justly described as "the first great theologian."[15] He is a man who has left his mark on the entire Christian tradition, East and West, in biblical scholarship, homiletics, spirituality, and systematic theology. His ideas inspired controversy even during his lifetime. Condemnations after his death, especially those en-gineered by the emperor Justinian in the sixth century, resulted in the loss of many of his writings. Enough have survived in the original Greek and in Latin translations, though, to give us a good idea of his theology. Even so, scholars today debate the accuracy of the condemnations, which frequently involved Origen's teachings on matters that had not yet been formally defined by the Christian tradition, such as the doctrine of the Trinity.[16]

Another such unsettled subject was the origin and nature of the soul. In the preface to *On First Principles*, his most important work of speculative theology, Origen claims (correctly) that apostolic tradition has no clear teaching on the origin of the soul. He lists three possibilities: the "traducian" materialist theory held by Tertullian; the soul's direct creation by God in the womb of the mother; and the preexistence of the soul in heaven prior to its entry into the body.[17] Origen favors the third and makes it a basic thesis of his theology. The theory of preexistence owes much to Plato, but Origen believes it is compatible with Scripture, citing passages such as Jeremiah 1:5 and Ephesians 1:4. Even more controversial are Origen's speculations on the resurrection. Ancient accusations that he denies the resurrection of the body are almost certainly wrong. In fact he is wholly committed to a faithful understanding of Paul's teaching in 1 Corinthians 15, trying to express, in a way comprehensible to the best opinion of his day, both the *identity and continuity* of the risen body and also its *transformation* into its glorified state.[18]

Only God, Origen thinks, was truly immaterial. God first created pure intelligences (*noes*) or souls who had ethereal bodies. All these souls except that of Christ grew cold in their love of God and fell away from God to lesser or greater degrees; some became angels, some became human beings, and some became demons. God created the physical world as a habitation for the human souls, a world in which they could find their redemption. Thus created beings find themselves arrayed in a vast hierarchy, some closer to God, some more distant. But all this was according to their own choice, which they made in the precosmic fall.

Origen believes that the purpose of human existence is to become increasingly like God, to participate ever more deeply in the divine life. This process begins in the Christian life on earth and continues after death. Brian Daley writes: "For Origen himself, eschatology was simply part of a larger picture: the grace filled finality of the mystery of growth towards God that is already at the heart of Christian faith and practice."[19]

Origen's idea of afterlife includes both an interim state for "souls unclothed by bodies"[20] and a resurrection. Like Tertullian, he seems to think[21] that the place for disembodied souls includes a "bosom of Abraham" for the just and a place of punishment for the wicked. He suggests that the soul in the afterlife is in some sense material, composed of a subtle wraithlike body. Like Clement of Alexandria, he believes that the punishments of God are educational and meant to improve the state of those being punished. Therefore he holds out the possibility that in the end all persons might be saved—another very modern position, known as "universalism." Here he appeals to Paul's idea in 1 Corinthians 15:24–28 that Christ will destroy every enemy, even death, and hand over the kingdom to the Father so that God "may be all in all." Because he sees all of life and history as a movement back into God, a recovery of the state of original contemplative union, he conceives of the period between death and resurrection as a long period of instruction and preparation for full reunion with God. So he suggests that after death human souls will be sent to a "school for souls."

It is the soul, therefore, not the matter of the body, that provides the continuity between this life, life after death, and the resurrection. Origen thinks of the soul as the form or *eidos* of the body. It is the organizational principle of the body, animating it and organizing it into a unitary whole. This is what ensures personal identity through time. It is obvious to Origen that the matter of the body changes over time but that the form remains the same.[22]

In the resurrection, the *eidos* of the body reconstitutes a resurrected body. This is recognizably the same person. But in the resurrection the person possesses a spiritual and glorified body, *because the soul forms for itself a body suitable to its new environment.*

> And just as we would . . . need to have gills and other endowments of fish if it were necessary for us to live underwater in the sea, so those who are going to inherit [the] kingdom of heaven and be in superior places must have spiritual bodies. The previous form does not disappear, even if its transition to the more glorious [state] occurs, just as the form of Jesus, Moses and Elijah in the Transfiguration was not [a] different [one] from what it had been.[23]

Origen's idea of the form of the body being the principle of continuity and of the body fitting its resurrected environment anticipates modern ways of understanding the resurrection.

Origen's idea, however, was strongly opposed by Methodius of Olympus. In *On the Resurrection*, Methodius argues that the resurrected body will be just like the body we now possess. The risen body of Christ had flesh and bones, and so will our resurrected bodies.[24] As a consequence, the saints will enjoy beatitude on this earth. For Methodius, then, and for most other ancient thinkers, the principle of continuity between the natural body and the resurrected body is the *matter* of the body. This physicalist idea was difficult to defend in ancient times and is difficult to defend today.[25] Even in ancient times, defenders of the physicalist position had to argue that God would somehow miraculously gather all the material particles that had been part of one's body and reassemble them in the resurrected body. Origen alone seems to appreciate the point that matter is always flowing through the body, like water through a river or fountain. Any attempt to make the matter of the body a person's identifying principle is doomed to failure. The principle of its continuity, therefore, has to be the form or pattern. Sophisticated modern thinkers, like John Polkinghorne, argue this very point today.[26] As Carolyn Walker Bynum asserts: "Origen thus solved the problem of identity more successfully than any other thinker of Christian antiquity."[27]

Origen also understood that the resurrected body must have a different *kind of matter* than the natural body. As we saw, this was Paul's idea as well. It was much easier to maintain this position in ancient times, when it was thought that the heavens were composed of a different kind of matter than the earth. Nonetheless, I will argue that any viable concept of the resurrection in contemporary times must also hold that the resurrected body will have a different kind of materiality than our earthly bodies.

Gregory of Nyssa

Gregory (ca. 335–ca. 395) was born in Cappadocia and became bishop of Nyssa, an auxiliary see of Caesarea in Cappadocia. Considered one of the greatest theologians in the Eastern church, he is recognized as one of the fathers of mystical theology in both the East and the West. In his theology, Gregory follows Origen and others—such as his brother, Basil of Caesarea—but he differed from Origen on certain points. He denies that souls were created before "falling" into various degrees of materiality, for example.

Gregory holds that the soul is "an intellectual essence which imparts to the organic body a force of life by which the senses operate."[28] In other words, the soul was immaterial, not material. But he also holds that in the end all human souls will be drawn into the salvation of God. His reason for this is his belief that evil is the corruption of the good and thus has no substance in its own right (this theme is also central to Augustine's theology). Evil, therefore, cannot be permanent; only good, which has real being, can be permanent.

Gregory therefore imagines an eternal progress in knowing and loving God. This mystical ascent into God has no end:

> This truly is the vision of God: never to be satisfied in the desire to see him. But one must always, by looking at what he can see, rekindle his desire to see more.

Thus, no limit would interrupt growth in the ascent to God, since no limit to the Good can be found nor is the increasing of desire for the Good brought to an end because it is satisfied.[29]

The full ability of humans to know and love God has been damaged but not destroyed by original sin, which engendered in humans the "habit of sinning." And so the return to God involves a difficult and painful cleansing or purgation, both on this earth and after death.

Gregory insists on the resurrection of the body and advances the argument that in the resurrection the soul will regather all the material particles that once constituted its body. Thus the body will be identical to the natural body but transformed into a subtle and ethereal body of far greater beauty.[30] "You will behold this bodily envelopment, which is now dissolved in death, woven again out of the same atoms, not indeed into this organization, with its gross and heavy texture, but with its threads worked up into something more subtle and ethereal."[31] Gregory thus unites two strands of ancient thought: the physicalist strand argued by Tertullian, Athenagoras, Methodius, and others, which sees the resurrected body to be composed of the same matter as the earthly body, and the spiritualist tradition coming from Origen, which sees the resurrected body as spiritualized.

The key to Gregory's thought is the idea of mystical ascent into God, the everlasting journey into the infinity of God's love and knowledge. This is a very attractive idea, especially today, when many people think of heaven as "static" and "boring." Gregory's belief that in the end all will be saved was not accepted in the mainstream of Christian tradition, but that very question has been raised again in recent times with renewed urgency; for many people, the idea of an eternal hell where the souls of the damned suffer forever is radically inconsistent with a God of love. Gregory's thought thus remains strikingly relevant today. Indeed, though I will not endorse his universalism (the idea that all are eventually saved), I believe his idea of heaven as an endless growth into fuller participation in God is one of the best ways to think of heaven. We will therefore return to Gregory's ideas in chapter 9.

Augustine

Augustine was born in Thagaste, North Africa, in 354. He was influenced first by Manichaeism, then Neoplatonism, and later converted to Christianity and became bishop of Hippo in North Africa. He lived in troubled times; the Roman Empire had been declining for years, and in 410 Rome itself was sacked by the Western Goths. Augustine died in Hippo in 430, as the Vandal invaders were besieging the city. Augustine's thought and writings dominate the theological tradition in the West, and his later works, particularly *City of God* and *Enchiridion*, had an enormous influence on the shape of medieval Christianity.

Augustine's view of human nature is much more pessimistic than that of Irenaeus, Origen, or Gregory of Nyssa. For Augustine, all humans, even infants, are under the sin of Adam, whose original transgression was communicated to the whole human race. Unless persons convert to Christ, they will go to hell. Even unbaptized infants fall under this condemnation. "Nevertheless, that one sin . . . was of so heinous a character, that in one man the whole human race was originally . . . condemned; and it cannot be pardoned and blotted out except through the one Mediator between God and men, the man Jesus Christ."[32] This pessimistic legacy has been passed on to the medieval West.

Following St. Paul, Augustine argues that physical death itself is the result of Adam's sin. Paul had written: "Therefore, just as sin came into the world through one man, and death came through sin, and so death spread to all because all have sinned" (Rom. 5:12). But the worst death, according to Augustine, is the "death" of the soul, which is incurred through sin and which cuts off the soul from God, its source of life. This does not mean that the soul is annihilated, for the soul is immortal. It means, rather, that the soul suffers apart from God for eternity.[33] Augustine calls the death of the body "the first death." The "second death" is that of the souls of the damned after the last judgment, when their souls will be irrevocably cut off from God. This is the most terrible death because it is eternal.

In the *City of God*, Augustine considers at length the state of the damned in hell. They will be burned with everlasting fire, he thinks, though the intensity of their pain will be proportional to the degree of their sins. He argues from Scripture, and against his more tender-hearted Christian brethren, that the punishment of the wicked in hell will be eternal. He quotes Jesus's words in Matthew 25:46—"And these will go away into eternal punishment, but the righteous into eternal life"—and vigorously rejects Origen's speculation that all might be saved. Accordingly, from the medieval period to modern times the doctrine of the Western church has followed Augustine: the punishments of hell are eternal. Only recently has this teaching been questioned.

For Augustine, there is no doubt that the soul survives bodily death. The "first death" is precisely the separation of the soul from the body. The souls of the martyrs, he thinks, are already in heaven. The souls of the wicked go to a state of punishment: "For the souls which have been separated from the bodies of the godly are at rest, but those of the ungodly suffer punishment until their bodies rise again: those of the godly to eternal life, and those of the ungodly to the eternal death which is called the second death."[34] Some, however, will go to heaven after a period of purgation.

> However, not all men [sic] who endure temporal punishment after death come into those everlasting punishments which are to follow after that judgment. As I have already said, some will receive forgiveness in the world to come for what is not forgiven in this; and these will not suffer the eternal punishment of the world to come.[35]

Augustine's basis for a period of purgation is his belief that the intercession of members of the church for the dead (a long tradition in the Latin church) cannot be in vain. Recall the prayers of Perpetua—a North African saint—for her dead brother Dinocrates. At the end of book 9 of Augustine's *Confessions*, he asks his fellow Christians to remember in their prayers at the altar his dead parents, Monica and Patricius. In a sermon he declares: "There is no doubt that the dead are helped by the prayers of the holy Church, by the saving sacrifice [i.e., the Eucharist], and by the alms given for their souls, in order that God may deal more mercifully with them than their sins have deserved."[36] This thinking laid the foundations for the Western belief in purgatory that is still held in Catholicism but was rejected by Luther and almost all Protestants.

At the resurrection, according to Augustine, the actual earthly material of the body will return to the soul, which will reanimate the body. However, all the material does not have to return to the same part of the body. Like a statue that has been melted down and recast, the same material will be in the body but perhaps in different locations.[37] Following Paul (1 Cor. 15), Augustine also insists that the resurrected bodies of the saints will be "spiritual bodies." "The flesh will then be spiritual, and subject to the spirit; but it will still be flesh and not spirit."[38] The matter of the bodies then will be transformed so that it is incorruptible. In addition, the body will be wholly submitted to the soul and the soul to the spirit so that the body will no longer be able to resist the will of the sanctified soul. So, like Gregory of Nyssa, Augustine integrates the physicalist and the spiritual traditions of the resurrection by insisting on both. The original material particles of the body are recombined but transformed into a spiritual body. Of the nature of that spiritual body, Augustine confesses ignorance: "But no experience that we have yet had enables us to know what the nature of that spiritual body and the extent of its grace will be; and so it would, I fear, be rash to offer any description of it."[39]

The last judgment, in which all the dead will appear and receive judgment "according to their works, as recorded in the books" (Rev. 20:12), will immediately follow the resurrection. Augustine's account of the judgment closely follows that found in Revelation. He even examines the nature of the book of life, which records the life and deeds of each person. We cannot think of this "book of life" literally, for any book that records all the events of a person's life would be too long to read. Instead, he thinks: "We must therefore understand this book to signify a certain divine power, by which it will be made possible for every man to recall to memory all his own works, both good and evil, and for the mind to review them all with miraculous speed, so that each man's knowledge will accuse or excuse according to his conscience."[40] As we will see (chap. 5), this is an amazingly accurate description of the "life review" that many people experience in NDEs.

As soon as the judgment has been accomplished, the present world will be cleansed by fire (see 2 Pet. 3:7) and transformed.

> By that conflagration . . . the qualities of the corruptible elements which were fitted to our corruptible bodies will wholly perish in the burning. Then, by a miraculous transformation, our very substance will take on qualities which belong to our mortal bodies, and the purpose of this will be to equip the world, now made new and better, with a fitting population of men [sic] who are themselves renewed and made even better in their flesh.[41]

The blessed shall live in heaven, in the presence of God and the angels, not in time but in eternal contemplation of God. But it must be remembered, the blessed (in Augustine's view) will be a minority of humankind. Overall, his vision is a somber one that stands in sharp contrast to the generally more optimistic vision of most Christian churches today.

Thomas Aquinas

Aquinas was a Dominican friar and university professor who lived from 1224 to 1274. Gifted with an encyclopedic memory and impressive powers of synthesis, he summarized much of the Latin tradition in theology up to his time. But he was also an innovator. In the first decades of the thirteenth century, Aristotle's physics and metaphysics became available in Latin translation. Aquinas synthesized Aristotle's philosophical framework with the traditional Neoplatonism he inherited through the Latin tradition, especially Augustine.[42] Aristotle's philosophy of form and matter allowed Aquinas to reconceptualize the traditional understanding of the soul and hence the resurrection.

Influenced by Aristotle's treatise on the soul, *De Anima*, Aquinas argues that the human, rational soul is the substantial form of the body. By this he means that the soul is the fundamental organizing principle of the body as well as its principle of life. It is also the source of intelligence or understanding in the human being. This will require some explanation.

The soul is, first of all, the primary organizing principle of the body, without which the body would disintegrate into simpler forms of matter. Explaining Aquinas's view, Etienne Gilson writes: "It is the soul which assembles and organizes what we call today the bio-chemical elements . . . in order to make a living body from them. In this complete sense, the soul is the *first act*; that is, is what makes it to be. Thanks to this first act, the living thing can exercise all its second acts, the vital functions which are its operations."[43] By form, then, Aquinas means the intrinsic organizing principle and structure of a thing, which makes it the kind of thing it is. This form or soul is an active integrating principle, not simply a static pattern. The soul makes the body a substance and an independently existing thing (rather than an accident, which is a characteristic that inheres in something else, like color). Hence Aquinas calls the soul the substantial form of the body.

Aquinas realizes that the matter in a person's body is constantly being replaced so that the identity of a person through time cannot be due to the continuity of the *matter* in that person's body. As he writes in his *Compendium of Theology*: "During the course of the present life, man evidently remains numerically the same from birth to death. Nevertheless the material composition of his parts does not remain the same, but undergoes gradual flux and reflux, in somewhat the way that the same fire is kept up although the logs are consumed and others are fed to the blaze."[44] A person's continuity and identity, therefore, are due to the soul, not the body. It is more correct, then, to say that the body is contained in the soul rather than that the soul is contained in the body. What perdures through time and makes us the same persons from one year to another is the form or pattern of organization of our bodies. For Aquinas, the soul is the principle and source of organization, which makes us the same person in adulthood that we were in infancy.[45]

Aquinas also insists that the human soul is capable of understanding. It is therefore intellectual or rational. Indeed, understanding is its most distinctive act. Aquinas thinks that the soul exercises most of its functions through the body. Sensation, for example, is an act of the soul using bodily organs. But the act of understanding—by which he means understanding a universal category, such as "tree," "triangle," "angel," "infinity," or "God"—does not depend on a bodily organ and is in its essence immaterial.

Understanding is proper to man [*homo*] beyond all other animals. Evidently, man alone comprehends universals, and the relations between things, and immaterial objects, which are perceptible only to the intelligence. Understanding cannot be performed by a bodily organ in the way that vision is exercised by the eye. . . . The intellect knows things in an immaterial fashion, even those things that are by nature material; it abstracts a universal form from its individuating material conditions.[46]

Because the act of understanding is essentially immaterial, Aquinas argues that the soul itself must be immaterial and incorporeal. Otherwise it could not perform an incorporeal act.

Aquinas thinks that the ultimate end of the intellectual soul, and hence of the perfection of the human person, is the beatific vision of God, or the *visio Dei*.[47] The souls of the saints, he affirms, are capable of the beatific vision immediately after death; they do not have to wait for the resurrection of their bodies. "Therefore as soon as the soul of the just man is separated from the body, it sees God, and this is final beatitude."[48]

However, it is only those souls who are entirely purified in their love of God who see God immediately after death. Those who have irrevocably turned away from God will go to hell immediately upon death. And those whose love of God remains to be purified will go to purgatory.[49]

As for the bodily resurrection itself, Aquinas remains firmly within the Latin tradition in holding that we will be resurrected with the same body we have now, including at least some of the same matter. But this matter will be transformed so that it is incorruptible and glorified. Aquinas realized, however, that not all the matter that has ever been part of our bodies could be part of our resurrected bodies in heaven. So we will be raised with "only so much [matter] as will be enough to constitute the species of the parts in integrity."[50]

Aquinas's theory that the soul is the form of the body allows him to arrive at a unique understanding of resurrection. Certainly the resurrection occurs only through the power of God, for it is beyond all powers of nature. But, Aquinas argues, the glorified properties of the resurrected body are mediated to it by the soul, which in heaven is in perfect unity with God and hence can communicate its perfection to the body.

> Therefore the bodies of the risen saints will not be corruptible and will not burden down the soul, as they do now. On the contrary, they will be incorruptible and will be wholly obedient to the soul, so as not to resist it in any way whatsoever. . . .
>
> Since the blessed soul, owing to its union with the first principle of all things, will be raised to the pinnacle of nobility and power, it will communicate substantial existence in the most perfect degree to the body. . . . And thus . . . the soul will render the body *subtle* and *spiritual*. The soul will also bestow on

the body a most noble quality, namely the radiant beauty of clarity. Further, because of the influence emanating from the soul, . . . the body will be *impassible*. Lastly, since the body will be wholly submissive to the soul . . . , it will be endowed with *agility*.[51]

Thus the resurrected body is, as it were, an *expression* of the purified soul, which is united with God. The soul is primary, but the soul is meant to inform a body and so would be incomplete without a resurrected body. In fact, it seems that the resurrected body might add a mode of knowing to the soul in heaven, because without the body, it can know things only "generally and indistinctly in the manner in which things are known through universal principles."[52] Through the risen body, the beatified soul is also able to know using the senses and thus know individual things. Even though Aquinas holds that the blessed soul in heaven possesses the full vision of God, he also holds that the resurrection of the body will add something to the happiness and knowledge of that soul in heaven.[53]

Finally, we might ask if Aquinas envisions a resurrected creation as a complement to the resurrected body. For what would be the point of a resurrected body without a resurrected environment? In Romans 8:21, Paul writes that "the creation itself will be set free from its bondage to decay and will obtain the freedom of the glory of the children of God." The belief that creation itself will be transformed and glorified in the resurrection has been held by the Eastern Orthodox churches. But Aquinas, reflecting the more narrow focus of the Latin tradition, holds that the entire creation will be purified with fire in the last days and that only the four elements and the resurrected bodies of the saints will survive, though both will be transformed into a better existence.[54] (We will consider this problem of a resurrected creation in chapter 7.)

Aquinas's ideas concerning the soul and resurrection were challenged in his own time, and some of his propositions were even condemned because he seemed to undermine the solidity of the resurrected body by making primary the soul and the form of the body.[55] Yet his ideas have stood the test of time and fit much better with contemporary theories of the soul and resurrection than do the ideas of his predecessors. We will return to a consideration of Aquinas's ideas when we discuss the nature of the soul in chapter 6 and the resurrection in chapter 7.

Martin Luther

Martin Luther (1483–1546) was an Augustinian monk and a professor of Scripture at the University of Wittenberg. Though it was not his intention to split the church, Luther's theological ideas and reforms became the basis for the Lutheran church and for the Protestant Reformation. Central to Luther's theology was what he called his theology of justification, that is, how one becomes justified or righteous before God (see chap. 8).

Luther emphasizes Paul's teaching that we are justified by faith: "For we hold that a person is justified by faith apart from works prescribed by the law" (Rom. 3:28). We can never be justified by works, Luther argues, but only by faith in Christ, who has paid the price for our sins. Works, therefore, are useless for salvation; justification is through faith in Christ alone. Luther put this article of faith front and center in the Smalcald Articles, which he wrote in 1537, nine years before his death.

> The first and chief article is this, that Jesus Christ, our God and Lord, "was put to death for our trespasses and raised again for our justification" (Rom. 4:25). He alone is "the Lamb of God, who takes away the sin of the world" (John 1:29). . . . Moreover, "all have sinned," and "they are justified by his grace as a gift, through the redemption which is in Christ Jesus, by his blood (Rom. 3:23–25) . . . it is clear and certain that such faith alone justifies us, as St. Paul says in Romans 3, "For we hold that a man is justified by faith apart from the works of the law" (Rom. 3:28), and again, "that he [God] himself is righteous and that he justifies him who has faith in Jesus (Rom. 3:26)."[56]

Luther believes that no human work can contribute to salvation, and he is reluctant even to admit that we cooperate in our own salvation. Salvation comes entirely as a gift from Christ. Though humans are free to decide small things, they cannot decide to be saved, for even their will to be saved comes from Christ. As Luther writes, "I believe that by my own reason or strength I cannot believe in Jesus Christ, my Lord, or come to him."[57] This leads Luther to reject the importance of pious works. Even works of charity do not avail us for salvation, though a Christian once justified by faith should do good works.[58] Luther therefore rejects both the teaching on purgatory and the belief in the intercession of the saints as a form of salvation by works. The individual, he says, is saved by faith in Christ alone, not by any intercession or by the prayer of others or by the work of priests or sacraments. "Consequently, purgatory and all the pomp, services, and business transactions associated with it are to be regarded as nothing else than illusions of the devil, for purgatory, too, is contrary to the fundamental article that Christ alone, and not the work of man, can help souls."[59]

What, then, did Luther teach about the state of the soul or the person after death? Actually, he says little on the subject. He strongly affirms the last judgment and the resurrection of both the blessed saints and the damned. "In this Christian church he [Jesus Christ] daily and abundantly forgives all my sins, and the sins of all believers, and on the last day he will raise me and all the dead and will grant eternal life to me and to all who believe in Christ."[60] But he says very little about the state of the saints in the resurrection. As for the souls of the dead before the resurrection, he thought of the souls as "asleep."

> Luther generally understands the condition between death and the resurrection as a deep and dreamless sleep without consciousness and feeling. When the dead are awakened on the Last Day, they will—like a man who wakes in the morning—know neither where they were nor how long they have rested. "For just as a man who falls asleep and sleeps soundly until morning does not know what has happened to him when he wakes up, so we shall suddenly rise on the Last Day; and we shall know neither what death had been like or how we have come through it."[61]

The most obvious way to interpret this doctrine is that the soul survives the death of the body and carries with it into the resurrected state the personal identity of the one who has died, even though that person is not aware of the interval between death and resurrection. The soul, then, is not nonexistent between death and resurrection; it continues, but as it were, in a state of sleep, so that the person has no consciousness of the interval.

This, then, is very different from the Catholic conception of the saints enjoying heaven directly after death, but it is also different from much of the teaching of the early church and even from parts of the New Testament (for example, Rev. 6:9–11).

Luther's theology, especially his teaching on the centrality of faith for salvation and the centrality of Scripture, formed the basis for much of modern Protestantism (though the Anabaptist tradition continued to emphasize the importance of works in salvation). Luther's rejection of purgatory and of the intercession of the saints was (and is) followed by virtually all Protestant denominations. And even within the Roman Catholic Church, which still teaches a doctrine of purgatory, purgatory is not much discussed. (We will consider purgatory in chapter 9, as a part of heaven.) However, Luther's doctrine of soul sleep, which was followed in some Anabaptist traditions, was discarded in Lutheranism itself in the seventeenth century. During this period, Lutheranism "once again adopted the medieval tradition and continued it. Before the resurrection, souls live in a blessed condition with Christ even though they are without bodies."[62] Luther's theology also formed the basis for modern individualism, inasmuch as Luther saw the individual as standing alone before

God without intercessors, the benefit of communal prayer, or intermediaries such as priests. Much of his theology was carried on in the teachings of John Calvin, to whose work we now turn.

John Calvin

John Calvin (1509–64), the most important Protestant reformer after Luther, largely followed Luther in his teachings. He was well educated in Greek and Latin, in the Bible, and in the patristic theologians, whom he cites frequently in his main work *Institutes of the Christian Religion*. Even more than Luther, he made Scripture the foundation of his teachings. The Reformed and Presbyterian churches take their origin from Calvin's work, as did the English Puritans and the Pilgrims in New England.

Arguably, the central doctrine in Calvin's theology is the absolute sovereignty of God. God's grace, according to Calvin, is irresistible. Consequently, those God has willed to save—the elect—are infallibly saved, and those God does not will to save are infallibly damned. In Calvin's view, humans possess no free will in matters of ultimate salvation. This gives rise to Calvin's famous, or infamous, doctrine of double predestination: humans are predestined either to heaven or to hell from the first moments of their lives. One would think that this terrible doctrine is depressing, but in practice it is not. The elect do not have to worry about their salvation, which is assured, and so they busy themselves with the work of being Christians in the world.

In discussing the Christian attitude toward death, Calvin focuses on the vanity and unhappiness of life in this world and urges his readers to meditate on death and to lift their hearts and hopes to the next world.

> If heaven is our country, what can earth be but a place of exile? . . . Wherefore, if it becomes us to live and die to the Lord, let us leave the period of our life and death at his disposal. Still, let us ardently long for death, and constantly meditate upon it, and, in comparison with future immortality, let us despise life. . . . Shall the lower animals and inanimate creatures themselves, even wood and stone, as conscious of their present vanity, long for the final resurrection, that they may with the sons of God be delivered from vanity (Rom. 8:19); and shall we . . . enlightened by the Spirit of God . . . rise no higher than the corruption of this earth? . . . Let us hold as fixed, that no man has made much progress in the school of Christ who does not look forward with joy to the day of death and final resurrection (2 Tim. 4:18; Titus 2:13), for Paul distinguishes all believers by this mark.[63]

Note in this passage that Calvin apparently believes the prophecy of Paul in Romans 8 that not only humans but also all other creatures—even wood and stone—will participate in the resurrection.

Calvin argues strongly for the immortality of the soul and adduces many scriptural passages in support of this doctrine, for example, Paul's saying "while we are at home in the body we are away from the Lord" (2 Cor. 5:6). He also argues strongly for the resurrection of the body, both for the just, who will be raised to blessedness, and for the unjust, who will be raised to judgment and torment. The body that is raised, he is sure, will be the same body that died, though the quality of the body will be different. Calvin is less sure about the nature of the intermediate state, though he is sure that the blessed reside in a place of joy and the wicked in a place of gloom:

> Let us be contented with the limits divinely prescribed to us—viz., that the souls of the righteous, after their warfare is ended, obtain blessed rest where in joy they wait for the fruition of promised glory, and that thus the final result is suspended till Christ the Redeemer appear. There can be no doubt that the reprobate have the same doom as that which Jude assigns to the devils, they are "reserved in everlasting chains under darkness, unto the judgment of the great day (Jude 6)."[64]

Calvin, therefore, does not follow Luther in his idea of "soul sleep" but adheres to the larger Christian tradition in assigning places of reward and punishment to the souls immediately after death and in strongly affirming the resurrection of the body. Like Luther, he rejects the Catholic belief of purgatory. Calvin's system of theology was widely influential, perhaps more so than Luther's. Reformed, Presbyterian, and Congregationalist churches take their direction from Calvin, though most of these have renounced the belief of double predestination.

Descartes and the Modern Period

Luther and Calvin belonged to the sixteenth century but in many ways were medieval in their outlooks, particularly in their belief that theology is the supreme science. The early seventeenth century saw the development of modern natural science, which was so successful in its explanations of physical phenomena that it rapidly became the model for all other sciences. Thus the development of modern science marked a decisive break between ancient and medieval thought on the one hand and modern thought on the other. During and after the time of Galileo, Descartes, and Newton, Aristotelian physics was displaced by a mathematical and mechanistic physics that explained natural processes by appealing to mechanical processes alone and eliminated substantial form, formal cause, and purposes (final causes) from scientific explanations.[65] This changed the entire landscape of physics, philosophy, and theology. It also held important implications for the explanation of God, the soul, resurrection, and afterlife. We will study briefly Rene Descartes (1596–1650)—often called the father of modern philosophy—whose thought reflected these changes.

Descartes began his philosophy by doubting everything except what he could prove by certain reason, such as logical or mathematical demonstrations. Like a geometer (for example, Euclid), he sought to build his philosophy on a few simple axioms he thought were self-evident or could be proved by certain reason.

Descartes found that he could not doubt he existed, for in the very process of doubting, he was thinking, and to think he had to exist. Therefore the foundation of his philosophy became "I think, therefore I am." Likewise, his analysis of the soul put the emphasis on thinking rather than on the soul, as Aristotle and Aquinas had done, as the life principle and the principle of organization of the body and the self. Practically speaking, for Descartes the soul became the *mind*. Thus the great problem for his philosophy was how the mind related to the body. Adopting the new science, Descartes concluded that the body was nothing but a collection of atoms organized on mechanical principles. Human bodies and animals were also complex machines, governed by the new scientific laws of mechanics. The mind, Descartes thought, was a "thinking substance" and the body an "extended substance" (that is, it took up space). They were connected, according to Descartes, through the pineal gland. This explanation of how the mind and the body are interconnected was seen as inadequate, even in Descartes' own lifetime, and has no supporters today. What has endured of Descartes' thought is his formulation of a basic problem: if humans are composed of minds and bodies, how are these two aspects interrelated? Indeed, this problem occupies a entire sector of philosophy, namely, the philosophy of mind. So, starting with Descartes, philosophy became concerned with minds and bodies rather than with souls and bodies. Except in some Thomist and Aristotelian philosophies, souls as the life force and organizational principles of bodies have dropped out of contemporary philosophy. Descartes' philosophy was the turning point in this shift. Beginning with Descartes, talk of the "soul" has been increasingly relegated to religion and theology and has been eliminated from the sciences, and largely from philosophy as well.

Many of the challenges to traditional beliefs, including beliefs about God, the soul, and resurrection, were anticipated by Descartes. After his time, nature was increasingly explained mechanistically by the new sciences. Essences, forms, and final causes or purposes were left behind in this new method. This meant that the soul could no longer be understood as the "form of the body." Nor could one appeal to the end or goal of natural entities to prove God, as Aquinas had done, because in scientific thought there were no intrinsic ends or goals of entities. Furthermore, if the matter in the heavens and the matter on earth were the same, as both Galileo and Newton showed, then it became much more difficult to argue for the resurrection. Where was the resurrected body of Christ in the new cosmos? We will consider these objections, and more, in the next chapter.

4

SCIENTIFIC CHALLENGES TO AFTERLIFE

> What we call "mind" today is considered to be nothing more
> than brain activity; put simply, the mind is what the brain
> does.
>
> James S. Nairne[1]

In the last century there has been a mounting challenge to the credibility of traditional notions of afterlife, both the reality of the resurrection of the dead and the existence of the human soul after death, as well as other traditional beliefs, such as the reality of heaven and hell. In this chapter we will deal primarily with the challenges from the natural and social sciences. Then, in the following chapters, we will discuss how these challenges can be answered.

The first challenge comes from physics and cosmology. Whereas ancient and medieval thinkers believed that the heavens and the earth were composed of different types of matter, Galileo and Newton showed that the heavens and the earth are composed of the same matter and are subject to the same laws of nature. This raises the question: where could the resurrected body of Jesus be in our universe? If it really is a different kind of matter, subject to different laws, where would it be? And again, if the dead are to be raised, will it be in this universe or another?

A second challenge comes from the science of history, which began during the Renaissance but was only fully developed in the nineteenth century.

At that time (the nineteenth century), scholars were applying the so-called historical-critical method to the study of the Bible. It was recognized that the stories and the words of Jesus had been passed down orally for decades before they were written down. This raised questions about the authenticity of Jesus's sayings and deeds as reported in the New Testament. In particular, the historical accuracy of the miracle accounts and of Jesus's resurrection were widely doubted by scholars. These questions are still with us.

The development of the theory of evolution forms a third challenge to the traditional Christian story. Evolutionary theory claims to explain the emergence of species, as well as the emergence of humans, by an entirely natural process and so challenges the traditional account that humans were created directly by God. As knowledge of human origins expanded in the twentieth century, it became more difficult to defend the Genesis story of an original paradise and an original couple from whom the whole human race descended. This in turn challenges the traditional Christian teaching on original sin, particularly in its strong form, as developed by Augustine.

Fourth, and most recent, is the challenge from psychology, evolutionary psychology, and the neurosciences. Psychologists no longer talk about the soul but rather speak of the mind. Psychology textbooks do not discuss free will, a topic that is left to philosophy. Evolutionary psychology explains emotions and attitudes, such as love, as the product of evolution and genetics. Finally, modern neuroscience has shown a strong correlation between brain events and mental events.[2] Every thought or experience in our minds seems to be based on a corresponding physical process in some part of our brains. This raises the question: can the mind and personality—and a fortiori the soul—survive the death of the brain? The answer coming from neuroscience is: "No."[3]

We will take up these four challenges sequentially in this chapter.

The Challenge of Physics and Cosmology to the Resurrection

There are at least five areas in which modern cosmology challenges traditional understandings of the resurrection of the body—both the resurrection of Jesus and the resurrection of all the dead at the end of history.

First, the universe is vastly larger than previously conceived, and all the matter in it appears to be of the same type. The stars we see at night are made of the same kind of matter—mainly hydrogen and helium—that we also have on the earth, not a different kind of matter, as the ancients thought. This is evident because the spectral lines of light coming from distant stars are the same as that of light from matter on earth. Furthermore, we can see the various effects of gravity on and in very distant galaxies. So the laws of physics appear to be uniform throughout the observable universe. This raises two sets of questions: Where is the resurrected body of Jesus now (would we find it if we searched every star and planet in the universe)? And where would the bodies of the dead reside when they are resurrected? Recently, some physicists have written about the possibility of other universes, or other domains of this universe, that might have different sets of physical laws.[4] None of these other universes or domains, however, has been observed, and it is questionable whether they even could be observed by our instruments. So their existence is speculative. The consequence of all this is that almost no one who defends bodily resurrection thinks that the resurrected body of Jesus could be found some place in our universe. If it exists, it would have to inhabit a very different kind of universe from ours. Either our universe would have to be transformed in the resurrection or the resurrected dead (including Jesus) would have to inhabit another, parallel universe, which perhaps intersects with ours. We will consider these possibilities in chapter 7.

A second challenge is related to the first. The laws of physics are very well established in the sciences. But the resurrection and ascension of Jesus and the resurrection of the dead seem to go beyond these laws, especially the law of conservation of matter and energy, which is one of the most firmly established laws. Therefore the resurrection must be a miracle, or at least would have to entail a transformation of the laws of nature. But miracles have been widely doubted recently, not only in the sciences but also in much biblical scholarship. It seems that to make a case for the resurrection (of both Jesus and all the dead), then, we will need to make a case for miracles and for the possibility of transforming the laws of nature (see chap. 7).

Third, time and change, or process, are now understood to be intrinsic qualities of matter and bodies as we know them. Matter is always in motion, except at absolute zero. Even elementary particles change. Organic bodies too are always changing—growing, flourishing, dying, and decomposing. So the traditional Christian belief in a resurrected body formed of "incorruptible matter" seems to be an oxymoron and an impossibility in our universe. In light of this, would an incorruptible and therefore changeless body even be a possibility? We now understand that the body takes in and consumes energy continuously. It is like a fountain; it maintains its form, but energy is always passing through it. If the energy stream ceases, the body dies almost immediately. So change seems to be an essential feature of the body as we know it. And so the question: is an incorruptible body even a possibility? This raises the larger question about time in the resurrected state. Will there be time in heaven or will heaven always be the same? Some modern thinkers have argued that time in some form will be a feature of heaven and that heaven is better thought of as an infinite process of growing in knowledge and love than as a static state of timelessness.[5] By contrast, eternity can be thought of as containing yet transcending all time. It could be that heaven is some combination of both these possibilities.

Fourth, we now realize that our human bodies are not isolated from their larger physical environments. They are made of the same matter as the rest of the universe and are constantly exchanging matter with the environment—bringing in food and water and excreting waste. So it is hard to even imagine a resurrection of the dead that does not also entail a resurrection of a much larger environment, perhaps of the whole universe. This possibility is hinted at by Paul, who speaks of the "hope that the creation itself will be set free from its bondage to decay and will obtain the freedom of the glory of the children of God" (Rom. 8:20–21). This would seem to entail a transformed creation, including a transformed kind of materiality, space, and time as the context for the resurrected body. Is this credible? Or should we think of the resurrection as occurring in a parallel universe with very different conditions from our own?

Finally, we must consider the eschatological challenge from cosmology. What does the far future hold for our universe?[6] Presently, the evidence points to a universe that is expanding, and not just expanding but accelerating. If that is the case, the universe will expand forever. After billions of years, the stars will eventually burn out and cool, leaving a universe without light or heat. Life as we know it could not survive in such a universe. An alternative theory suggests that the universe will stop expanding and that gravity will cause it to collapse. In a process that would take billions of years, the universe will collapse into a singularity in which all matter would be compressed into a virtually infinite density. Here again, no life could survive.

There are no better prospects in our own local region of the galaxy. After five billion years or so, our sun will cool and expand, turning into a red giant like the star Betelgeuse. It will expand out to about the orbit of Mars. In this process the earth will be incinerated (note the similarity of this scenario to the biblical prediction in 2 Pet. 3:7 in which the earth will be destroyed and purged by fire). Perhaps human life could move to other planets or moons, but that would only prolong the dying process, because the sun will eventually burn out and go black, leaving the solar system heatless and lightless.[7]

Thus scientific scenarios of the future leave no hope for the survival of life as we know it. The only way out of the eschatological cul-de-sac into which our universe seems to be headed is to imagine resurrected life occurring in some other kind of universe in which the condition of matter and time are quite different from our present universe. We will explore this possibility in chapters 6 and 7.

The Challenge of Historical Science

Ancient and medieval biblical exegetes tended to read Scripture as if it were the direct word of God. Little attention was paid to the human authors, the historical contexts in which particular books were written, or the literary genres of the books. The focus was on the divine message. This unquestioning approach began to change in the Renaissance and accelerated dramatically during the nineteenth century with the advent of historical criticism. The use of such historical scholarship was a major factor in the Reformation. Luther, who had studied the Bible in its original languages, used these methods to challenge a number of traditions that had developed in the Western church, for example, the authority of the papacy and the existence of purgatory. Indeed, a return to the original texts of the Bible, studied in their original languages, became the hallmark of Protestantism. Universities such as Harvard and Yale were set up by Protestants partly to teach the study of Scripture in its original languages.

By the time of the Enlightenment, and even more during the nineteenth century, historical methods were used to study the biblical texts themselves. The aim of biblical historians was to discover as much as possible about the formation of the biblical texts and the cultural contexts in which they were written. The scholarly focus, then, was on the human authors rather than on the divine author. Early on, for example, it was realized that because the Pentateuch contained a number of duplicate passages, it must have been composed from several earlier documents rather than being written by one person, Moses. A landmark book in English was *Essays and Reviews*, published in England in 1860, in which prominent Anglican theologians defended scientific methods of biblical interpretation. Among them was Benjamin Jowett, a professor of Greek at Oxford, who argued that Scripture should be interpreted like any other book, that is, by specialist scholars trained in the original languages.[8]

The emerging science of archaeology also contributed to the historical understanding of biblical texts. For example, the great ancient city of Nineveh, the capital of Assyria, had been destroyed by the Medes in 612 BCE and was later lost to history. Even the knowledge of its whereabouts had been forgotten. But in 1847, the British adventurer Austen Henry Layard discovered the remains of the great palace of Sennacherib in Nineveh and the lost library of Ashurbanipal, which contained twenty-two thousand cuneiform tablets and was one of the largest libraries in the ancient world. Among these tablets was the Akkadian creation myth the *Enuma Elish*, a text which is similar to, and which probably influenced the writers of, the creation account in Genesis. This and the discovery of other ancient creation accounts, such as that of the Egyptians, allowed scholars to re-create the human and cultural contexts in which the Genesis creation accounts were written. For example, the picture of the physical universe we find in Genesis 1–11 is similar to that of other ancient cultures, such as Akkadia and Babylonia: a flat earth, resting on pillars, surrounded by sea, and covered with a dome or firmament, above which were also waters. These waters above the firmament came down as rain, snow, and hail. But they were also the waters released during the great flood, which threatened to overwhelm the earth.

This picture of the physical cosmos does not look anything like the modern one. Rather, it is that of the common culture in which the authors of Genesis 1–11 wrote. If we ask why God didn't reveal a modern picture of the cosmos to these ancient peoples, the answer is obvious: no one in the ancient audience would have believed it (or even understood it). Like good teachers everywhere, the authors of Genesis began with the students where they were. But their writings also contain profound revelations about God and God's relation to humanity, for example, that humans are made in God's image. The point of the Genesis writings is not to reveal the truth about the physical cosmos, which humans can figure out with their own reason and is not relevant to their salvation anyway. Rather, the point is to reveal the truths of faith about God and God's relation to humans. Understood in this way, however, Genesis 1–11 is no longer read as literal history or science but as a symbolic story, a creation myth, which reveals spiritual truth about God and humanity. But for many Christians, this reassessment is a profound challenge; it is the challenge of historical science.

Similar challenges emerged when biblical scholars turned the use of historical-critical methods on the New Testament. An excellent example of this is found in Rudolf Bultmann's 1951 lectures published as *Jesus Christ and Mythology*.[9] Bultmann's thesis is that the fundamental message of Jesus was the preaching of the kingdom of God. But this message was eschatological. The kingdom would not emerge slowly through history but suddenly and supernaturally, through the direct intervention of God: "God will suddenly put an end to the world and to history, and He will bring in a new world of eternal blessedness."[10] Jesus expected this to happen "in the immediate future." Yet, Bultmann writes:

> The hope of Jesus and the early community was not fulfilled. The same world exists and history continues. The course of history has refuted mythology. For

the conception "Kingdom of God" is mythological. . . . Just as mythological are the presuppositions of the expectation of the Kingdom of God, namely the theory that the world, although created by God, is ruled by the devil, Satan, and that his army, the demons, is the cause of all evil, sin, and disease. The whole conception of the world which is presupposed in the preaching of Jesus as in the New Testament generally is mythological; i.e., of the world as being structured in three storied, heaven, earth, and hell; the conception of the intervention of supernatural powers in the course of events; and the conception of miracles. . . . This conception of the world we call mythological because it is different from the conception of the world which has been developed by science . . . and which has been adopted by all modern men . . . modern science does not believe that the course of nature can be interrupted or, so to speak, perforated by supernatural powers.

The same is true of the modern study of history, which does not take into account any intervention of God or of the devil or of demons in the course of history. . . . Modern men take it for granted that the course of nature and history . . . is nowhere interrupted by the intervention of supernatural powers.[11]

One could hardly ask for a better summary of the challenge of modern historical science to Christianity. On the one hand, modern historians have attempted to recover the original meaning of the Scriptures in their original context. This resulted in the recognition that Jesus's message was eschatological and supernatural. On the other hand, modern history incorporates the assumptions of modern naturalistic science—that events can be explained by natural causes—without the need of supernatural causes. Bultmann makes this clear in his critique of miracles:

Modern man acknowledges as reality only such phenomena or events as are comprehensible within the framework of the rational order of the universe. He does not acknowledge miracles because they do not fit into this lawful order. When a strange or marvelous accident occurs, he does not rest until he has found a rational cause.

The contrast between the ancient world-view of the Bible and the modern world-view is the contrast between two types of thinking, the mythological and the scientific.[12]

This critique is obviously relevant to our inquiry in this book because in rejecting miracles, Bultmann also rejects bodily resurrection as mythological and hence no longer credible to modern persons.

Bultmann states the challenge of modern natural science and historical science to traditional Christianity with exceptional clarity. To leave it at this, however, would not be fair to him. His aim is to separate the core of Jesus's message from the mythological conceptions with which it was originally clothed precisely so modern persons can once again hear the real challenge of Jesus's message, which is "to be open to God's future in the face of death and darkness."

> This, then, is the deeper meaning of the mythological preaching of Jesus—to be open to God's future which is really imminent for every one of us; to be prepared for this future which can come as a thief in the night when we do not expect it; to be prepared, because this future will be a judgment on all men who have bound themselves to this world and are not free, not open to God's future.[13]

I agree with this eloquent advice. As I will argue later, it is a mistake to expect eschatological establishment of God's kingdom in our lifetime. Too many people have been mistaken in the past, including Paul and most of the early church. Jesus himself said that no one knew when the last day would come, "neither the angels of heaven, nor the Son, but only the Father" (Matt. 24:36). If Jesus did not know, how can we? We believe, however, that each of us will be summoned into the presence of Christ and God when we die, and we do not know when that will be. So we need to be prepared.

We need to be aware of one more aspect of the challenge of historical science to traditional Christianity. One of the early achievements of historical criticism was the recognition that many of the books of the Bible—Genesis, Exodus, and the four Gospels, for example—were composed in stages and compiled by editors or redactors who used earlier materials. Take, for example, the Gospel of Mark, thought to be the earliest Gospel. Mark is usually dated somewhere between 65 and 70 CE, that is, some thirty-five to forty years after Jesus's death. Mark, if he was the author of the Gospel, was not an immediate disciple of Jesus but a follower of Peter. So Mark, in writing his Gospel, made use of the sayings and deeds of Jesus that were passed on through the oral teaching of Jesus's earliest followers, such as Peter. He may also have used an early written narrative of the passion story that is now lost. This means that the teachings and deeds of Jesus, as recorded by Mark, had been handed down orally for decades and that these sayings and deeds may have been modified in this process of oral transmission, as well as being modified by the final author. That this was the case can be shown by comparing similar passages in different Gospels. The Lord's prayer, for example, is found in both Luke 11:2–4 and Matthew 6:9–13. But Luke's version is about half as long as Matthew's, though recognizably the same prayer. To arrive at Jesus's actual words in the Lord's prayer, we have to attempt a scholarly reconstruction, using both Luke's version and Matthew's version and translating back from Greek into Jesus's original language of Aramaic. Even in this critical instance, we don't have an exact record of what Jesus taught, because his words were not written down by eyewitnesses but were preserved and possibly modified in the oral tradition before being written down by two different authors (Matthew and Luke), each of whom had differing theological agendas (and so may have modified what they wrote accordingly).

This raises the problem: can we recover what Jesus truly said and did during his lifetime? There is now an entire industry of scholars writing their versions of the "historical Jesus." Writers in the Jesus seminar have reconstructed their versions of the historical Jesus, and in the process they have rejected most of the sayings recorded in the Gospels. Typically, the so-called nature miracles, including the resurrection of Jesus, are rejected for the reasons given by Bultmann. The resurrection of Jesus has been reinterpreted to mean that the early Christian community experienced the presence of Jesus in a new way. But Jesus's body did not rise from the dead. The resurrection, in this interpretation, is something that happened to the early community more than it is something that happened to Jesus. And without the resurrection of Jesus, doubt is cast on the Christian belief in an afterlife. Such is the challenge of scientific biblical criticism to traditional Christianity. We will respond to these objections in chapter 7.

The Challenge of Biology and Evolution

The theory of evolution has changed considerably since Darwin's *Origin of Species* was published in 1859. Evolutionary theory has incorporated modern genetics, population statistics, and other disciplines to become a very complex theory or set of theories sometimes called neo-Darwinism. Not all understandings of neo-Darwinism are materialist and atheistic. Some evolutionary biologists are Christians and argue for the compatibility of evolutionary theory with Christianity, a view called "theistic evolution."[14] But most understandings of modern evolutionary theory reinforce a materialistic and naturalistic understanding of humanity and strongly challenge the credibility of belief in a nonmaterial soul.

The first challenge of neo-Darwinist theory is the claim that natural evolution is a complete account of how humans emerged. But this means that nature alone produces humans; God has no role to play. This line of thinking has become much more prominent in recent decades, but we find its beginning in Darwin's own writings. For example, at the end of *The Descent of Man* Darwin considers the origin of human moral beliefs. These, he argues, derive from human social instincts that are themselves the product of natural selection. That is to say, they arose from nature, not from God's revelation (as Jewish, Christian, and Muslim theologians would argue). It is striking how contemporary much of Darwin's writing sounds today. The reason is this quality of naturalism. Darwin occasionally adverts to Christian beliefs, mainly out of concern for Victorian propriety, but Christian beliefs play no part in his explanation of the origin of species or of humanity. What was a tendency or an attitude in Darwin's writings has now become a generally accepted practice and assumption. Whole disciplines, such as evolutionary psychology, are devoted to explaining every human trait naturalistically through evolutionary processes. Religion itself is viewed as contributing to group bonding and thus conferring an evolutionary advantage on groups that are religious. Therefore evolution, naturalistically explained, has become an alternative story for how nature and humans were created. In intellectual circles, it has displaced traditional religious explanations almost entirely.

A second challenge is related to the first. Genesis 1:27 states that human beings were made by God in "the image of God." This has traditionally been interpreted to mean that there is a similarity between God and humans, such that humans can know and love God and participate in God's Spirit. The goal or end of human life is understood by Jews, Christians, and Muslims as knowing and loving God and being with God in the afterlife. But a naturalistic evolutionary understanding of humanity leaves no place for a supernatural end or goal of human life. Hence the Christian teaching that humans have a supernatural destiny of knowing and loving God is undercut by naturalistic evolutionary theories.

A third challenge is this: if humans emerge or evolve gradually from primate ancestors, at what point does the soul develop? Is there a point in evolutionary history at which the first humans appear? It is hard to determine such a point, and so this also undermines the Christian belief in a soul and afterlife.

A fourth major challenge concerns the shift in perception of suffering, death, and evil in nature. In the Genesis story, it is not clear that humans or even animals were mortal until after the fall. Death is one of the penalties imposed on the first man and woman after they ate the forbidden fruit: "you are dust, and to dust you shall return" (Gen. 3:19). Paul taught that death was the penalty for sin and that sin and death came into the world through the sin of Adam (Rom. 5:12). But the new geological knowledge of nature, and Darwin's theory especially, shows that death and extinction played an extensive role in nature eons before the human race appeared on the scene. Darwin wrote: "The extinction of species and of whole groups of species which has played so conspicuous a part in the history of the organic world, almost inevitably follows from the principle of natural selection; for old forms are supplanted by new and improved forms."[15] After Darwin, the view of nature in the Western world became more somber. Natural selection and the Darwinian emphasis on the struggle for existence throughout nature gradually replaced the older Romantic view that nature was a vast sign of both harmony and the Creator, a view that is strikingly portrayed in the paintings of the Hudson River School, especially those of Frederic Church.[16] The Romantic sense of the sublime in nature—"a sense sublime / Of something far more deeply interfused, / Whose dwelling is the light of setting suns, / And the round ocean and the living air, / And the blue sky, and in the mind of man" (Wordsworth, "Tintern Abbey")—gave way to a view of nature as the "survival of the fittest" (Herbert Spencer's phrase) and "nature red in tooth and claw" (Tennyson's phrase).[17] Perhaps we can still see nature as a sacred cosmos, but not without a deep awareness of the conflict, suffering, pathos, and death that are intrinsically woven throughout nature's tapestry.

We will consider these challenges in chapters 5 and 6.

The Challenge of Psychology and Neuroscience

Just as the biblical understanding of human origins is being supplanted by scientific alternatives, so too traditional Christian understandings of psychology are being seriously challenged by recent scientific theories of psychology and neuroscience.

Etymologically, *psychology* means the study of the soul, psyche, or mind. Such study in the West goes back at least to Aristotle or Plato. Psychology textbooks, however, typically state that psychology as a science dates only from 1879, when Wilhelm Wundt established the first psychological laboratory in Leipzig. Before this period, psychology was a branch of philosophy and theology.

Ancient psychology differs in important ways from modern psychology. Philosophers from Plato on, as well as theologians influenced by Platonic thought (for example, Augustine), held that at least part of the mind was spiritual and could know spiritual reality, including God, directly. This knowledge was not mediated through concepts but came through participation in divine grace and contemplation of the goodness and beauty of God. A famous passage from Plato's dialogue *The Symposium* describes the mind contemplating beautiful things and so ascending to the contemplation of perfect Beauty.

> He who has been instructed thus far in the things of love, and who has learned to see the beautiful in due order and succession, when he comes to the end will

suddenly perceive a nature of wondrous beauty . . . which is everlasting, not growing and decaying, waxing and waning. . . . And the true order of going, or being led by another, to the things of love, is to begin from the beauties of the earth and mount upwards for the sake of that other beauty, using these as steps only, and from one going on to two, and from two to all fair forms, and from fair forms to fair practices to fair notions, until from fair notions he arrives at the notion of absolute beauty, and at last knows what the essence of beauty is. This . . . is that life above all others which man should live, in the contemplation of beauty absolute.[18]

Centuries later, Augustine, influenced by Neoplatonism, described the ascent of his own thought from created things to the vision of God:

I had discovered that above my changing mind was the unchangeable and true eternity of truth. And so I went on by stages from bodies to soul, and from this to the inner power of the soul to which the senses present external things. The faculties of animals extend as far as this, and from this point I went on to the faculty of reason to which sense data are referred for judgment. This also found itself in me to be something subject to change. It then . . . raised itself up to the level of its own understanding, freed my thought from the power of habit, and withdrew itself from those crowds of contradictory phantasms, so that it might discover what was that light with which it was illumined when . . . it cried out that the unchangeable is to be preferred to the changeable, and how it was that it had knowledge of the unchangeable itself: for unless it had knowledge in some way of the unchangeable, it could in no way prefer it with certainty to the changeable. And then, in the flash of a trembling glance, my mind arrived at That Which Is. Now, indeed, I saw your *invisible things understood by the things which are made*, but I had not the power to keep my eye steadily fixed; in my weakness I felt myself falling back and returning again to my habitual ways.[19]

Much like Plato's description of the ascent to perfect beauty in *The Symposium*, Augustine lays out the way of ascent to the mystical knowledge of God. Note that for Augustine, the light with which the intellect is illumined is the light of God. Ordinarily the mind is lost in a crowd of contradictory images. So the illumination of divine "light" (a metaphor) is required to arrive at the mystical knowledge of God. This "light" is a grace, a gift of God, and goes beyond the natural powers of the mind. It cannot be known by natural analysis or natural science because it goes beyond the powers of nature. But it can be known in the experience of mystical ascent. Thus, according to Augustine and generations of Christian mystics, it is possible for the human mind to know God directly through the light of divine illumination.

The whole of traditional Christian psychology assumes that we can come to know God not as an *object* but as a *subject* through an intuitive and contemplative process that differs from discursive reason but is more akin to love. And this kind of knowledge of God, the knowledge born of love,[20] is essential to the whole process of Christian dying, because in dying (hopefully) we surrender to and die into the presence of God. We cannot do this if we do not know God intimately, as lover to lover.

This idea is also found in the New Testament, particularly in John's Gospel, in which our interior knowledge of God is mediated through God's love:

> If you love me, you will keep my commandments. And I will ask the Father, and he will give you another Advocate, to be with you forever. This is the Spirit of truth. . . . You know him, because he abides with you, and he will be in you. I will not leave you orphaned; I am coming to you. In a little while the world will no longer see me, but you will see me. . . . On that day you will know that I am in my Father, and you in me, and I in you. . . . Those who love me will keep my word and my Father will love them, and we will come to them and make our home with them. (John 14:15–23)

Paul also speaks of the indwelling of the Spirit: "God's love has been poured into our hearts through the Holy Spirit that has been given to us" (Rom. 5:5). In a famous passage in 1 Corinthians 13 that is often read at weddings, Paul writes of the virtue of love (*agapē*) and says that love never ends, even in heaven. He finishes the chapter with these words: "For now we see in a mirror, dimly, but then we will see face to face. Now I know only in part; then I will know fully, even as I have been fully known" (1 Cor. 13:12). We know God directly through love, but in this life we do not have the full vision of God, which comes in heaven. But even then it will still be a vision mediated by love and by the Holy Spirit, who is the Spirit of love. In this life we participate—that is, share in a part—of the life of the Spirit. This participation is the fruit of faith and results in an intuitive knowledge of God not mediated by concepts or discursive reason.

Yet this idea that we can know God directly through participation and illumination has completely vanished from contemporary scientific psychology, in which the soul has been reduced to the mind, the mind to the brain, and the brain to the product of natural selection.

The challenge of psychology, then, is that as a science it necessarily deals with only what can be observed, measured, and tested. This excludes free will, which is left to philosophy; it excludes the soul, which cannot be measured or tested; it excludes mystical knowledge and spirituality, which is usually assigned to theology. So what traditional Christianity understands as the spiritual capacities of the soul are eliminated in modern psychology. Contemporary psychology typically analyzes mental behavior in terms of social causes, environmental causes, and physiology but not in terms of spiritual factors, which cannot be measured and tested. Alcoholism, for example, is typically considered to be a product of genetic and social factors or upbringing. Free will typically does not figure into the professional scientific literature on alcoholism; nor do spiritual factors, although Alcoholics Anonymous, which urges alcoholics to seek help from a "higher power," has had a long history of successfully treating alcoholism.

Psychology textbooks define psychology as the scientific study of behavior and mind.[21] Thus James Nairne's textbook on psychology defines mind as follows: "What we call 'mind' today is considered to be nothing more than brain activity; put simply, the mind is what the brains does."[22] But this, of course, means that when the brain dies, the mind dies; there can be no soul that survives death. The view that the mind is the brain also raises problems with the reality of free choice. Jeffrey Schwartz, a neuropsychiatrist at UCLA, writes: "It is not merely that the will is not free, in the modern scientific view; not merely that it is constrained, a captive of material forces. It is, more radically, that the will, a manifestation of mind, does not even exist, because a mind independent of brain does not exist."[23] This is the challenge of psychology and neuroscience.

We will consider this challenge in chapters 5 and 6.

5

Near Death Experiences

Death is a lie.

Pam Reynolds[1]

As we have seen, the evidence from evolutionary biology and neuroscience strongly challenges the traditional Christian belief in a soul that survives bodily death. But there are other streams of evidence, usually ignored by those in the sciences, that do support the claim that the mind survives physical death. These are the so-called near death experiences (NDEs).[2]

Near death experiences entered the popular literature in 1975 with the publication of Dr. Raymond Moody's book *Life after Life*. Moody collected accounts for some one hundred fifty persons who nearly died but were resuscitated or revived and reported extraordinary experiences. These persons claim to have been outside their physical bodies, seeing the scene of their accident or operation; they felt themselves pulled into a dark tunnel and encountered at the end of it a brilliant and wonderful light, which radiated love and peace. Moody describes this as a "being of light, a personal being of great love who knew them intimately and questioned them about what they had done with their lives." One woman put it this way: "The first thing he said to me, that he kind of asked me, if I was ready to die, or what I had done with my life that I wanted to show him."[3] Another common feature of NDEs is the so-called life review. People who experience NDEs often see their whole life flash before them in great detail. They see not only the events themselves but also the effects of their actions on others. Often they also encounter dead loved ones in this out-of-body state, including, sometimes, loved ones whom they did not know were dead or relatives they never knew existed. They either choose to or were told to return to their physical bodies because their work on earth was not finished. These experiences, Moody found, were usually life-transforming: people lost all fear of death and became less materialistic, more altruistic, and more spiritual.

These accounts are important to our quest in this book: if people really can perceive, think, remember, and retain their personalities outside of their bodies, as NDE patients claim, then that would constitute powerful evidence for an afterlife. But the claims of NDE patients are contested, especially by scientists who deny that consciousness can exist outside the body and brain. No one denies that many people have these extraordinary experiences near death; the issue is how these experiences are explained. Skeptics usually explain them as due to some physical condition in the brain: lack of oxygen, endorphins, hallucinations, or the dying brain process. Yet those who have had NDEs almost unanimously explain them as genuine out-of-body encounters with spiritual reality, a reality that is much more real than our earthly reality. In this chapter, we will consider the arguments for and against the various interpretations of NDEs and evaluate these experiences as evidence for afterlife.

Out of the Body?

Many near death experiencers claim to perceive events, such as their own resuscitation, from a perspective outside their physical bodies. A striking report of this appears on a BBC-produced DVD titled *The Day I Died*. This video records interviews with a number of near death experiencers, NDE investigators, and NDE critics. One story, that of Pam Reynolds, is particularly relevant to the questions concerning out-of-body experiences.[4] In 1991 Reynolds, a songwriter from Atlanta, began experiencing severe dizziness and head pain. She was diagnosed as having a very large aneurysm at the base of her brain and was given a short time to live. She was referred to Dr. Robert Spetzler, director of the Barrow Neurological Institute in Phoenix, for an experimental surgery nicknamed "operation standstill." In this operation, the patient's body is chilled to between 50 and 60 degrees, all heart and brain activity is stopped, the blood is drained from the brain, the aneurysm is repaired, the blood is pumped back into the patient, and the heart is restarted. This is what happened to Reynolds.[5] She was fitted with instruments to measure her brain waves, heart rate, blood pressure, core body temperature, brain temperature, and blood oxygen levels. Her eyelids were taped shut, and speakers were placed in her ears, which emitted repeated loud clicks to test the responsiveness of the auditory nerve in her brain stem. Thus even if she had been conscious, she could not have seen or heard anything. She was placed under general anesthesia through the use of pentathol, her skull opened with a saw, and the brain cut into so as to gain access to the aneurysm. At the same time, the blood was drained from her body and her body chilled. Her heart was arrested and brain function stopped—the instruments indicated no measurable brain activity. Dr. Spetzler was able to locate the aneurysm, clip it out, and replace it with a healthy blood vessel. The surgical wounds were closed up, the blood warmed and pumped back into her body, her heart restarted, and she was revived. The operation took about four hours.

During this operation, Reynolds had an experience of being pulled out of her body. From outside her body she observed the scene in the operating room. Then she moved through a dark tunnel into an extremely bright light, where she met dead relatives: her grandmother, grandfather, uncle, and cousin. They made it clear to her that she had to return to her body. Here is her story in her own words:

I remember seeing several things in the operating room when I was looking down. I was the most aware that I think I have ever been in my entire life. . . . It was not like normal vision. It was brighter and more focused and clearer than normal vision. . . . There was so much in the operating room that I didn't recognize, and so many people.

I thought the way they had my head shaved was very peculiar. I expected them to take all of the hair, but they did not. . . .

The saw thing that I hated the sound of looked like an electric toothbrush . . . and the saw had interchangeable blades, too, but these blades were in what looked like a socket wrench case. . . .

Someone said something about my veins and arteries being very small. I believe it was a female voice and that it was Dr. Murray, but I'm not sure. She was the cardiologist. I remember thinking that I should have told her about that . . . I remember the heart-lung machine. I didn't like the respirator. . . . I remember a lot of tools and instruments that I did not readily recognize. . . .

There was a sensation like being pulled, but not against your will. . . . It was like the Wizard of Oz—being taken up in a tornado vortex, only you're spinning around like you've got vertigo. . . . The feeling was like going up in an elevator real fast. . . . It was like a tunnel, but it wasn't a tunnel.

At some point early in the tunnel vortex I became aware of my grandmother calling me. But I didn't hear the call with my ears. . . . It was a clearer hearing than with my ears. I trust that sense more than I trust my ears. The feeling was that she wanted me to come to her, so I continued with no fear down the shaft. It's a dark shaft that I went through, and at the very end there was this little pinpoint of light that kept getting bigger and bigger and bigger. The light was incredibly bright, like sitting in the middle of a light bulb. It was so bright that I put my hands in front of my face fully expecting to see them and I could not. . . .

I noticed that I began to discern figures in the light . . . they began to form shapes I could recognize and understand. I could see that one of them was my grandmother. I don't know if it was reality or projection, but I would know my grandmother, the sound of her, anytime, anywhere. Everyone I saw, looking back on it, fit perfectly into my understanding of what that person looked like at their best during their lives. I recognized a lot of people. My uncle Gene was there . . . my grandfather was there. . . . They were specifically taking care of me, looking after me.

They would not permit me to go further. . . . It was communicated to me—that's the best way I know how to say it, because they didn't speak like I'm speaking—that if I went all the way into the light something would happen to me physically. They would be unable to put me back into the body. . . . I wanted to go into the light, but I also wanted to come back. I had children to rear. . . .

My grandmother didn't take me back through the tunnel. . . . My uncle said he would do it. . . . But then I got to the end of it and saw the thing, my body. I didn't want to get into it. . . . It looked terrible, like a train wreck. It looked like what it was: dead. I believe it was covered. It scared me and I didn't want to look at it. It was communicated to me that it was like jumping into a swimming pool. . . . I didn't want to. . . . I felt a definite repelling and at the same time a pulling from the body. . . . It was like diving into a pool of ice water. . . . It hurt![6]

What makes this account extraordinary is the detail, including her descriptions of the scene in the operating room. Dr. Michael Sabom, who was involved in the case, testifies that he at first thought her description of the tool the surgeon used—the bone saw—must be wrong. But he sent for a picture of the saw and in fact it looked just like an electric toothbrush (or a high-rpm handheld drill). It also had many attachments, which were contained in a case that looked just like a socket wrench set. Reynolds's description of this tool and its attachments, therefore, was accurate. She had expected to see a saw, but the tool she actually observed did not look like a saw. But at the time she observed the tool in use, her body was under general anesthesia, her eyes taped shut, her ears plugged, and her brain was inactive. She also described a conversation in the operating room when the surgeons were trying to drain the blood through her femoral artery. She heard the female surgeon say that her artery was too small. In fact, surgeons first tried to access the right femoral artery, but it was too small, so they had to move to the left femoral artery.

Again, her report was accurate. Dr. Spetzler testifies that Reynolds could not have known what the saw and what its attachments looked like before the operation, because these instruments were locked up until just before use to retain their sterile conditions. Nor could she have heard the conversation about her arteries being too small through normal sensory channels. "I don't know how it's possible for it to happen considering the physiological state she was in," Dr. Spetzler said.[7]

Reynolds's account has many of the features that are often found in NDEs: the out-of-body experience, including being able to describe scenes from an out-of-body perspective; the passage through a dark tunnel; the encounter with the light; entering the light; meeting dead relatives; experiencing nonverbal or telepathic communication; a profound sense of peace and love; the desire to remain in the light; and the reluctance to return to the "dead" physical body while at the same time feeling a sense of obligation to return. Also typical is her feeling after recovery: she testifies that she now has no fear of death and thinks that death is a lie.

The ability of NDE patients to accurately describe events going on in the operating room or elsewhere outside the range of their senses is important in the interpretation of NDEs. Among scientists, at least, these experiences are typically explained in terms of physical causes in the brain rather than as actual encounters with spiritual reality. But if NDE patients can accurately describe events they could not have witnessed—either because they were comatose at the time or because these events were outside the range of their senses—then it would seem that NDEs cannot be explained as simply the product of the physical brain. There are hundreds, perhaps thousands, of anecdotal accounts of NDE patients describing events beyond the reach of their senses when they were comatose. Reynolds's account is striking because at the time she was undergoing the NDE, she was connected to monitoring instruments that showed no measurable brain activity.

Some scientific studies support Reynolds's story. One such study was conducted by Dr. Michael Sabom, a cardiologist in Atlanta. Sabom first encountered NDEs in a church discussion of Raymond Moody's famous book *Life after Life*. His initial reaction was skeptical: "I don't believe it."[8] But when he began talking to his patients who had been resuscitated from cardiac arrest, he was astounded to find that some of them indeed had had experiences like those Moody described. So he decided to conduct his own study. He collected accounts from thirty-two patients who were able to accurately describe their own resuscitations, all of which occurred at a time when they were comatose. Some of their accounts contained specific details they could not have known. For example, one patient described the movement of the needles (one fixed, one moving) on the defibrillator; another patient described in detail the defibrillator paddles and equipment; another described his wife, son, and daughter crying in the hall outside the hospital room, at a time when he was unconscious and they were not expected to be there (they had made a surprise visit). Sabom also organized a control group of twenty-five seasoned heart patients who had not been resuscitated or had NDEs. He asked these patients to describe a resuscitation. Twenty of the twenty-five made major errors in their description (for example, they thought that mouth to mouth breathing was used instead of artificial ventilation). Three gave only limited and vague descriptions of CPR procedure that were without error, and two could not describe CPR at all. Thus whereas the control group of seasoned cardiac patients, who might have been expected to be able to describe a resuscitation from their general knowledge, mostly failed, the thirty-two patients who claimed to have seen their own resuscitation during an NDE gave accurate accounts and in some cases provided visual details that they could not have known.[9]

Another study is described by Dr. Pirn van Lommel and others in an article in the British medical journal *The Lancet*. This study reported on the frequency and characteristics of NDEs in 344 patients who were successfully resuscitated from cardiac arrest in ten Dutch hospitals over a period of time.[10] One such patient was brought into the hospital already comatose. A coronary care unit nurse reports:

> During a night shift an ambulance brings in [sic] a 44 year old cyanotic, comatose man into the coronary unit. He had been found about an hour before in a meadow by passersby. . . . When we went to intubate the patient, he turns out to have dentures in his mouth. I remove these upper dentures and put them into the "crash cart." Meanwhile, we continue extensive CPR. After about an hour the patient has sufficient heart rhythm and blood pressure, but he is still ventilated and intubated, and he is still comatose. He is transferred to the intensive care unit to continue the necessary artificial respiration. Only after more than a week do I meet again with the patient, who is by now in the cardiac ward. I distribute his medication. The moment he sees me he says: "Oh, that nurse knows where my dentures are." I am very surprised. Then he elucidates: "Yes, you were there when I was brought into the hospital and you took my dentures out of my mouth and put them onto that cart; it had all these bottles on it and there was a sliding drawer underneath and there you put my teeth." I was especially amazed because I remembered this happening while the man was in deep coma and in the process of CPR. When I asked further, it appeared the man had seen himself lying in bed, that he had perceived from above how nurses and doctors had been busy with CPR. He was also able to describe correctly and in detail the small room in which he had been resuscitated as well

as the appearance of those present like myself. At the time that he observed the situation he had been very much afraid that we would stop CPR and that he would die. And it is true that we had been very negative about the patient's prognosis due to his very poor medical condition when admitted. The patient tells me that he desperately and unsuccessfully tried to make it clear to us that he was still alive and that we should continue CPR. He is deeply impressed by his experience and says he is no longer afraid of death. Four weeks later he left the hospital as a healthy man.[11]

These accounts are particularly well authenticated since they occurred under medical observation. But there are hundreds of similar stories in the literature on NDEs. Indeed, out-of-body experiences are a frequently reported feature of NDEs. In van Lommel's study of 344 patients, 62 reported NDEs, and of those 62, 24 percent reported out-of-body experiences.[12]

Seeing Dead Loved Ones

That persons sometimes during their out-of-body experiences encounter dead relatives whom they had never known or even known about is another striking feature of NDEs. Here is one such story, summarized from P. M. H. Atwater's *The New Children and Near Death Experiences*.

Lynn, from Michigan, had open-heart surgery when she was thirteen. There were complications in the surgery and she experienced herself leaving her body. She moved into the waiting room, where she saw her father crying, which was very unusual. She then moved through a tunnel into a bright light where she encountered the being of light, who told her it was not time for her to die and that she had work to do. But she also encountered a man whom she had never seen before. He told her he was her uncle Franklin. He told Lynn to tell her aunt Dorothy that he was okay and that "the baby is with me. Tell her that I never stopped loving her and that I am glad she got on with her life. Tell her that when her time comes, I will come for her."[13] Sometime after Lynn recovered, she relayed her experience to her family. The reaction was shock and dismay. Her aunt Dorothy, it turned out, had married Franklin years before and had become pregnant. But Franklin left for World War II and was killed in the Italian landings. Dorothy was so upset she had a miscarriage. A year later she married George, to whom she had been engaged before marrying Franklin. George had insisted that Franklin's name never be mentioned and that all pictures of him be destroyed. The relation between Dorothy and Franklin was therefore unknown to her niece, Lynn, until she encountered Franklin in her NDE.

A researcher who has had extensive experience with children and death is Elizabeth Kubler-Ross, who began her psychiatric career investigating the dying. One of her first books on the subject was *On Death and Dying*.[14] In this book she laid out her well-known stages of death: (1) denial, (2) anger, (3) bargaining, (4) depression, (5) acceptance. In this early book, Kubler-Ross thought that a belief in afterlife was a form of denial, that is, a way of not accepting one's mortality. But she changed her opinion completely as a result of her research with children and NDEs. In her later book *On Children and Death*, she writes:

> I have studied thousands of patients all around the world who have had out-of-body or near-death experiences. . . . Many of these people were not ill prior to the life-threatening event. They had sudden unexpected heart attacks or accidents. . . . The common denominator of these out-of-body experiences is that these people were totally aware of leaving their physical body. . . . They found themselves somewhere in the vicinity of where they were originally struck down: the scene of an accident, a hospital emergency room, at home in their own bed. . . . They described the scene of the accident in minute detail, including the arrival of people who tried to rescue them from a car or tried to put out a fire, and the arrival of an ambulance. Yes, they described accurately even the number of blowtorches used to extricate their mangled bodies from the wrecked car. . . . We, naturally, checked these facts out by testing patients who had been blind with no light perception for years. To our amazement, they were able to describe the color and design of clothing and jewelry the people present wore. . . . When asked how they could see, people described it with similar words: "It is like you see when you dream and you have your eyes closed."
>
> The third event they shared was an awareness of the presence of loving beings, who always included next of kin who had preceded them in death. . . .
>
> How does a critical and skeptical researcher find out if these perceptions are real? We started to collect data from people who were not aware of the death of a loved one, and who then later shared the presence of that person when they themselves were . . . at the "gate of no return."

She provides examples, among them the following:

> "Yes, everything is all right now. Mommy and Peter are already waiting for me," one boy replied. With a content little smile, he slipped back into a coma from which he made the transition which we call death.
>
> I was quite aware that his mother had died at the scene of the accident, but Peter had not died. He had been brought to a special burn unit in another hospital severely burnt, because the car had caught fire before he was extricated from the wreckage. Since I was only collecting data, I accepted the boy's information

and determined to look in on Peter. It was not necessary, however, because as I passed the nursing station there was a call from the other hospital to inform me that Peter had died a few minutes earlier.

In all the years that I have quietly collected data from California to Sidney, Australia; from white and black children, aboriginals, Eskimos, South Americans, and Libyan youngsters, every single child who mentioned that someone was waiting for them mentioned a person who had actually preceded them in death, even if by only a few moments. And yet none of these children had been informed of the recent death of the relatives by us at any time. Coincidence? By now there is no scientist or statistician who could convince me that this occurs, as some colleagues claim, as a result of "oxygen deprivation" or for other "rational and scientific" reasons.[15]

Seeing dead loved ones is a frequent event in NDEs. In van Lommel's study, 32 percent of the patients who reported NDEs also reported seeing dead loved ones.[16]

How Are People Transformed by Near Death Experiences?

One of the most frequent consequences of an NDE is a radical change in attitude and lifestyle. NDE patients typically become less materialistic, less selfish, less competitive, more altruistic, and more concerned with persons and with spiritual things. A striking example is the story of Gordon Allen given in the BBC video referenced above. Allen was a very successful but ruthless financier in Seattle when he was taken to the hospital with pneumonia and had an NDE. He separated from his body and traveled into the light, where he felt a profound sensation of love "so totally unconditional that it was overwhelming to me." He was met by a "high spiritual being" who welcomed him as if he were an old friend or a brother. He realized that there was a purpose to everything, that "whatever happened had a point to it." With this came the realization that he had been given his organizational skills and talents for a greater purpose than just making money. He had not fulfilled the purpose of his own life. As he says in the video (twice), "At that moment my life changed." When he recovered, and even as he spoke before the video camera, he claimed that his heart felt as if it were on fire with love. That feeling did not leave him. He determined to leave the business world and pursue another career. Before he left his previous career, however, he contacted the many persons he had known professionally and apologized to them. He said: "I wanted to call you and ask for your forgiveness for what I have done to you." He comments: "If you ever want to hear dead air on a phone, try that." Allen is now a qualified counselor who lives in a small apartment and drives a modest car. But, he says, the richness of his life now compared to what it was is like that of the Sistine Chapel compared to a simple room.

A similar, though not so dramatic, story was given to me by one of my students. His father had been a police officer in St. Paul, Minnesota. In his semiretirement, he had worked part time for the police department whenever the police lieutenant would call him in. He told his wife always to wake him if the lieutenant called. One night he had a serious heart attack and was taken to the hospital. Medical personnel could not revive him, so they called his wife in to speak to him in a last hope of trying to revive him. His wife called to her dying husband: "Mike! Mike!" She told him how much she loved him and pleaded with him not to die, not to leave her alone. But there was no response. Then, in an inspired moment, she yelled at him: "Mike, the lieutenant is on the phone!" And Mike responded; he came back and revived. Later he told his wife that he had heard her calling to him, but that it was so beautiful over there that he did not want to leave. Yet his sense of duty to the lieutenant and the police force persuaded him to return. But his life thereafter changed. He had held grudges, but he quietly made up with all the people he had disliked. He spent his time making wooden lawn ornaments, which he could have sold for profit but instead gave away. He died five years after his heart attack, but those last five years with his wife were the happiest of their lives.

According to Dr. Bruce Greyson, a psychiatrist and NDE researcher, this life-changing behavior is common among survivors of NDEs.[17]

Do Nonreligious People Have Near Death Experiences?

It is not only Christians or religious people who have NDEs. These experiences are reported by people from across all religious and cultural backgrounds, and even from atheists. A particularly striking account is given by Howard Storm. Storm was a professor of studio art at Northern Kentucky University. At thirty-eight years old, he was ambitious and beginning to find some fame as an artist. He despised religion and religious people as being weak. In his words: "They had bought into a fantasy in order to justify their mediocrity."[18] His belief was that "if you are born into this dog eat dog world you might as well be a winner instead of a loser. . . . Being an artist was a way to get what I wanted. You win eternal fame as an artist. . . . I didn't believe in life after death. When you died, it was like having the switch turned off."[19] On a trip with students to Paris in 1985, Storm collapsed in pain and was taken to a Parisian hospital. He had a hole in his duodenum, so that his stomach acids were leaking into his abdomen. He needed surgery immediately (normally people with this condition have a life expectancy of about five hours). But it was a weekend in Paris (June 1, 1985), and there was only one surgeon on duty in the hospital. Storm lay in his hospital bed in intense pain for more than nine hours before a surgeon arrived. During that time he had an out-of-body experience.

He found himself standing next to his bed, looking down at his body. "'Could this be a dream?' I kept thinking. . . . But I knew it wasn't. I was aware that I felt more alert, more aware, and more alive than I had ever felt in my entire life. All my senses were extremely vivid. . . . I had never viewed the world with such clarity and exactness."[20] He screamed and swore at his wife, Beverly, but she could not hear him. Rather, "she remained frozen in the chair next to the bed. I screamed and raged at her, but she just ignored me. No matter how loudly I yelled or cursed at her, there was no reaction."[21] He heard voices calling to him just outside the hospital room door. Not knowing what else to do, he followed them. The way became increasingly cloudy and dark, and there was a profound sense of timelessness. Storm felt increasingly "frightened, exhausted, cold, and lost"; he realized that these terrible beings had promised him help as a ruse to get him to follow them. He refused, and they turned on him and attacked him, tearing his "body" apart.

> To my horror, I realized that I was being taken apart and eaten alive, methodi-
> cally, slowly, so that their entertainment would last as long as possible. . . . These
> creatures were once human beings. The best way I can describe them is to think
> of the worst imaginable person stripped of every impulse of compassion. . . .
> Simply, they were a mob of beings driven by unbridled cruelty.[22]

Even twenty years later, Storm could not bring himself to describe this experience completely: "I haven't described everything that happened. . . . In fact, much that occurred was simply too gruesome and disturbing to recall. I've spent years trying to suppress a lot of it."[23]

In his destitution, and out of his body, Storm began to pray for the first time in his adult life. He didn't know any prayers, so he prayed fragments from Psalm 23, "God Bless America," and the Lord's Prayer. As he prayed, the evil beings drew away, cursing at him. He saw a light like a distant star approaching him as he prayed. Soon the light was upon him and he was within it. It was a living being of perfect love. "This loving, luminous being who embraced me knew me intimately. He knew me better than I knew myself. He was knowledge and wisdom."[24] Storm experienced a painful review of his past life, seeing not only his actions but also their effects on others, what others thought at the time, and so on. He spoke with the luminous being, whom he thinks of as Jesus, and with angels about the many questions he had, such as why does God allow war, what happens to people when they die, and the like. He woke up in his body, still in the Parisian hospital room, just before the surgeon arrived to perform an emergency operation. He barely survived the operation and flew home to the States, where he was hospitalized for an additional five weeks, hovering between life and death. He eventually recovered. Few people believed his story, however. (One who did was a Roman Catholic nun whom he discovered had been praying for him for thirteen years.) He joined a United Church of Christ congregation and continued with his job as a professor of art, even serving a three-year term as chair of the department. His art changed and became more Christian but was turned down by galleries and did not sell. Because he wanted to serve God and Christ, he resigned from his faculty position, went to seminary for several years, and became a pastor of a United Church of Christ in Cincinnati, Ohio, where he now works. His life has been utterly transformed, and that transformation is detailed in his book.

A frequent question concerning NDEs is, Why aren't there more negative near death experiences? Storm has an answer for that:

> Over the years many people have shared their near death experiences with me, many of which were negative experiences. Most of these people have told me that they have not really shared their experiences with anyone because of the shame and ridicule they felt when they did attempt to tell about them. Based on the number of people who have told me about their negative experiences, it appears that these are not uncommon, and it is highly unlikely that anyone will ever hear about them.[25]

Historical Parallels

Another question concerning NDEs is, Are these experiences new, or have they occurred throughout history? In fact world religious traditions and literature are full of encounters of the living with the world of the dead.[26]

Journey to the land of the dead is a central theme in the epic stories of heroes. In *The Epic of Gilgamesh*, Gilgamesh, the legendary ruler of ancient Uruk, searches for immortality by journeying through the underground realm to speak with Utnapishtim, the only human granted immortality by the gods.[27] Odysseus, in book 11 of Homer's *Odyssey*, visits the land of the dead and there speaks with the dead shade of the seer Teiresias, who tells him of the future trials he will endure on his journey home to Ithaca. Aeneus, the hero of Virgil's *Aeneid*, journeys to the underworld, where he sees the punishment of the wicked, the Blessed Groves of the just, the generations of his future descendants, souls yet to be born, and the future of Rome (*Aeneid*, book 6). Dante's great medieval epic, *The Divine Comedy*, is a fictional narrative of Dante's journey through hell, purgatory, and heaven, that is, through the realms of the dead. Finally, even in modern times, if we turn to J. R. R. Tolkien's epic *The Lord of the Rings*, we find that in *The Return of the King* the hero Aragorn journeys to the land of the dead to recruit an army to help him in his battle against the evil forces of Sauron. In these epics, the journey to the land of the dead is difficult, fraught with peril, and terrifying, but it ultimately brings insight, wisdom, life, and victory to the hero. The journey to the realm of the dead reveals the ultimate purpose structure and meaning of life to those who make that journey. Carol Zaleski writes: "These traditions [of the West and the East] . . . see death as a journey whose final goal is the recovery of one's true nature. . . . They agree, moreover, that awareness of death is a precondition for wisdom and that it is necessary to prepare—morally, spiritually, or imaginatively—if one is to die well."[28]

Some accounts in ancient literature claim to report actual NDEs.[29] A vivid account of a near-death vision is given in Bede's *Ecclesiastical History*. A Northumbrian man named Dryhthelm died early in the night. At dawn, however, he came to, terrifying those who were mourning around the "corpse" so that all but his wife fled. Dryhthelm relayed to her the visions he had had of the world of the dead. He had been guided by a man of brilliant countenance to a huge valley with fire on one side and ice and hail on the other. There the souls of men were tossed from one side to the other, enduring first deadly heat then freezing cold. He then entered a place of darkness and saw a pit of terrible flame in which were human souls, like sparks, being tossed up then sucked back into the pit. From there he was taken to the top of an enormous wall, above which he saw a meadow with many groups of people in white robes. Beyond them he saw a more beautiful region of light, which he was not allowed to enter. So shaken by this vision was Dryhthelm that he distributed all his goods among his family and the poor and joined the monastery at Melrose, where he passed the rest of his life in prayer and severe penances (bathing in icy water once a day, etc.). Bede comments that this man's story was a miracle, meant "to rouse the living from spiritual death."[30]

There are many other such stories in ancient and medieval literature. Gregory the Great, for example (in *Dialogues* 4) tells several stories of persons who recovered almost miraculously from death and told stories of seeing the dead and of hellish and heavenly regions. These stories are similar to contemporary NDEs in many ways. The "dead" leave their bodies and meet a being of light or a guide who ushers them through hellish and heavenly regions where they see scenes of judgment. It is in death and the journey to the other world that they come to understand the true goal of their lives and the true moral and spiritual structure of the universe, which had not been apparent to them in their earthly lives.

But the ancient and medieval accounts differ from modern accounts. Concerning this difference, Carol Zaleski writes: "Most striking . . . is the absence from most twentieth century near-death accounts of postmortem punishment: no hell, no purgatory, no chastening torments or telltale agonies at the moment of death."[31] Zaleski thinks this indicates that "near-death experiences and the literature that describes them, are profoundly shaped by cultural expectations."[32]

While I agree that NDEs are shaped by cultural expectations, I also believe that the lack of reports of postmortem punishment in contemporary accounts is due to the fact that people are unwilling to talk about these experiences (as Howard Storm notes) rather than to a general lack of such negative experiences. Indeed one researcher, cardiologist Maurice Rawlings, did find many accounts of hellish experiences but noted that an NDE researcher had to interview the patients as soon as they recovered or they would suppress the memory of these experiences. Furthermore, persons who experience a life review, in which they see all the events of their lives, also experience an intense judgment in which they are very ashamed of many of their actions.[33] (I do not think this "judgment" is the same as either the individual judgment that people undergo at their deaths or the general judgment at the end of history. These are both final judgments [see chap. 8]. But the judgment people receive during NDEs is not final—they can change the course of their lives upon reviving, and they usually do. Therefore I think of these "judgments" during NDEs as anticipations or previews of final judgment.)

Near Death Experiences in Other Cultures

It seems to be true that the explanation and expression of NDEs is culturally mediated so that people explain them in terms of their own culture. Karlis Osis and Erlendur Haraldsson, for example, found that those experiencing NDEs in India often describe the beings they encounter as Hindu deities.[34] Nevertheless, there is a striking similarity in the themes and structures of these experiences from culture to culture and across historical periods. People experience leaving their bodies, traveling through a dark tunnel, and encountering a being (or beings) of light who communicates not with words but through thought transfer; they witness a flashback of their lives (the life review); they witness scenes of intense joy and love but also sometimes witness hellish scenes, and sometimes judgment; they either choose to return to their bodies or are sent back; and after their recovery, their lives are profoundly transformed, namely, they become more concerned with spiritual things, less concerned with material things, and more altruistic and less selfish. Here is one example from Tibet, told by Sogyal Rinpoche:

> A curious phenomenon, little known in the West, but familiar to Tibetans, is the délok. In Tibetan dé lok means "returned from death," and traditionally déloks are people who seemingly "die" as a result of an illness and find themselves traveling in the bardo [the state after bodily death but before reincarnation, in Tibetan Buddhism]. They visit the hell realms, where they witness the judgment of the dead and the sufferings of hell, and sometimes they go to paradises and Buddha realms. They can be accompanied by a deity, who protects them and explains what is happening. After a week the délok is sent back to the body with a message from the Lord of Death for the living, urging them to spiritual practice and a beneficial way of life.[35]

This passage illustrates the point made above: the themes and structures of the NDE appear to be the same in Tibet as in the United States and Europe, but they are interpreted in Buddhist, rather than Christian, terms.

Questions and Objections

The startling experiences and claims indicated above raise all kinds of questions and objections. We will deal with the most common ones in this section and refer the reader to more extensive treatments in the notes.[36] First, are these people really dead? This depends on one's definition of death. Medically, death refers to an absence of vital signs, or "clinical death": no pulse, no breathing, pupils unresponsive to light, and no measurable brain activity. In many cases of NDEs and out-of-body experiences—for example, the case of Pam Reynolds given above—no vital signs are present. But clearly patients who have reported NDEs have been capable of resuscitation; their brains had not decomposed or been shattered by violent trauma. So they are in what we might call an in-between state, neither alive nor irretrievably dead. And this corresponds to their own descriptions. They are not in their bodies, and they feel no pain, even when given electric shocks to resuscitate them.

Could NDEs be due to fraud or deception? It may be that some recently published accounts have been embellished, now that near-death stories have gained a lot of publicity. But when these experiences were first coming to light in the 1970s, people would not talk about them for fear of ridicule and because they were so deeply personal. Moody writes: "I have witnessed mature, emotionally stable adults—both men and women—break down and weep while telling me of events that happened up to three decades before. . . . So to me . . . the notion that these accounts might be fabrications is utterly untenable."[37] It is also noteworthy that many of the investigators—such as Moody, Kubler-Ross, Sabom, and others—initially were very skeptical about the veracity of these accounts and came to accept them only as a result of the testimonies they heard from their own patients.[38] Furthermore, as we have seen, the lives of those experiencing NDEs often change dramatically after their encounter with death. Finally, there are so many similarities among these accounts— such as the out-of-body experiences, the experience of unconditional love, and the encounters with dead relatives—that one would have to suppose a worldwide conspiracy among investigators and experiencers, all of whom have nothing to gain from such a conspiracy but have a lot to lose, namely, their professional credibility.

Could these experiences be due to patients picking up visual or auditory cues from their surroundings either just before they become unconscious or just after they emerge from unconsciousness? The problem with this explanation is that many persons experiencing NDEs report events in the operating room that occurred when they were in deep coma, like Pam Reynolds and the resuscitated Dutch man in van Lommel's study. Or they report on events that occurred out of the range of their senses, and these reports are later corroborated by independent witnesses. Dr. Melvin Morse, for example, reports the case of Katie, a seven-year-old girl who drowned in a pool and was brought into the hospital in a comatose state. She was later revived and reported details of what her family was doing in their home: "she shocked them with her vivid details about the clothing they were wearing, their positions in the house, even the food her mother was cooking."[39] Kubler-Ross describes how patients can describe details at the scene of an accident when they were unconscious. There is some evidence that persons blind from birth can see, for the first time, when they are out of the body in an NDE.[40] The theory of patients picking up visual and auditory cues via their physical senses also does not explain how patients can encounter dead loved ones whom they did not know were dead or in some cases did not know existed. Finally, if NDEs are nothing more than residual memories of events before and after a person passes into unconsciousness, why would patients' lives change so drastically after NDEs?

For all the above reasons, NDEs cannot simply be dismissed as hallucinations. Hallucinations are enormously varied, whereas NDEs share a structural similarity. It should also be noted that patients who have experienced both NDEs and hallucinations say these events are not the same.

Concerning NDEs, a variety of medical explanations are advanced: NDEs are a result of drugs; of a lack of oxygen in the brain; of endorphins; or of the process by which the brain dies, that is, the so-called dying brain hypothesis. We will consider these in order.

Initially, many people dismissed NDEs as the result of drugs. But Moody and many others have noted that, in most cases, no drugs were administered.[41] Dr. Melvin Morse conducted a study in Seattle in which he interviewed children who had experienced cardiac arrest over the previous ten years. Seventy percent of these had had NDEs. "Many of the patients who had full-blown near-death experiences were not being treated with any hallucinogenic medications at all."[42] As a consequence of these studies, and others, skeptics usually do not try to explain NDEs as being caused by drugs but advance different explanations, such as a lack of oxygen in the brain or cerebral anoxia.

Van Lommel, however, notes that only 12 percent of those patients studied—all of whom experienced cardiac arrest—actually had NDEs. If cerebral anoxia were the cause of NDEs, then more of their patients, all of whom suffered interrupted blood flow to the brain, should have reported NDEs. "With a purely physiological explanation such as cerebral anoxia of the experience, most patients who have been clinically dead should report one."[43] Finally, lack of oxygen to the brain cannot explain how patients are able to describe what is going on in the operating room when they are comatose or what is occurring at distant locations. Nor does it explain how these patients can encounter dead relatives whom they did not know were dead.

Could NDEs be due to endorphins? B-endorphin is a substance found within the brain that provides dramatic relief from pain. Sabom cites an article in *The Lancet* that describes the injection of B-endorphin into cerebrospinal fluid of fourteen cancer patients suffering from intractable pain.[44] All experienced complete relief in one to five minutes. This relief lasted from twenty-two to seventy-three hours. As Sabom points out, however, this is at variance with near-death reports, in which relief from pain lasts only as long as the patient experiences being out of the body—usually a period of a few minutes—and returns as soon as the patient is back in the body. If the painlessness associated with NDEs were a result of endorphins, then the effect should last much longer than a few minutes. Furthermore, patients dosed with B-endorphin can still feel light touch. For example, they can feel an IV needle being inserted. One woman who from an out-of-body perspective was "watching" her physician insert an IV noted: "I can remember I couldn't feel when they were putting the needle in. That was unusual because you can usually feel that."[45] Patients out of the body feel nothing whatsoever happening to their physical bodies, even when the doctor is pounding their chests in CPR. For these reasons, endorphins cannot be the explanation for NDEs.

Some researchers think that NDEs are simply the result of the physiological processes that occur when the brain begins to "die." The most detailed account of such processes comes from the British psychologist Susan Blackmore.[46] The crucial question, according to Blackmore, is when NDEs occur. She believes they occur while the brain is still functioning and that the experiences people have are the residues of what their senses picked up as they were entering into or recovering from the comatose state. Yet all such hypotheses fail to explain how people can perceive events occurring while their brains and senses are inactive, as in the case of Pam Reynolds (see above). So the crucial question is whether persons undergoing NDEs actually can perceive events that occur when their senses and brains are inactive.

The final question is, how can people perceive when their body, brain, and normal sensory pathways are not functioning? This appears to me to be the strongest objection to the statements of those who claim to have NDEs. How can they see without using their eyes, hear without using their ears, and so on? When questioned about this, they say it is like seeing when you dream. But this does not really answer the concern, because in dreaming we are still using the brain, though not the eyes. I think we do not have an answer for this objection. Somehow, the mind seems to be able to function outside the body. Van Lommel advances the theory that consciousness is not generated by the brain but received by it, a notion also found in William James. The brain, then, is not the generator and source of consciousness but its receiver, just as a radio receives radio waves. This is a question I will take up in the next chapter when I discuss the soul. I would point out, however, that there was no explanation for gravity when Newton first proposed it. How can any force act across empty space? Newton had no answer, nor was any answer forthcoming until Einstein's theory of general relativity. But gravity was accepted nonetheless after 1683 when Newton published his *Principia*, even though there was no explanation for how it could possibly work until about 1920. The first principle in science is to be open to evidence and not reject evidence because it does not fit with reigning theoretical paradigms. Only in this way can science progress. If evidence is rejected because it does not fit the current explanatory framework, then of course we will never be able to advance beyond the current explanatory framework, and the progress of scientific knowledge will be frozen. This is precisely the charge that scientists have leveled against religion for centuries: religion looks at issues dogmatically, ignores contravening evidence, and so never progresses. But we find the same phenomena in many of the sciences today, where good researchers are simply not open to the possibility of something so radical as near death, out-of-body experiences.

Evaluation of Near Death Experiences

The question of NDEs is not whether they exist; no one denies that at this point. The question is, How are they to be explained? Can materialist or naturalistic causes, such as a lack of oxygen to the brain, endorphins, or the experience of the dying brain, sufficiently explain these experiences? Or, if materialist explanations do not suffice, are these experiences evidence that conscious awareness, perception, and memory can survive outside the body when the brain is inactive? These questions are germane to our inquiry in this book. Any good explanation must be evaluated by how well it explains all the evidence. In courts of law, as in everyday life, an explanation that leaves some of the evidence unaccounted for is a poor explanation.

Scientific explanations, however, are restricted to causes that can be observed, tested, and measured. Any cause—for example, God or the soul—that cannot be observed, tested, and measured is not considered a scientific explanation. This, of course, poses a problem for science in the case of NDEs, because if materialist explanations do not account for all the evidence, then scientists qua scientists have nothing else to rely on to explain them. As scientists they cannot appeal to a disembodied "soul" as an explanation of NDEs, because such an explanation would not be empirically testable.

Thus there are at least two unique problems in trying to evaluate the evidence for NDEs. First, most of the accounts are anecdotal, although there are some scientific studies, such as that of van Lommel.[47] There is, however, an enormous amount of anecdotal evidence. This means one can't evaluate NDEs fairly by referring to only a few scientific studies. One has to read through quite a lot of accounts and evaluate their credibility. Second, the causes of these phenomena may lie outside the purview of natural science. And anyone who is not open to the possibility of such extra-scientific causes will conclude that these must be caused by some materialist factor or another, no matter how strained such an explanation might be. Causal factors like the soul will be excluded a priori.

In the end, therefore, you, the reader, will have to decide on how best to interpret the phenomenon of NDEs. Given the evidence presented above, my own conclusions are as follows: Materialist explanations simply do not account for all the evidence presented by NDEs. At least four types of evidence point beyond materialist or naturalist explanations to the conclusion that the human mind, including perception and memory, can exist outside the body, even when the brain is not functioning.

First, the evidence is wide ranging that persons in out-of-body states can describe events, either in the operating room or elsewhere, that they could not have known through their natural senses. The case of Pam Reynolds, given above, is a good example of this. So is Michael Sabom's study on patients describing their own resuscitations. There are just too many examples, scattered through a wide range of literature, that testify to the ability of NDE patients to describe events occurring outside the range of their senses to not take them seriously. And if these patients did experience this, then their experiences cannot be explained from a materialist perspective.

Second is the change in values, behavior, and lifestyle of the many persons, such as Gordon Allen, who have gone through NDEs. These changes are also not adequately explained by the usual materialist theories. The people who come through NDEs almost unanimously think of these experiences as more real, more "objective," than anything else they have ever experienced, and they change their lives accordingly.

Third is the phenomena of meeting dead loved ones, especially dead persons whom the NDEers did not know were dead. There are many such accounts in the NDE literature, but no materialist explanation seems adequate to explain this phenomenon.

Finally, there is the sheer wealth of testimony, from men and women of all ages, classes, and nations, that attest to these experiences as going beyond what can be explained by present materialist explanations. Almost no one among those actually experiencing NDEs comes back and thinks that his or her experiences were just a result of lack of oxygen to the brain or of endorphins or of a dying brain experience. Reading through hundreds of NDE testimonies and accounts, what is striking is the near-unanimous conviction on the part of NDE patients that their personal consciousness and perceptions do not die with the body. Moreover, these experiences are common enough so that anyone who has the interest can ask around among relatives or friends and probably find a few examples for him- or herself, as I have. That is, interested readers can do some of their own research into NDEs.

The final question we have to ask, To what extent do these NDEs confirm or clash with traditional Christian beliefs about death and afterlife? Clearly there is a great deal of similarity: the consciousness is capable of experience separate from the body; experiencers encounter a being of light and perfect love, like Christ himself. Indeed, many experiencers (for example, Howard Storm) identify this being with Jesus. There is not a judgment in the traditional sense—hearing one's deeds read from the book, as in the book of Revelation, or seeing souls weighed on scales. However, people undergo a profound sense of judgment in experiencing the review of their life and seeing the effects of their actions on others. But it is not the being of light who judges them; it is their own consciences (in the light of a being of perfect love). People often see their dead relatives or friends, which is just what one would expect based on Christian teaching on afterlife. They witness scenes of heavenly beauty, which also fits with Christian descriptions of the afterlife. The lack of hellish visions has bothered some more fundamentalist Christian commentators. Such visions are, however, found in the literature—Howard Storm's testimony is particularly poignant in this regard. Cardiologist Maurice Rawlings also records a number of hellish experiences, as does Margot Grey in *Return from Death*.[48] George Ritchie's book *Return from Tomorrow* contains an appalling vision of hell that does not seem to depend on biblical portraits.[49] Both Storm and Rawlings explain that people are extremely reluctant to describe their hellish experiences and repress them shortly after the experience. This is not surprising in our culture, where the reality of sin, judgment, and hell are widely doubted and ridiculed. In this respect, our culture differs markedly from medieval and ancient cultures, in which the existence of hell and final judgment were widely believed. Finally, and most importantly, people who return from NDEs are convinced that love and the knowledge of spiritual realities are what really count in life. They are also convinced of the unimportance of material pleasures and of money. This is exactly what Jesus taught. I find these experiences, then, to be on the whole profoundly supportive of Christian teaching on death and afterlife.

It is noteworthy that a number of books by Christians, including evangelical Christians, have appeared that strongly assert the veracity of NDEs and their compatibility with Christianity. Howard Storm's is one such book; so is Michael Sabom's *Light and Death*. Evangelical philosophers Gary Habermas and J. P. Moreland's book *Beyond Death* devotes several chapters to NDEs and argues strongly that they support the Christian teaching on the immortality of the soul.[50] Maurice Rawlings is a conservative evangelical who has written several books supporting the compatibility of NDEs and Christianity,[51] and George Ritchie, a psychiatrist who experienced extensive near-death visions in 1943, became a Christian as a result of those visions.[52]

It is true that NDEs are culturally mediated and to some extent reflect the cultural expectations of the experiencers. But it is also true that in many respects the experiences do *not* reflect cultural expectations. Howard Storm's experience of hell is not what one would have expected from the general beliefs of the culture; he saw no demons, devils, flaming pit, and the like, only human beings stripped of all love and compassion and reduced to incarnations of hatred and cruelty. In a culture whose image of judgment is one of an angry God who flings souls into hell, the life review is not what we would have expected; it's a judgment to be sure, but it is very different from the cultural stereotypes and biblical images found in the book of Revelation, for example. Also, the being of light does not, unexpectedly, identify itself as Jesus Christ even to Christians. This is not what Christians expect, and it raises problems for some Christians.[53] If NDEs simply reflected cultural or religious expectations, that would be a strong argument that they were simply occurring in the minds of the experiencers. But they don't. People tend to explain them in the terms of their cultures, but many of the elements are not at all what we would expect if they were simply cultural projections. And that, also, is an argument for their veridicality.

One last point. Many of the people involved in NDE research seem to believe in reincarnation. And some of the experiences do mention this. But many other accounts testify to the vision of dead relatives who died long ago, sometimes forty years or more.[54] This would argue against reincarnation, especially reincarnation as conceived by Mahayana and Tibetan Buddhists, for whom the Bardo state, that is, the state between death and reincarnation, lasts only forty-nine days. Sabom, Ritchie, Rawlings, Habermas and Moreland, and others find no correlation between NDEs and reincarnation. So I think that it is not true that NDEs entail a belief in reincarnation.

Near Death Experiences bring us to a consideration of the nature and state of the soul. Can we counter the arguments against an immortal soul stemming from modern science? If it exists, what is the nature of the soul? These are questions we will consider in the next chapter.

6

ON THE SOUL

But the souls of the righteous are in the hand of God, and
no torment will ever touch them.

Wisdom 3:1

The belief that each human person[1] is composed of an immortal soul and a perishable body is part of the traditional teaching of the Christian church. Thus the Athanasian Creed states: "For just as the reasonable soul and flesh are one man, so God and man are one Christ."[2] The Westminster Confession (1646) declares:

> The bodies of men, after death, return to dust, and see corruption; but their souls (which neither die nor sleep) having an immortal subsistence, immediately return to God who gave them. The souls of the righteous, being then made perfect in holiness, are received into the highest heavens, where they behold the face of God in light and glory, waiting for the full redemption of their bodies; and the souls of the wicked are cast into hell.[3]

The *Catechism of the Catholic Church* states: "The Church teaches that every spiritual soul is created immediately by God . . . and also that it is immortal: it does not perish when it separates from the body at death, and it will be reunited with the body at the final resurrection."[4]

Furthermore, belief in the soul is widespread in Christian popular piety. Catholics pray for the dead (who are presumed to be in purgatory) and pray to the saints (who are thought to be in heaven, but not yet resurrected). Orthodox Christians also pray to the saints. Protestant and evangelical Christians, though they follow Luther in the rejection of purgatory and prayer to the saints, nonetheless have a widespread sense that the souls of their dead survive the death of the body. Indeed, it is rare to meet a Christian who does not believe in the soul. Moreover, belief in some sort of soul is widely held by religions as diverse as African and American native traditions, Chinese religions, Hinduism, and even Buddhism (as we shall see below), which seems to deny the existence of a self.

Thus the widespread rejection of the existence of the soul among academics, especially those in the sciences and in philosophy, is striking. Here, more than elsewhere, there is a wide gulf between popular and academic culture. For example, in the *Stanford Encyclopedia of Philosophy*, a standard in philosophy, there is an entry titled "Soul, Ancient Theories of," but no entry dealing with theories of the soul after the ancient Greek period.[5] Philosophers working in the area of philosophy of mind discuss theories of the mind but not of the soul, which is regarded as an antiquated theory and thus of historical interest only. Recently a number of authors have published books or articles denying the existence of the soul, while others have written to defend the soul. Thus there is an extensive range of opinions about the soul, as well as a very large body of scholarly literature, especially if one includes the closely related area of philosophy of mind.[6] In a short chapter, it is not possible to cover all opinions or positions on the soul. Therefore, after short summaries of the views of the soul in the Bible and the Christian tradition, the challenge of neuroscience, and the evidence of near death experiences, I shall lay out five representative positions on the soul and discuss the strengths and weaknesses of each. In the last part of the chapter, I shall attempt to make a case for a traditional Christian view of a soul that survives bodily death and carries personal identity through an intermediate state to the resurrection at the end of human history.

Views of the Soul in the Bible and in Christian Tradition

We saw that there is a range of views on the soul in the Old and New Testaments. Furthermore, especially in the Old Testament, the understanding of the soul developed over time. In the early texts we find the notion that the shade of the dead person survives in the underworld (usually called Sheol). The shades are ghostly survivals of persons that possess no life force but are sufficient to carry on personal identity in the underworld. In late Jewish apocalyptic literature, Sheol was regarded as an intermediate state where the dead await the resurrection, where the good are rewarded, and where the wicked are punished. In Judaism of the New Testament period, generally, the Pharisees and the Essenes taught that the soul survived bodily death and was reunited with the body in resurrection, whereas the Sadducees denied both the resurrection and the survival of the soul.

There are a variety of beliefs in the New Testament also, and notions of the soul are not well developed. A number of texts, however, point to the widespread New Testament belief that personal identity can survive bodily death. This is the most natural interpretation of Jesus's saying "Do not fear those who kill the body but cannot kill the soul; rather fear him who can destroy both soul and body in hell" (Matt. 10:28). It is the most natural way to interpret the parable of the rich man being punished in Hades and Lazarus resting in Abraham's bosom, and of the souls of the dead martyrs in Revelation 6 calling out for justice. It is the most natural way of interpreting Jesus's promise to the dying thief on the cross: "Truly I tell you, today you will be with me in Paradise" (Luke 23:43). When the risen Jesus appears to his disciples in Jerusalem (Luke 24:37), his disciples think they are seeing a ghost or spirit: "They were startled and terrified, and thought they were seeing a ghost" (*pneuma*; RSV: "spirit"). Even Joel Green, who generally denies the existence of a soul, comments: "It is difficult not to see in the disciples' responses a dualist anthropology; accordingly, in their imaginative categories, they were encountering a disembodied spirit, a phantasm."[7] The disciples' reaction, then, is evidence for the prevalence of the view in the New Testament period that personal identity could exist in a disembodied state. There are many other such passages, especially if we acknowledge that the word "spirit" (*pneuma*) can sometimes, like "soul" (*psyche*), refer to the spirit of a person that survives bodily death. Thus while dying, Stephen prays: "Lord Jesus, receive my spirit" (Acts 7:59). At least two passages in Paul's letters imply the possibility of personal existence outside the body (see chap. 2, above).[8] In sum, then, there is considerable evidence in the New Testament that there was a widespread belief that persons can survive as souls or spirits outside the body, even though the nature of that state was not clearly worked out.[9]

Again, there is a range of views about the soul in the Christian tradition. Some thinkers, such as Tertullian, thought of the soul as composed of a subtle material substance. Most thinkers, however, thought of the soul as immaterial. Origen and Aquinas thought it was the form or formative principle of the body. What is clear, however, is that from very early times, at least by ca. 200 CE, there is a widespread belief that the soul survives bodily death and awaits the resurrection. Perpetua, in 202 CE, had a vision of her dead brother, Dinocrates, and prayed for him. Afterward, she had another vision in which he was comforted. The *Letter to Diognetus*, dated about the end of the second century or the beginning of the third, states: "The soul dwells in the body, but is not of the body. . . . The soul, which is invisible, is confined in the body, which is visible. . . . The soul is enclosed in the body, but it holds the body together."[10] Thinkers as diverse as Tertullian and Aquinas held that the soul was the seat of reason and of free will in the person. Virtually all thinkers thought of the soul as carrying the identity of the person from the death of the body until the resurrection. Finally, from early times it was thought that the souls of the martyrs enjoyed the full presence of God in the afterlife. Aquinas held that the blessed in heaven enjoyed the beatific vision, and therefore a direct vision of God.

Thus from the Bible and the Christian tradition, we can gather several affirmations concerning the soul:

1. It is the seat of consciousness and awareness.
2. It is the seat of personal identity and carries personal identity forward from the death of the body into the resurrection.
3. It is the seat of intelligence, reason, and understanding.
4. It is the seat of freedom (i.e., free choice).
5. It is capable of knowing God directly, at least in heaven. This is evident in the affirmation that the souls of the martyrs behold God in heaven.

We will consider all of these as we develop a theology of the soul in the remainder of this chapter.

Challenges to the Existence of the Soul

We considered a number of challenges to afterlife in chapter 4. The strongest challenge to the soul comes from contemporary neuroscience. Simply put, neuroscience claims that everything that was once explained by an immaterial soul can now be, or soon will be, explained by neuroscience. Since every experience in the mind depends on a brain state, it follows that if the brain dies, no experiencing subject remains. Therefore all experience is explainable by brain states; we don't need to bring in a ghostly soul. Both neuroscientists and philosophers influenced by neuroscience make these claims. Some Christian physicalists, who hold that there is no nonphysical soul in human beings, also claim this and deny the existence of a soul but affirm a resurrection of the body in the end times.[11]

The following statements are representative. Neuroscientist Michael Arbib writes: "Mind has properties (self-consciousness, wonder, emotion, reason) which make it *seem* more than merely material. . . . Yes, people have religious longing; yes, they have a sense of soul. Nonetheless, I believe that all of this can be explained in terms of the physical properties of the brain."[12] Philosopher Daniel Dennett writes: "But this idea of immaterial souls, capable of defying the laws of physics, has outlived its credibility thanks to the advance of the natural sciences."[13] Philosopher Owen Flanagan writes:

> First, we will need to demythologize persons by rooting out certain unfounded ideas from the perennial philosophy. Letting go of the belief in souls is a minimal requirement. In fact, desouling is the primary operation of the scientific image. "First surgery" we might call it. There are no such things as souls, or non-physical minds. . . . There are no angels, nor gods, and thus there is nothing—at least no higher beings—for humans to be in-between.[14]

Christian philosopher Nancey Murphy writes: "The physicalist thesis is that as we go up the hierarchy of increasingly complex organisms, all of the other capacities once attributed to the soul will also turn out to be the products of complex organization, rather than the properties of a non-material entity."[15]

These are formidable challenges to the traditional Christian doctrine of the soul, but we will attempt to answer them in the latter part of this chapter.

Near Death Experiences

In chapter 5, we looked at near death experiences. The evidence from these phenomena points in exactly the opposite direction from that of neuroscience: it indicates that persons can survive the death of their bodies with consciousness intact, something most neuroscientists would say is impossible. My argument concerning NDEs is not that they prove the possibility of out-of-body experiences but that they provide substantial first-person testimony to that effect. By now thousands of persons have testified to having out-of-body experiences in which they claim to be able to perceive their own resuscitation, or other events, from a perspective outside their bodies and therefore not available to their senses. Some scientific studies also support these claims. Also, I noted that almost all of these reports come to us from persons practicing in the applied sciences: mainly medicine and psychology.

Still, the preponderance of scientific evidence at this time strongly favors the challenge of neuroscience. So if we want to say that only scientific studies be accepted as evidence, we will have to reject the evidence for out-of-body experiences. But if we also include testimonial evidence, which is primary in areas such as law and history, then we should take seriously the evidence coming from NDEs.

Five Representative Positions on the Soul

Given this review, then, what can we say about the soul? Here I will present five representative or typical positions. Some positions on the soul, however, don't fit easily into any of these categories; that is unavoidable in any typology, especially in an area as complex as this one. The categories are as follows: (1) metaphysical materialism (sometimes called reductive physicalism); (2) nonreductive physicalism, or emergent monism; (3) substance dualism; (4) holistic or emergent dualism; and (5) reincarnation. One can find many Christians in categories 2–4 and a few Christians in category 5. Category 1, metaphysical materialism, is incompatible with Christianity and most other religions because it holds that the only reality is matter, and therefore no spiritual God could exist.

The last position I will discuss is my own proposal, in which the soul is understood as "subject-in-relation." This is a variant of position 4 (holistic dualism). I propose this as a synthesis of the biblical and traditional Christian positions that also incorporates the findings of neuroscience and near death experiences. It is, I believe, quite close to the position of a majority of Christians, since it argues both for a soul that is created by God and that survives bodily death in an intermediate state and for a resurrection of the dead at the end of time.

Let us consider these categories in order.

Metaphysical Materialism (or Reductive Physicalism)[16]

This position holds that there are no souls, gods, spirits, or angels; only physical beings exist, and everything in the human person will eventually be explainable by purely physical processes. Even our higher states—reason, moral commitments, religious experiences, free choice (if it exists), and so on—will turn out in the end to be nothing but brain processes and the interaction of molecules in neural networks. Biologist and neuroscientist Francis Crick sums up this view forcefully: "The Astonishing Hypothesis is that 'You,' your joys and your sorrows, your memories and your ambitions, your sense of personal identity and free will, are in fact no more than the behavior of a vast assembly of nerve cells and their associated molecules."[17] Not all reductive physicalists would be as radical as Crick; some would make a case for free choice, for example. Generally, this position is aligned with atheism. It is hard to see how a proponent could make a case for God, or any other nonmaterial being, including a soul.

The strength of this position is that it adheres closely to scientific explanations and, indeed, typically holds that only scientific explanations can yield knowledge (a position known as scientism). It is also very simple: only matter exists, and everything in the universe can be explained by matter and its interactions.

The weakness of this position is in what it leaves out. For a start, it has no explanation for what are called *qualia*. Qualia are subjective experiences, such as pain, fear, intentions, beliefs, mental images, mental events, and consciousness itself. Everyone experiences these—indeed, what we experience first of all and most certainly is our own consciousness and mental states. But the problem is that these experiences are accessible only to the person experiencing them and to no one else; they are not publicly accessible. A neuroscientist examining a patient's brain will not find in the brain pain, fear, intentions, beliefs, mental images, or consciousness. Take a simple example: you are searching for your car in a parking lot. You have a mental image of what your car looks like, otherwise you would not find it. But the image in your mind does not exist in your brain as an image; there is no screen where an image appears, there is no light inside the brain, and there is no viewer separate from the brain itself. So where is the image? It exists in your mind, but not in the brain, even if it is correlated with some neural state in the brain. Or consider another, standard example. Mary is a distinguished neuroscientist who is colorblind. She specializes in the neurology of brain states dealing with color and knows everything there is to know about color, except the experience itself: she cannot know what it is like to experience "red." This illustrates that the experience of color cannot be reduced to a state of neural networks in the brain. But this means that the mind cannot be reduced to the brain. Leibniz's law states that if two things are identical, they share in all their properties or characteristics. But the mind experiences states—images, beliefs, intentions, consciousness—that do not appear as such in the brain. Therefore the characteristics or properties of the mind are different from the brain, and the mind is not identical with or reducible to the brain.

Other things are left out of reductive physicalism as well; for example, purpose. Science can discern function—the eye and heart have functions, but science cannot discern intrinsic purpose in human life or in nature. So according to reductive physicalism, there are no purposes in human life or nature; we can construct our own purposes, of course, but there is no objective purpose outside ourselves of which we can be a part.

Finally, there is the question of free choice. Libertarian free choice means that persons can choose one alternative over another, one course of action over another. It does not mean that we are free to do anything. The most basic freedom, according to Jeffrey Schwartz, is the freedom to shift our attention.[18] Even if we are completely paralyzed, we would still be free to change our attention and change our way of thinking. Schwartz has developed this idea into a therapy for obsessive compulsive disorder. The therapy consists in getting the patients to shift their attention from an obsessive thought to another thought. In this way, new neural pathways are formed—simply by shifting attention—and the old, obsessive pathways are gradually de-energized. The question is, Can reductive physicalism give an explanation for true libertarian freedom? Where does the freedom come from? Human free choice carries with it an intention and a purposiveness; I choose to do this and not that. But intentions and purposes cannot be explained on the reductive physicalist model. Perhaps we could say that in human beings freedom is the equivalent of quantum indeterminacy and randomness. But freedom is not random—even physicalists like Owen Flanagan agree on that.[19] If I behave randomly, I am likely to turn randomly in the middle of the block and drive into a house. We would not say that is free choice; it is madness. While some physicalists such as Flanagan do defend free choice, what they actually end up defending is not libertarian freedom but so-called compatibilist freedom, which really means that we are not constrained to do something not that we can freely choose between alternatives. In fact, many reductive physicalists such as Crick do not believe in libertarian free choice. My argument against this position is as follows: one can deny libertarian free choice, but one cannot live and act as if one does not have free choice. So there is a performative contradiction.

There are other arguments to be made against reductive physicalism, and admittedly the arguments given here are just sketches because this is a short chapter. A full cumulative argument against materialism and reductive physicalism would take a book.[20] But enough has been said to give the reader a sense of what is at stake and why many find this position unconvincing. It leaves out too much of what it means to be human. For this reason, some thinkers have moved to another position, described in the following paragraphs.

Emergent Monism or Nonreductive Physicalism

There is a wide range of positions that can be considered emergent monism or nonreductive physicalism, including some atheistic positions.[21] Here I will focus on the Christian version of these positions, particularly as espoused by Nancey Murphy. Murphy defines nonreductive physicalism as follows: "The person is a physical organism whose complex functioning, both in society and in relation to God, gives rise to 'higher' human capacities, such as morality and spirituality."[22] Nonreductive physicalism (as defined by Murphy), then, is first of all physicalism: it holds that there is no nonphysical component, such as an immaterial soul, to the human person. The person is entirely composed of physical material. Nonreductive physicalism differs from reductive physicalism, however, because it denies that all human capacities can be reduced to the physical; human beings possess emergent capacities and powers, such as consciousness, rationality, a moral sense, and spirituality, that cannot be reduced to the physical activities of the brain. Murphy explains emergent properties as follows:

> While emergent properties (such as full-scale language) are dependent on lower-level abilities, they cannot be totally accounted for in terms of lower-level abilities. Thus [Warren] Brown suggests that we use "soul" to designate not a separable part of the person but rather the person's emergent property of capacity for personal relatedness. This capacity, then, is dependent on but not reducible to the neurological features enabling higher forms of cognition.[23]

A similar position to nonreductive physicalism is emergent monism, as explained by Philip Clayton.[24] Like Murphy, he rejects the existence of a soul and argues that persons are only one physical system. But within persons, consciousness and mind emerge and cannot be reduced to physical laws or to physical explanations. Therefore neuroscience will never be able to give a complete explanation of consciousness, which is an emergent property of the brain that must be understood and described using first-person language instead of third-person descriptions. Clayton especially argues that while the brain and neural events influence the mind, the mind as an emergent property of the brain can also influence the brain: "The causal line seems to move 'up' from the physical inputs and the environment to the mental level, then along the line of mental causation—the influence of one thought on another—and then 'down' again to influence other physical actions, to make new records and synaptic connections within the brain, to produce new verbal behaviors, and so on."[25]

Also similar to emergent monism is the view of process thinkers such as Ian Barbour. Process thought, unlike emergent monism, argues that there is a subjective aspect or pole, as well as an objective aspect or pole, to all entities from atoms to organisms. Barbour therefore describes process thought as "dipolar monism."[26] He writes: "We agree that consciousness and mind are emergent new properties found only at high levels of complexity. . . . However, process thinkers diverge from emergent monism by holding that at least a rudimentary form of subjectivity is present actually, and not just potentially, in integrated entities at all levels."[27]

Thus nonreductive physicalism and emergent monism seek to integrate the findings of biology, psychology, and neuroscience with philosophy and Christian theology. In Murphy's view, neuroscience and nonreductive physicalism will eventually be able to explain all that traditional Christianity sought to explain by the soul: mind and consciousness, free choice, a moral sense, and the personal relation with God. This makes the concept of the soul superfluous.

The strength of these positions is their attempt to fully integrate the findings of contemporary science, especially neuroscience, with philosophy and theology. A number of Christian scientists, psychologists, and neuroscientists, such as Warren Brown and Malcolm Jeeves, support some variant of these positions.[28]

There are a number of weaknesses of or challenges from this view, some philosophical, some specifically Christian. Murphy has addressed most of these,[29] and they tend to be very complex, so I will cite only a few of them here. We will begin with a philosophical challenge: Can libertarian free choice be explained as an emergent property of the brain? Let us grant that all or almost all the properties in nature with which we are familiar are emergent properties. Chemical properties are examples of this: what makes water, water and different from a mixture of hydrogen and oxygen is its emergent properties, that is, properties that are true of the whole water molecule and not of its parts. And these emergent properties have emergent causal powers—water can dissolve substances, for example. Granted all this, does that explain libertarian free choice? For all the emergent properties we observe in physical nature are subject to the laws of physics and chemistry. But libertarian free choice seemingly is not; if it is determined by the laws of physics, it is not free, in the libertarian sense. In the technical parlance of philosophy, if a physical system is causally closed, that means any event can be explained by previous physical causes, so to affirm libertarian free choice would seem to deny the causal closure of the physical. Free choice is not a physical cause, so how can it affect the workings of the brain? Thus I (and others) question whether libertarian free choice can be adequately supported by both reductive and nonreductive physicalism or emergent monism.[30] (I will propose below that free choice is due to our interrelationship with God and is not a naturally emergent property.)

There are some specifically Christian concerns with nonreductive physicalism as well. First, the obvious: if there is no soul, how do we account for the continuity of personal identity between death and the resurrection, which is traditionally understood to take place at the end of history? Secondly, this position implies that to have a mind we must have a brain. This would seem to mean that there cannot be angels—because they have no brains and therefore no minds. But this would also seem to be true of God: God does not have a brain; how could God, therefore, on a nonreductive physicalist account, know anything at all? A third problem is overall credibility of this position among the vast majority of Christians (as well as other theists). Most Christians cannot understand believing in God and the resurrection but not believing in a personal soul. Most Christians, at all times, so far as I can see—certainly almost all Catholic and Orthodox Christians—have thought and still think that the whole transcendent spiritual world of angels, saints, and the beloved dead exist *now*, in a spiritual realm, and that they can be addressed in prayer. But on a nonreductive physicalist account, they do not exist now at all but will exist again at the resurrection, in the far future (unless we admit immediate resurrection, a difficult position—see the next chapter). I think this will be very difficult for most Christians to accept. And if it does become Christian doctrine, it will mean, I fear, not that most Christians will become nonreductive physicalists or emergent monists but that they will cease to believe in afterlife at all, much as Reformed Jews have done.

One further point: Christians have typically held that those in heaven could know God directly, face to face as Paul puts it (1 Cor. 13:12). But Murphy holds that our knowledge of God is mediated through the brain: "The physicalist response is to say that all human experience is mediated by the nervous system, and so religious experience must be as well."[31] This would seem to be true even in the resurrected state. But then even in heaven we could not know God directly, through intuition; for that to happen, we would need a spiritual receptor, a faculty by which we could perceive the spiritual God. This is precisely one of the functions of the soul (I argue below). Without such a faculty, we can know God only indirectly, mediated through concepts, images, and feelings, even in the resurrection. But this does not accord with Christian teaching either in the Bible or in the tradition, which has typically held that the blessed in heaven behold God directly, in the beatific vision.[32]

Finally, it is obvious that on a nonreductive physicalist or emergent monist account, the mind cannot exist outside the brain. Therefore, according to this perspective, they would have to hold that there is no truth in the many NDE reports that persons can, on occasion, view events from an out-of-body perspective.

Substance Dualism

Substance dualism is the belief that human beings are composed of an immaterial soul—which is an independently existing entity or substance—and a material body. The soul, being immaterial, does not occupy space, whereas the material body is extended in space and is locatable in space. In the view of substance dualists, it is the soul that thinks and has mental, emotional, and spiritual experiences. And in most views of substance dualism, the soul survives bodily death. Something like this view was held by Plato and his followers, by Augustine (who was influenced by the Neoplatonists), and by those in the Augustinian tradition, including most thinkers up through the medieval period. In the modern period, this view is strongly associated with the philosophy of René Descartes. Descartes came to the conclusion that a human being is composed of a thinking substance, or the mind, which is immaterial and nonspatial, and a body, which is extended in space. His thought is often caricatured as if these two substances—the soul or mind, and the body—scarcely interact with each other, but in fact Descartes held that they were closely connected. "Nature also teaches me by these feelings of pain, hunger, thirst, and so on that I am not only residing in my body, as a pilot in his ship, but . . . that I am intimately connected with it, and that the mixture is so blended . . . that something like a single whole is produced."[33] There is a range of substance dualist positions, however, depending on who is doing the classifying—even Aquinas is sometimes classified as a substance dualist (though I think he is better considered a holistic dualist).

The strength of this position is that it corresponds with a common-sense view of ourselves; most Christians are probably substance dualists. This is because we are all aware of the fact that we have mental events—thoughts, intentions, beliefs, and so on—and we can easily imagine our consciousness as existing outside the body. Substance dualism fits with the testimony from NDEs. Some prominent philosophers are substance dualists, notably Oxford philosopher Richard Swinburne.[34] Some scientists have identified with this position, such as neurologists Wilder Penfield and John Eccles.[35]

Nonetheless, this position has come under heavy attack in recent years; it has almost no support in the sciences and very little in philosophy. It is often caricatured as "the ghost in the machine." One objection is that of neuroscience: we can account for all human experience by the neurology of the brain, so talk of an immaterial soul is superfluous. Another objection is that substance dualists cannot explain how an immaterial soul can influence the material body or how the material body can influence an immaterial soul. If they are so unlike, they should not be able to influence each other at all.[36] If, as substance dualists often argue, reason is an act of the soul, then damage to the brain, drugs, alcohol, and so on should not affect the soul's reasoning power. Substance dualists do have answers to this objection. Most say that there is a high degree of interaction between the soul and the brain, that the soul uses the brain for its functions (this is Swinburne's argument), and so on. But they cannot explain how this is so. Therefore, even though substance dualism has widespread popular support, it has fallen out of favor in academic circles.

Holistic or Emergent Dualism

This position includes an assorted group of thinkers who believe that the person in this life is a psychophysical unity but who also believe that the soul can survive bodily death. I have space to describe only a few of these thinkers here.[37]

HOLISTIC DUALISM

This position seems to fit the biblical view fairly well, with its emphasis on resurrection, which implies that it is the whole person who is resurrected, and its view that the soul can survive bodily death. John Cooper, after an extensive survey of the biblical texts, calls this position "holistic dualism."[38]

It seems fitting to place the view of Thomas Aquinas in this category. Aquinas held that the immaterial soul was the form, that is, the organizing principle and intrinsic pattern, of the body. Consequently, for Aquinas the body and the soul are an integrated entity, in this life at least: "man is not a soul only, but something composed of a soul and body."[39] He also held that the soul could survive the death of the body, but in a deficient state, because it lacked a body. But how, for Aquinas, could the soul survive bodily death at all if its nature is to be the form of a body? Aquinas's answer here is not so clear; the soul, he says, is created by God as a subsistent entity and so subsists after death, even though it needs the body for its full operation. So, in Aquinas's view, God can hold an immaterial form in existence even after death. (He also contends that angels are immaterial yet are held in being by God as immaterial forms.)

The real question for Aquinas's position is, What exactly does he mean by saying that the soul is the "form" of the body? The tradition he is drawing on is Aristotelian philosophy, which analyzed substances as compounds of substantial form and matter. Form was what makes any substance this kind of thing rather than another. This is easy to see in the case of an artifact such as a statue: it is the form or pattern of the marble that makes the statue a statue and another piece of marble a building block or a piece of a marble floor. According to Eleonore Stump, for Aquinas, "The complete form . . . of a non-human material object is the arrangement or organization of the matter of that object in such a way that it constitutes that object rather than some other one."[40] So the form of a molecule would be the arrangement or organization or configuration of its constituent parts. In the case of the soul, Aquinas holds that the soul is also an active organizing principle—it also configures the matter of which it is the form. Hence Stump refers to it as "the soul as subsisting form configuring matter."[41] However, how the soul configures or organizes the matter of the body is an extremely difficult question, which I will leave aside for another time.[42] For our purposes here, it is sufficient to consider the soul as the form or pattern or configuration of the body. This is similar to John Polkinghorne's idea that the soul is the "almost infinitely complex, dynamic, information bearing pattern, carried at any instant by my animated body."[43] (But as well as being an information pattern, the soul has a subjective dimension: it is a subject.) That pattern or form develops as the person matures through life. In this sense then, the soul develops in and through the body and is intimately integrated with the body. But according to Aquinas (and Roman Catholic church teaching) it can survive outside the body as well, if God holds it in existence. This, then, qualifies as a kind of "holistic dualism."

Emergent Dualism

Philosopher William Hasker, in a number of writings, has presented a view that he characterizes as a "middle way" between materialism (including nonreductive physicalism), and (Cartesian) dualism.[44] Hasker's central idea is that the mind, and therefore the soul, emerges as the brain and the self develop in this life. He states: "The human mind is produced by the brain and is not a separate element 'added to' the brain from the outside."[45] God therefore does not create the soul; consciousness develops naturally as the brain develops. This is true in animals as in humans; Hasker's philosophy is therefore easily able to account for animal consciousness in a way that Cartesian dualism does not. So far, then, Hasker's position resembles emergent monism or nonreductive physicalism or property dualism: as the brain develops, the mind develops. But Hasker is not content with saying that emergent powers develop; he thinks this is insufficient. It is insufficient because of what he calls the "unity of consciousness" argument, which posits that our experience of consciousness is that it is a unity, not a collection of parts or powers distributed in different parts of the brain. "A conscious experience simply is a unity, and to decompose it into a collection of separate parts is to falsify it. So it is not enough to say that there are emergent properties here; what is needed is an emergent individual, a new individual entity which comes into existence as a result of a certain functional configuration of the material constituents of the brain and the nervous system."[46] So, a person can be a new emergent substance. Hasker uses the analogy of a magnetic field, which is generated by a magnet but extends past the magnet itself. Under certain conditions, he claims, the magnetic field can even exist if the magnet is destroyed. So also the brain generates a field of consciousness, a "soul field," which is an emergent person. Hasker also thinks that there is a real possibility that persons, so formed, can be kept in being after the death of the body by a miraculous act of God and that they can be resurrected. This seems to be the view of British theologian Keith Ward, who also holds an emergentist view of the soul: "The soul . . . like a butterfly emerging from a chrysalis, . . . may be able to disentangle itself from the public spatial properties of the brain and exist either alone or in a different form of materialization."[47]

Emergent dualism seems close to that of Catholic theologian Karl Rahner, who theorized that in the process of development, the human being developed into something ontologically greater than a material being with social relations; in the process of development, the human being developed into a being who could self-transcend and come to know God.[48]

The strength of this position is that it is consistent with all the neurological evidence and the evidence of biological evolution; it does not require that we import an immaterial soul created by God. It can also explain animal consciousness—at least as much as any theory can. It is consistent with the obvious fact that the brain and the mind develop gradually. We do not think that newborn infants have fully developed powers of free choice or reasoning; these powers develop gradually as the brain and the person matures. And this position allows for survival of the soul after death, for resurrection, and for the continuity of personal identity between death and resurrection.

The weakness, of course, is that it posits the emergence by biological evolution—sometime after conception, when the brain becomes more or less developed—not only of a causal power, say free choice or reasoning, but also of a whole new entity, an individual person. For many, this will be hard to believe. Again, can this position admit that a human being with an undeveloped brain—a fetus or a Down syndrome infant—is fully a person?

Reincarnation or Rebirth

This position is mainly held by Hindus and Buddhists, though many in the West, particularly those influenced by so-called New Age thought, have embraced reincarnation. In classical Hinduism, the "subtle body," the personal soul (*jiva*), and the ultimate self (*atman*) transmigrate from life-form to life-form, depending on one's karma. An evil person could take on a life-form in a hell state or a highly greedy person that of a "hungry ghost." It could also be that someone who cultivated little higher consciousness could be reincarnated into an animal on earth. In contrast, a deeply meditative and loving person could take on the life-form of a god (*deva*) or perhaps a human being whose life status is very comfortable. Ultimately, the goal is to escape (*moksha*) the wandering from lifetime to lifetime (*samsara*) and achieve union with ultimate reality, known as Brahman.[49]

While Buddhists claim to reject an eternal, unchanging self, they embrace something similar to Hindu reincarnation.[50] For them, the human being is composed of five impersonal collections: matter, sensations, perceptions, mental formations, and consciousness. Upon death, one's consciousness re-forms into another life based on one's karma. Buddhists claim that what they believe is radically different from Hindus in this regard. For example, Buddhists deny that there is a "self" to reincarnate and affirm that everything that references a human being is impersonal and ever changing. On the other hand, the relationship between oneself, karma, and rebirth is similar to Hinduism. It is also the case that the Buddha was notoriously silent about ultimate questions. He claimed only to teach that which assisted in liberation, and he distinguished conventional truth (*sammuti-sacca*) from ultimate truth (*paramattha-sacca*).[51] So for our purposes here, both traditions embrace reincarnation, but their understandings of reincarnation differ.

Contemporary Western beliefs in reincarnation seem to vary somewhat from those of classical Hinduism or Buddhism. First, reincarnation is typically seen as hopeful, as another opportunity at life and another learning experience, not as something to be escaped as it is in classical Hinduism. Second, not many people in America seem to believe that they might be reincarnated as anything other than a human life-form.

The strengths of reincarnation are several. It has an explanation for the fact that most people make very little spiritual progress in the course of one lifetime: it answers that people need many lifetimes to achieve spiritual transcendence. Again there is the all-too-obvious fact of severe inequality in human life: some are born, live, and die in wretched circumstances while others live in luxury. Why? Because, according to reincarnation, each is living the life they deserve, based on past karma.

There are several problems with the theory of reincarnation. For one thing, many of the objections to substance dualism given above also apply to theories of reincarnation. Secondly, most people don't recall past existences, and the few who claim to do so live almost exclusively in Eastern cultures. Finally, it is hard to understand how the same soul could have been at one time an animal and at another time a human. So the case for reincarnation has not been widely persuasive, at least in the West and certainly not in academic circles. The traditional Christian argument against reincarnation (as it was known from Plato and Pythagoras) has been that it is incompatible with the resurrection,[52] especially if the resurrection is conceived as a reassembly of the same matter that the individual had in earthly life. But if we think of the resurrection as occurring in a renewed creation of God's choosing (see next chapter), then this objection may lose some of its force. Again, Christianity has held that we have only one life, not a series of lives. A frequently cited passage from the Bible against reincarnation is Hebrews 9:27: "it is appointed for mortals to die once, and after that the judgment." There is some similarity between reincarnation and the Catholic doctrine of purgatory in that both assume the possibility of development after bodily death. Karl Rahner has cautiously speculated that the Catholic notion might "be a starting point for coming to terms in a better and more positive way with the doctrine of the 'transmutation of souls' or of 'reincarnation.'"[53] But the Catholic church has also held firmly to the Christian belief that we are given only one lifetime, and it has condemned reincarnation as heretical.[54]

The Soul as Subject-in-Relation

In the following paragraphs, I shall lay out my own perspective on the soul, a perspective that attempts to synthesize the biblical and traditional under-standing, incorporate the findings of neuroscience, and also incorporate the evidence from NDEs. This position argues that the person in this life is an integrated unity of body and soul but that, nonetheless, the soul can survive bodily death and carry personal identity from the death of the body into the resurrected state, in which the soul is united with a resurrected body.

In this view, the soul is defined as the subject of personal consciousness (or personal identity) and of one's mind, intentions, memories, reason, and free choice. To be a subject is to be capable of personal subjective experience, that is, to be capable of a first-person perspective on reality. But the soul, as subject, is always in relation to the body, to others in society, to its physical environ-ment, and to God.[55] I place the soul as subject-in-relation in the category of "holistic dualism" as described above. It is holistic because the soul is integrated with the body (to the extent that the body's development allows) at all stages of its bodily existence. Thus for the soul to exercise its powers—free choice, for example—it depends on the brain. But the causality is in two directions. First, the brain and the brain states influence the mind and the soul.[56] This is brought out pointedly in contemporary research in neuroscience. On the one hand, if there is damage to the brain in one or another area, the abilities of the mind are damaged. For example, damage to the brain may mean that a person cannot recognize even familiar faces. But on the other hand, free choices taken by the mind or soul, ideas, or intentions can affect brain neurons. Thus the physical, in my view, is not causally closed. In other words, ideas and free choices can affect how the neurons and neural networks behave in the brain. And we would have to say that a free choice, though expressed through the material brain, is not a physical cause in the sense that it could be detected by scientific instruments.[57]

Like Aquinas, I think of the soul as the form, that is, the formative or organizing principle, of the body. In this view, without the soul the body would disintegrate into its component molecules. I take "form" in this sense as more than the pattern of arrangement or organization of the molecules in the body; I take it as an active, forming principle, a kind of holistic cause. However, there is little support for this in contemporary science, so I do not insist on it. It is sufficient for my theory to consider the soul as the form of the body in the sense that it is the total informational pattern of the human individual, which develops throughout life, as John Polkinghorne has proposed.

The idea that the soul is integrated with the body to the extent that the development of the body allows raises a potential problem for this theory. How could the soul be integrated with the body when the body is only a few cells or only a fertilized zygote? At that point in time, there is no developed brain to serve as the basis for mental awareness or free choice or intentions. I do not conceive of the soul in this state as a tiny homunculus waiting for the zygote or fetus to develop. Rather, what I think happens is this. At conception, a new human individual is formed, possessing the potential to develop into a fully grown adult human being. That individual develops in relation to its mother, and after birth in relation to others as well. But it also develops in relation to God. There are two ways it can be in relation to God. One is that it is related to God as is every other created thing: hydrogen atoms, molecules, stars, planets, asteroids, rocks, trees, and so on. God holds all these in existence. But another we might describe as "election": God initiates a personal relationship with the emerging individual human from the first moments of its existence. This has some biblical basis. Jeremiah 1:5 reads: "Before I formed you in the womb I knew you, / and before you were born I consecrated you." And in Ephesians 1:4 the author writes: "just as he chose us in Christ before the foundation of the world to be holy and blameless before him in love." This is what I believe happens with each emerging human person. It is God's election of that person that constitutes the person as a person, as more than a biological entity, as a unique soul/person, with the potentiality for relationality, for free choice, and eventually for eternal life with God.

This, I think, is one way of understanding what it means for God to "create" the soul. When God creates a soul, it is not separate from its body, as an extrinsic "thing" waiting to be inserted into a body. God's act of creating the soul means that God constitutes the newly emerging person as an entity-in-personal-relation-to-God. "To be is to be substance-in-relation," as Father Norris Clarke has written, so when the soul comes into being,[58] it is as a subject in relation to God. And during the whole course of her embodied life, the person chooses and develops her relations with the world, with others, and with God. In this sense, then, the person co-creates herself in cooperation and interrelation with the physical environment, with other persons, and with God. The whole point of an embodied life is to allow the human being to choose for or against God, for or against others, and for or against her own deepest nature.

Because persons are elected by God, they develop with an intrinsic purpose: to come to know and love God and others in the course of this life and onward, into the afterlife and resurrection. They may choose other purposes as well, but this I take to be an intrinsic purpose given with the relation to God.

This is a dualist theory because according to this theory the soul can survive with its mental faculties intact the death of the body. This ability to survive the death of the body is not due to physical nature but to God's grace.[59] It is only because of its relation to God that the soul can survive death. I take it that the relation to God, in the sense of election, carries with it a quality of permanence. Once God has entered into a personal relationship with a human person, that relationship does not perish but lasts into eternity: "for the gifts and calling of God are irrevocable" (Rom. 11:29). Thus the immortality of the soul is a gift from God and is due to its relation to God; it is not a property that evolves or emerges through nature by itself (indeed, hardly anyone would claim this). How God holds the soul in existence, especially in the intermediate state, is hard to explain. John Polkinghorne writes that the soul exists after death and before resurrection as an informational pattern in the mind of God: "It is a perfectly coherent hope that the pattern that is a human being could be held in the divine memory after that person's death."[60] I believe that God can hold the soul in existence not merely as an idea in God's mind, and not merely as an informational pattern, but as an existent entity that continues to have a subjective life of its own, even in the intermediate state. But perhaps this is not that different from saying that the soul survives in the mind of God.[61]

Because of its personal relation to God, the soul/person has other capacities besides immortality that animals do not have. One is the capacity for libertarian free choice—that is, the ability to choose freely between alternatives. This understanding of free choice is more than an absence of external constraint; it is also an absence of internal constraint. At bottom, a truly free choice, though it occurs within an embodied person and hence within a brain, is not physically caused because if it were physically caused it would either be determined according to the laws of physics or be random, as quantum events are random. But it is neither. I cannot understand how the capacity to make truly free decisions, which differs from a random decision, can emerge or evolve from nature on its own. Thus I contend that the capacity for free choice can only come from the relation to God, who, after all, is perfect freedom.

Another ability or capacity of the soul that comes from its relation to God is the capacity to know God personally and directly. This differs from the capacity to know about God through concepts or have feelings or images about God. Rather, it is to experience a personal relationship with God directly, to some extent in this life and fully in the next (Catholics call this the beatific vision). Again, this comes from the personal relation to God. It certainly would, however, require the development of self-awareness and consciousness, so it would not be available to the zygote or undeveloped fetus; in this sense then, it is a capacity of the whole person, but it is a capacity that continues on after death.

Finally, the soul, in this view, is a bridge between the world of matter and the world of spirit—God being understood as pure spirit. There has to be some kind of a bridging principle if humans are to be able to relate to God, know God personally, and participate in the Spirit of God. Otherwise the gulf between God as pure spirit and humans as material beings would be unbridgeable. For this reason, Karl Rahner has argued that there is a continuity between spirit and matter. Matter, Rahner thinks, is as it were "solidified" spirit.[62] Another way to consider this same point is that if human persons are able to know God directly (rather than as mediated through concepts, images, and feelings)—obscurely in this life,[63] clearly in the next—they have to possess some kind of a receptor so they can relate to and know the world of spirit. Just as to see light, humans have to have eyes and a brain, which translates the nerve impulses from the eyes into visual images, so also if humans are to be able to perceive the world of spirit, they must have a spiritual receptor or sensor. Otherwise the dimension of spirit would be opaque to us. And that spiritual receptor or sensor is the soul, which has the capacity to relate to both matter and spirit. The analogy of spiritual "seeing," by the way, is found throughout the works of Aquinas and Augustine, both of whom speak of the spiritual light that enlightens the mind, allowing it to perceive spiritual things. But it goes back further to Paul, who speaks of seeing God face to face (1 Cor. 13:12), and back even to the Old Testament, to Moses, "whom the LORD knew face to face" (Deut. 34:10).

This, then, is my proposal about the soul. It affirms the characteristics of the soul affirmed in the Christian tradition, namely, (1) it is the seat of consciousness and awareness; (2) it is the seat of personal identity and carries personal identity forward from the death of the body into the resurrection; (3) it is the seat of intelligence, reason, and understanding; (4) it is the seat of freedom (i.e., free choice); (5) it is capable of knowing God directly. In addition, my theory affirms two other characteristics: (6) it affirms that the mind and soul are integrated with the body and brain in this life and hence that damage to the brain will affect the mind and the power of the soul to function; and finally, (7) it is consonant with the testimony of NDEers that consciousness can survive outside the body because it is intrinsic to the soul's relation to God that the relation is permanent, and hence that God will hold the soul in being, even after the demise of the body.

What are the challenges to this theory? First, many in the sciences will simply say that the tight correlation between the brain and mind prove that the mind cannot exist outside the brain. But the tight correlation does not prove this; it only shows that as embodied the mind is dependent on and expresses itself through the brain. It does not show that the mind cannot exist outside the brain. Secondly, what about animal consciousness? If higher animals are conscious, does that mean they have souls? I take it as obvious that higher animals have feelings and experiences. They experience pain; dogs whimper in their sleep, indicating they are probably having dreams; and so on. How animal consciousness emerges is a mystery. Process philosophers and theologians theorize that there is a subjective pole to all matter, even simple matter like atoms (a position known as "panpsychism"), and that as matter becomes more complex, consciousness emerges, and, in humans, becomes self-consciousness.[64] This would make sense if we think of matter and spirit as fundamentally continuous, as Rahner has proposed. So, then, higher animals are capable of subjective experiences, and if the soul is the subject of subjective experiences, then they have souls. Whether these souls continue after the deaths of their respective bodies is known only to God; if God chooses to hold them in being, then they can survive. My argument is that there are certain capacities of the human soul—its immortality, its free choice, and its ability to know God directly—that do not simply evolve out of physical nature by themselves but that originate in the relationship of the human soul with God and that develop as the brain/body and its social relations develop. We might say, then, that these abilities co-evolve through the workings of God in nature.

The soul, in Christian tradition, is embodied in this life and will be embodied again in the resurrection. The next chapter considers how we can understand the resurrection.

7

RESURRECTION

If Christ has not been raised, then our proclamation has been
in vain and your faith has been in vain.

1 Corinthians 15:14

The Problem of the Resurrection

We saw in chapter 2 that the resurrection of Jesus[1] was central to early Christianity. Jesus's resurrection vindicated the disciples' belief that he was the
Messiah (Mark 8:29) and the Son of God (Mark 1:11); it confirmed his victory over sin and death and sealed the promise of eternal life with God; it
was interpreted by his followers as a promise of their own future resurrection
and fullness of life with God (1 Cor. 15:14). The resurrection of the dead was
also the central hope for afterlife in the Christian tradition (chap. 3). Given
all this, one might think there would be no problem with belief in the resurrection today. But it is widely doubted, even by some Christians. The reason
is that it does not fit with our contemporary view of the cosmos and the laws
of nature. The problem becomes clear if one asks: "Where is Jesus's risen
body right now?" No informed Christian claims that the risen Jesus is located
somewhere in our space-time universe. But if our space-time universe is the
whole of reality and the risen Jesus is not in our space-time universe, then
the resurrection must be a fiction. This is the contemporary problem of the
resurrection. This needs to be addressed first of all, because until it is resolved,

no particular arguments from Scripture will be persuasive. We can line up the case for Jesus's resurrection point by point, but if the listener is convinced that resurrection is impossible, no amount of argument from ancient texts will be convincing. For this reason, we need to consider the case *against* the resurrection before we can make the case *for* it.

The Case against the Resurrection

The case against the resurrection—either Jesus's resurrection or that of the dead at the end of time—can be stated in five points. (1) We never see resurrections happening today, therefore they did not happen in the past. (2) Resurrection violates the laws of nature, specifically the law of conservation of matter and energy, therefore it could not have happened. (3) No one claims that the resurrected body of Jesus exists now in our space-time universe; there is no other universe, so the resurrection is impossible. (4) The far future of our universe holds no promise for continuing life. Either the universe will continue to expand, the stars and galaxies will burn out, and the universe will die of heat death or it will contract in on itself and everything will be crushed together in a singularity. Either way, life cannot survive. (5) Given all this, it is most likely that the disciples made up the story of the resurrection or that they had a profound subjective experience of Jesus's continuing presence and interpreted this to mean that he was physically raised from the dead (when he really was not).[2] In the following pages, I will deal with each of these points. After that I will consider the evidence for Jesus's resurrection and then discuss the resurrection of the dead and the meaning it has for contemporary Christians.

1. *We don't see resurrections occurring today—dead bodies stay dead. Therefore they did not happen in the past.* How shall we respond to this? First of all, note that we do not hesitate to believe in very rare events in the past, which we never see today, as long as they fit with what we know can happen in our cosmos. For example, it is widely believed that a huge asteroid struck the earth sixty-five million years ago and wiped out the dinosaurs.[3] We don't see this happening today, but it is not hard to believe. Why? First, because experts have found physical traces of this event, and second, because it is the kind of event that fits with our understanding of our cosmos. We know there are asteroids and that they revolve around the sun, therefore it is not hard to believe that one of them could have struck the earth. So the real issue is not, Do we see similar events now, but rather, Does the past event seem possible or likely given our current understanding of the cosmos? So the issue is not,

How rare the event is; the issue is, Does it fit our conception of what kind of events can happen? This brings us to the second point.

2. *The resurrection could not happen because it violates the laws of nature, particularly the law of conservation of energy.* But this raises questions: What are the laws of nature? Do they simply describe what we usually observe or do they state what has to happen? That is, are they descriptive or prescriptive? It is true that in laboratory experiments we find that the amount of matter/energy is constant, that is, the quantity of matter/energy is neither increased nor decreased in isolated systems. For instance, in nuclear fission a small amount of matter is converted into heat, but the amount of heat energy released exactly equals the energy equivalent of the matter lost, where the energy equivalent is given by Einstein's famous equation e *(energy)* $= m$ *(mass)* c *(speed of light)*^{2}. But the laws of nature—as we have formulated them—are generalizations from what we have observed in the past; they do not necessarily prescribe what has to happen in nature. In fact, our formulations of the laws of nature have changed during the history of science, and it would be naive to think they will not change in the future. We find many surprises in the history of science, in which what were thought to be laws of nature had to be modified because of new facts (or new theories). For example, the discovery of superconductivity was inexplicable until physicists realized that the laws of physics behave differently under very different conditions, such as extreme cold. Another example is quantum theory. Some of its predictions seem impossible, such as the "tunneling effect," in which a particle such as an electron can "tunnel" through a wall of lead as if it were not there. Such an effect surely would have been said to be beyond the laws of nature before the discovery of quantum theory; now it is readily accepted and is routinely used by engineers. So the question is, Do we know all there is to know about nature, or is it likely that our present formulations of the laws of nature will change in the future? We certainly do not have a final theory of physics; consequently, it seems quite likely that the laws of nature as they are presently formulated will be changed in the future, as happened with the revolution in quantum physics only eighty years ago. Is it likely that we now know most or all of what there is to nature, or is it more likely that there may be states of matter and nature that go beyond what we presently know?

There is a good deal of speculation by leading physicists that our universe may be only a part of a much larger—and different—universe or may be one of a series of parallel universes or multiple universes.[4] String theory predicts a universe of ten or eleven dimensions. Lisa Randall, a physicist at Harvard, theorizes that our universe exists within a universe of many higher and unseen dimensions and that the laws of nature may be very different in different regions of this so-called multiverse.[5] If this (or something like it) is so, then we do not inhabit a closed universe with closed laws of nature. The larger hidden dimensions in which our universe exists may influence our own three-dimensional space-time world and its laws of nature at certain critical moments. Generally, this is part of contextual causality: events always occur in wider contexts and these contexts can influence the events themselves. Superconductivity is such an event; at ordinary temperatures, all conductors have some resistance to the passage of electricity, but at extremely cold temperatures, this resistance disappears in some conductors. The context influences how the physical law is manifested.

Another example is natural selection in biology. The environment favors some characteristics in species and selects against others. A radical change in the environment or context—such as would be caused by an asteroid hitting the earth—will cause changes in the direction of selection. If our universe is part of a much greater multiverse, it is possible that the laws of nature as we have formulated them can be very different within different contexts.

More generally, the question of the violation of natural laws raises the question of miracles. I have written about this at length elsewhere, and here will only summarize what I said there.[6] David Hume claimed that miracles were "violations" of the laws of nature. That is, however, a misleading caricature. If one actually examines cases of putative miracles, one finds that nature is not violated but rather enhanced and elevated. For example, consider the case of Joachine Dehant, a twenty-nine-year-old Belgian woman who in 1878 made a pilgrimage to Lourdes by train. She sought healing for a massive gangrenous ulcer (twelve inches by six inches) on her right calf. This ulcer had penetrated to the bone, destroying muscles and tendons and causing the foot to invert. The wound had been attended by local physicians for twelve years, but it had not healed; it had been years since Dehant had walked or worn a shoe on her right foot. Her trip to Lourdes was agonizing and humiliating; the stench from her wound sickened her companions on the train. Yet on her second bathing in the pool at Lourdes, the wound was healed; muscles, tendons, and skin were restored, leaving a well-formed scar. This cure was attested by physicians at Lourdes; by her traveling companions; by the townspeople of Dehant's hometown, Gesves, Belgium, who had known her for years; by the physicians who had treated her for twelve years at Gesves; and by her family. It was subsequently investigated by professors at the Catholic University at Louvain, who gathered testimony from all concerned, including physicians. Dehant enjoyed perfect health for more than thirty years after the cure.[7]

What is of interest here is that the healing ended in a scar. This indicates that the natural processes of healing were followed but were greatly accelerated. The miracle was certainly beyond what we normally see occurring in nature but not beyond the capacities of nature elevated by grace. Nature, including human nature, is capable of being elevated by the assistance of a higher power. And this was the traditional understanding of miracles. It was only after the scientific revolution, when the laws of nature came to be thought of as absolute, that miracles were taken to be "violations" of nature. But to absolutize the laws of nature above the power of God is to commit idolatry; it sets up nature as an absolute that not even God can influence.

The resurrection is similar to a healing miracle; the body of Jesus is transformed and ascends to a higher state. But its own nature is not violated; it is transformed and elevated.

3. *Where is the body of the risen Jesus now?* A materialist would say that if it does not exist in our spatio-temporal universe (and no one claims it does), then it does not exist. This assumes there is no higher state of being than this material universe. Such an assumption does indeed render the resurrection incredible. But do we have to accept this assumption? Could not our universe be part of a much more extensive universe of multiple unseen dimensions with very different laws and states of matter? If so, then we do not need to accept the assumption "This universe is all there is." And if there are states of reality beyond what we know in this universe, then the resurrection is at least a possibility (compare the discussion of Paul's idea of the "spiritual body" [1 Cor. 15:44] in chap. 2, above).

4. *In the far future, our universe will be dead.* Right now the best data indicates that our universe is expanding and will continue to expand indefinitely.[8] After tens of billions of years, the stars and galaxies will have exhausted their fuel, will burn out, collapse, and go cold. The far-future universe will be cold, dark, empty, and dead. An alternate scenario involves the force of gravity eventually overcoming the expansion of the universe, causing the universe to collapse in on itself. In this state, no life, or even separate planets to house life, could exist. As John Polkinghorne states: "However fruitful the universe may seem today, its end lies in futility."[9]

All this indicates that we cannot evolve naturally into the state of resurrection. Actually, we didn't need science to tell us this. Jesus entered the resurrected state only by first undergoing death, and that will be true for each of us as well. And it may be true for our planet and for the whole universe. Only through death can we reach the resurrection. But this does not mean that the resurrection cannot occur. As we saw above, the resurrected body, if it exists at all, must exist in a very different form of matter, space, and time from our present universe. This was already apparent in the resurrection of Jesus: according to John, he appeared to the disciples in a room where the doors were

locked (John 20:26); according to Luke, he disappeared from their sight suddenly (Luke 24:31), and after a time he ascended into heaven (Luke 24:51). If
we can trust the Gospel accounts at all, then his resurrected body existed in a
reality that transcended our space and time. Presumably this will be the case
with the general resurrection of the dead.

Though many early Christians seemed to imagine the resurrected state as
occurring on this earth as we know it, now it is hard to see how this could be
the case. In our universe, everything eventually decays and dies. Our universe
is under the signature of death. As Paul notes, creation is in bondage to decay
(Rom. 8:21). Paul, however, thought that this bondage to decay will be broken
and that "the creation . . . will obtain the freedom of the glory of the children
of God" (Rom. 8:21). For this to happen, the laws of nature in our universe—
including in all one hundred billion or so galaxies—would need to be changed.
Some Christians do argue for this; for example Robert John Russell, a leader
in the dialogue of science and theology, argues for a transfigured cosmos in
the resurrection.[10] So does N. T. Wright, if I understand him correctly.[11] And
the Eastern Orthodox have held this view for centuries. Yet most Christians
will find this very hard to believe. Thus while I do believe in Paul's vision of a
transformed creation freed from the bondage of death, I am wary of arguing
that it must be the very matter of *this* creation that is transformed. As I have
argued above, what carries identity is the form of a person, not the matter.
Thus I think it more likely that the context of the resurrection is a different
and more exalted state of space, time, and matter that intersects with our
universe but is not necessarily tied to the matter of our creation.

5. *The interpretation is widespread today that Jesus's resurrection was
made up by the disciples, so that it was an event that changed the disciples'
understanding of Jesus but did not change Jesus himself, who remained dead.*
We have seen above (chap. 2) that this was Rudolph Bultmann's interpretation.
Bultmann considered the bodily resurrection of Jesus to be "myth" because
he rejected the possibility of nature miracles. Not that he investigated the
evidence for such miracles, past or present—he simply assumed they were
not possible given the modern scientific understanding of the universe. But
the assumption that the disciples invented the resurrection is very hard to
square with the New Testament evidence. The Gospels, and also Paul, insist
that Jesus's resurrection was bodily. If the disciples thought otherwise, why
didn't they say so? Why did they go to their deaths defending what they knew
to be a lie? The main reason to assume that Jesus's resurrection was a myth
would be because one was convinced (like Bultmann) that nature miracles and
resurrections cannot happen because they violate the laws of nature. But this
ignores both ancient and modern evidence for miracles[12] and further assumes

that our understanding of nature is complete, which seems naive, given the changes in our understanding of nature in the last one hundred years.

The Case for the Resurrection

Ultimately, the case for the resurrection of Jesus rests on the witness of the apostles and disciples, and not just on their words but on their changed lives as well. What one would expect of a failed messiah is that his followers would scatter in despair. In fact the disciples did scatter during Jesus's crucifixion. After the resurrection and the coming of the Spirit (Acts 2), however, the disciples, who were "uneducated and ordinary men" (Acts 4:13), spoke out with boldness, courage, and conviction. Luke's rendition of Peter's first sermons in Acts 2 and 3 give us an idea of the content of the early Christian preaching. Peter calls on the Jewish audience to repent and be baptized. His clinching argument is that God had raised up Jesus from the dead, thus proving that Jesus, who had been crucified, was truly "both Lord and Messiah" (Acts 2:36). The apostles and disciples were imprisoned for this belief, persecuted (Acts 8:1), and put to death. Yet none of them, so far as we know, renounced their belief in Jesus's resurrection. None of them confessed that it was really a made-up conspiracy or an attempt at wish fulfillment dreamed up by Jesus's disappointed followers. They were convinced that God had raised Jesus from the dead. And they persuaded many others of this belief.

Probably the best witness is Paul. Paul was initially hostile to Christianity but was converted by a vision of the risen Lord. Paul's belief in the resurrection was therefore not a result of wish fulfillment or collaboration with the first apostles, whom he did not know until a few years after Jesus's death. He had not been a follower of Jesus, and as an educated Pharisee he had every reason to attack the new movement, which was heretical by Jewish standards. Yet Paul was converted, as he tells us in his letters (e.g., Galatians). Furthermore, he endured persecution, floggings, beatings, stonings, shipwrecks (2 Cor. 11:24–27), trials, and ultimately martyrdom (by beheading, according to Eusebius) for his witness to Christianity. As we saw in chapter 2, he makes his case for the authenticity of Jesus's resurrection in his first letter to the Corinthians (1 Cor. 15). He handed on to them what he had heard from the apostles a few years after Jesus's death (at the time of his own vision of the risen Christ): that Christ died for our sins, was buried, and was raised on the third day; that he appeared to Cephas (Peter), then to the twelve, then to five hundred brethren, then to James, then to all the apostles, and finally to Paul (1 Cor. 15:5–9). At the time Paul was writing this letter to Corinth, in the early 50s, almost all these witnesses were still alive, as Paul himself states (1 Cor. 15:6). Any of them, therefore, could have publicly contradicted him if he were lying about the resurrection. Yet there is no record that any of them ever did. It is very hard to believe that Peter, Paul, and all the other apostles and disciples endured torture, imprisonment, trials, persecution, and death for their faith if they had invented the story of Jesus's resurrection and knew all along that it was a lie.

There is other evidence as well. The first witnesses to the resurrection were women (Mary Magdalene in particular). But in ancient Judaism, the legal testimony of women was not highly valued; it took the testimony of two women to equal the testimony of one man. Therefore it is hard to believe that if the disciples made up the story of Jesus's resurrection they would have said that the first witnesses were women. This would be similar to making up a story today and claiming that the primary witnesses were children; no one would do it. Again, very early on, the first Christians changed the sabbath day of worship from Saturday to Sunday as a commemoration of Jesus's resurrection. They must have been motivated by what they regarded as more than a psychological event to make such a radical change in custom and tradition. Finally, there is the unanimous witness of the four Gospels that the tomb was found empty.[13] With the strong (but not exclusive) emphasis on embodiment in Judaism, being "raised from the dead" would mean being raised bodily from the dead. The Gospels (especially Luke and John) emphasize that the resurrection was bodily and that it was Jesus's own body that was raised. In both Luke's and John's accounts, Jesus actually eats with the disciples and they touch him. The point is that he was not a disembodied spirit or a ghost, a point that Luke in particular takes pains to emphasize (Luke 24:39–43).

The empty tomb is not itself evidence of the resurrection. By itself it could be explained in other ways—perhaps the body was stolen, perhaps it was never put in the tomb. But coupled with the appearances of the risen Jesus to the disciples, recorded in the Gospel tradition, the empty tomb indicates that the risen Jesus was not just a subjective vision or a transformed consciousness on the part of the disciples. Something happened to Jesus as well. That is the claim of the New Testament.

How Can We Understand the Resurrection Today?

The Christian hope for resurrection is based on the resurrection of Jesus. Hence I will consider first how we can understand Jesus's resurrection and then how we can understand the resurrection of the dead at the end of human history.

In the Gospel accounts of Jesus's resurrection, it is clearly Jesus's own body that is raised from the dead. Bodily resurrection is indicated by the empty tomb and also by the scenes in Luke and John in which the disciples see and touch Jesus, talk with him, and see the wounds on his risen body (Luke 24:40; John 20:27). However, Jesus's resurrection was not a resuscitation. He appears to the disciples in a room with locked doors (John 20:19), disappears from the sight of the two disciples eating with him after their walk to Emmaus (Luke 24:31), and apparently was not easily recognizable—the two disciples did not recognize him during the seven-mile walk to Emmaus (Luke 24). According to Acts 1, he ascended into heaven in plain sight of the disciples (Acts 1:9). Thus the New Testament accounts indicate that though the resurrected Jesus could appear bodily to the disciples, he was not bound by our universe of three-dimensional space and time. Perhaps we can think of the risen Jesus as existing in a higher dimension or a parallel universe that intersects with and is open to our universe. These, however, are metaphors; we don't really know what kind of space-time the resurrected Jesus exists in, only that it seems to transcend our space-time and gives him a great deal of freedom so that he can appear (and disappear) to the disciples at will. In attempting to describe the nature of the resurrected body, Paul contrasts it with the physical body that dies and implies that the resurrected body is still a body, but has been transformed: "What is sown is perishable, what is raised is imperishable. It is sown in dishonor, it is raised in glory. It is sown in weakness, it is raised in power. It is sown a physical body [*sōma psychikon*] it is raised a spiritual body [*sōma pneumatikon*]" (1 Cor. 15:42–44).

There is then both continuity and discontinuity between the body that dies and the body that is raised. The form and matter of the dead body continue on but are transformed into something clearly beyond nature as we know it: imperishable, glorified, powerful, of heaven. Paul uses the metaphor of a seed becoming a new plant and implies that the resurrected body has a different kind of flesh—and hence matter—than do physical bodies (1 Cor. 15:36–41). Clearly this is a mystery: we don't have other events with which to compare it because the resurrection of Jesus was a one-time event, difficult for many people to believe. In Paul's time it apparently was thought that there were different kinds of flesh for different kinds of animals (1 Cor. 15:39) and different kinds of "glory" for the sun, moon, and stars. Today, however, we know of only one kind of matter/energy in the universe. This matter/energy can take many forms but at bottom is the same matter/energy. So it is more difficult to accept the resurrection today, though it certainly was not easy in ancient times either. But, as noted above, physicists today are beginning to develop sophisticated theories of radically different kinds of universes, in which matter, space, and time would be different from this universe. Perhaps we can imagine the risen Jesus as present in one of these alternate universes. John Polkinghorne suggests the possibility of the resurrected "new creation" as existing in a different dimension:

> Mathematicians can readily think of the spacetime of the old creation and the "spacetime" of the new creation as being in different dimensions of the totality of divinely sustained reality, with resurrection involving an information-bearing mapping between the two, and the redemption of matter as involving a projection from the old onto the new. Such a picture offers some partial insight into the nature of the appearances of the risen Christ, as arising from limited intersections between these two worlds.[14]

The point is that if there are many different types of universes, it is more likely that the risen Jesus could exist in a very different kind of state from our own.

This state is clearly beyond the capacity of nature as we know it—in traditional language the resurrection was a supernatural event. But the traditional language of "supernatural" can be misleading. Yes, the resurrection of Jesus was due to the power of God because nature by itself does not produce resurrected bodies. That is why we don't see resurrections happening regularly; such events are beyond the capacity of *unaided* nature. But at the same time, Jesus's resurrected body was and is also an exalted state of nature—it is a body, after all, and this body was therefore capable of being transformed into a resurrected body. It is nature empowered and transformed by God's supernatural power—we might call it "supernaturalized nature." So it comes about both through nature, which is open to such a transformation, and through the supernatural power of God. It is nature supernaturally elevated by grace. It is therefore both a state of nature and a state of grace—nature transformed by grace. This is another and more precise way of speaking of the continuity and discontinuity apparent in Jesus's resurrection.

In this respect, the resurrection is like a healing miracle. In healing miracles, the natural course of the body's healing is followed but the healing itself is greatly empowered and accelerated. Miracles, like the resurrection, therefore, are not violations of the laws of nature. Instead they represent the laws of nature elevated to a new regime, operating in an environment in which they are empowered by grace. Just as the laws of electrical transmission behave in seemingly impossible ways in the extreme cold of superconductivity, so in the milieu of nature-transformed-by-grace the laws of nature, with which we are all too familiar, can behave in a seemingly impossible fashion.

As well as being God's vindication of Jesus, the resurrection of Jesus is a demonstration of possible states of nature that we could not have known about except through revelation. It is also a promise of our own resurrection and, as Paul assures us, of the possibility of a transformed creation (Rom. 8:19–21).

The Resurrection of the Dead

What then can we say concerning the resurrection of the dead at the end of human history? First, the early Christians took Christ's resurrection as a sign and a promise of their own resurrection, which they expected soon (because the resurrection of the dead was supposed to happen only in the end times). Paul writes: "But in fact Christ has been raised from the dead, the first fruits of those who have died" (1 Cor. 15:20). "First fruits" implies that there will be more fruit, namely, the resurrection of Jesus's followers. According to Brian Daley, "virtually all early Christian writers agreed . . . that the confession of the risen Jesus as Lord implies the hope that his disciples, too, will someday share in his resurrection."[15]

We have seen in chapter 3 that the early church's thinking on the resurrection tended to be paradoxical. On the one hand, many thinkers, such as Athenagoras, Tertullian, Gregory of Nyssa, and Augustine, insisted that the same material particles that make up our body in this life will be reassembled into the resurrected body. On the other hand, some writers, especially Origen, recognized that matter was always flowing through our bodies—like a river—and insisted that the resurrected body would be "spiritual." Origen thought that it was the soul, the *eidos*, that was the form of the body and that continued on into the resurrection, rather than the same matter that had been a part of the earthly body. And this soul would form for itself a new body suitable to its resurrected environment.

> And just as we would . . . need to have gills and other endowments of fish if it were necessary for us to live underwater in the sea, so those who are going to inherit [the] kingdom of heaven and be in superior places must have spiritual bodies. The previous form does not disappear, even if its transition to the more glorious [state] occurs, just as the form of Jesus, Moses and Elijah in the Transfiguration was not [a] different [one] from what it had been.[16]

Augustine tried to hold on to both ends of this spectrum:

> Whatever, therefore, has been taken from the body, either during life or after death, shall be restored to it, and in conjunction with what has remained in the

grave, shall rise again, transformed from the oldness of the animal body to the newness of the spiritual body, and clothed in incorruption and immortality.[17]

Given what we now know about our bodies, that they are constantly exchanging matter with their environments, it does not make sense to say that every particle of matter that at one time or another has been part of our bodies will be raised and transformed. Origen was right: the body is like a river. And yet if we say that none of the matter of our bodies will be carried over into the resurrection and transformed, then we are in effect saying that the empty tomb in the case of Jesus did not matter; even if his body had remained in the tomb, he still would have been resurrected. But this does not seem right. In the end, we cannot know for sure how the resurrection will take place. Our souls will survive death (through their graced relationship with God) and will be "reclothed" in bodies in a transformed state of matter, space, and time suitable to the resurrection. It seems that the matter of our bodies cannot be the principal element of continuity between this life and the next and that, as I have argued in the previous chapter, the principal element of continuity is indeed the soul, the form of the body.

Physicist-theologian John Polkinghorne argues a very similar point:

> It seems a coherent belief that God will remember and reconstitute the pattern that is a human being, in an act taking place beyond present history. . . . If human beings are psychosomatic unities, then the persons reconstituted by the divine act of resurrection must have new bodies to act as the carrier of the soul. It is not necessary, however, that the "matter" of these bodies should be the same matter as makes up the flesh of this present world. . . . That is because the material bodies of this world are intrinsically subject to mortality and decay. If the resurrected life is to be a true fulfillment, and not just a repeat of an ultimately futile history, the bodies of that world to come must be different, for they will be everlastingly redeemed from mortality. Science knows only the matter of this world, but it cannot forbid theology to believe that God is capable of bringing about something totally new.[18]

Aquinas presents an interesting argument about the role of the soul in the resurrection. The soul, he thinks, is the form or organizing principle of the body. In this life, the soul does not have complete control of the matter of the body, and so we age and die. But in the next life, the soul (of the righteous) will be perfectly united with God and hence will be empowered to render the body spiritual and glorified.

> Since the blessed soul, owing to its union with the first principle of all things, will be raised to a pinnacle of nobility and power, it will communicate substantial

existence in the most perfect degree to the body that has been joined to it by divine action. And thus, holding the body completely under its sway, the soul will render the body *subtile* [sic] and *spiritual*.[19]

In both resurrection and miracles the same principle is at work: divine action works through nature, empowering and elevating it.

The resurrection of the dead also involves a community; though we are resurrected individually, we are also resurrected in the community of the blessed. That is part of what heaven is (see below, chap. 9).

Immediate Resurrection?

Some theologians have proposed the idea of "immediate resurrection," that is, the belief that persons are resurrected immediately after their death. Karl Rahner, for example, writes: "No one is in danger of defending a heresy if he maintains the view that the single and total perfecting of man [sic] in 'body' and 'soul' takes place immediately after death; that the resurrection of the flesh and the general judgment take place 'parallel' to the temporal history of the world; and that both coincide with the particular judgments of individual men and women."[20] What are the strengths and weaknesses of this theory?

The strength claimed by its proponents is that immediate resurrection eliminates the need for a soul that survives separate from the body in an intermediate state. Therefore it avoids both substance dualism and holistic dualism because it is the whole person who is resurrected. It also avoids the problem of continuity of personal identity between death and resurrection because resurrection follows immediately upon death. This theory is mainly attractive to those who find the idea of a separated soul and an intermediate state untenable; and indeed, it was not advanced until the mid-twentieth century, when traditional theories of the soul came under attack.

What are the weaknesses of the theory? First, there is almost no support in either Scripture or tradition for this theory. Almost all the New Testament evidence points in the other direction, namely, that the dead will be raised on the last day, at the end of history, after a period of great tribulation (Mark 13). Thus Jesus says, "Those who eat my flesh and drink my blood have eternal life, and I will raise them up on the last day" (John 6:54). As N. T. Wright notes, in the world of second-Temple Judaism "nobody imagined that any individuals had already been raised, or would be raised, in advance of the great last day."[21] Perhaps two passages in the New Testament could be adduced to support immediate resurrection: Luke 16, which is the parable of the rich man and Lazarus,

and Jesus's words to the dying thief: "today you will be with me in Paradise."
Both of these we have discussed in chapter 2. It is clear in Luke 16 that the
resurrection has not yet occurred, because the rich man's brothers are still alive.
So it seems that the best interpretation is that the rich man and Lazarus are
envisioned, in this parable, as in an intermediate state, one that is after death but
before the resurrection. Jesus's words to the dying thief certainly indicate that
the thief will be in the presence of Jesus after death, but there is no indication
that he will be in a resurrected state. Furthermore, there is no support for this
theory in the Christian tradition until the mid-twentieth century.[22] In this it is
unlike the theory of purgatory, which also has scant New Testament support
but does have substantial support in the later Christian tradition.

Second, even Jesus was not immediately resurrected after his death, unless
we want to argue that the entire Christian tradition has been wrong and that
Jesus was really resurrected just after he died while his body was still on the
cross. Granted, one can argue that if it is the form of the body that persists
after death and is reclothed with a new materiality in the resurrection, then it
is not essential that the same matter from our present bodies continue in the
resurrected body. But the theory of immediate resurrection reverses the pattern seen in Jesus's own resurrection, in which his earthly body was raised and
caught up into a transcendent state. In the theory of immediate resurrection,
this earthly body would be left behind and a new resurrected body would take
its place. So there would be two bodies: the corpse and the newly resurrected
body. This, I think, poses a serious problem of credibility for this theory. How
many Christians are going to believe that their loved one has been resurrected
bodily when they can still see the corpse in front of them at the funeral?

I grant that one can make this theory work if we say that the time of the resurrection does not correspond with earthly time and that it is the form, not the
matter, of the body that carries over into the resurrection. But I think the burden of
proof is on those who propose this novel theory and that they will have to adduce
powerful reasons for it since it has so little support in the New Testament, and
none in the Christian tradition. Almost the only reason for holding this theory is
to avoid believing in a soul that survives bodily death. But I think we can provide
good reasons for believing in an immortal soul (chap. 6). In the end, though, I
leave it up to the reader to judge the merits of immediate resurrection.

A Transfigured Creation

We cannot imagine resurrected bodies floating by themselves in empty space.
The body in life is intrinsically part of a larger environment, and if it is cut off

from that environment it will die. Indeed, there would be no point in having a resurrected body if there were no resurrected environment. And so we must imagine the resurrection including not only other persons but also something similar to what we call nature, a resurrected environment. Thus Paul writes: "the creation itself will be set free from its bondage to decay and will obtain the freedom of the glory of the children of God" (Rom. 8:21). And the author of Revelation writes: "Then I saw a new heaven and a new earth; for the first heaven and the first earth had passed away, and the sea was no more" (Rev. 21:1). Revelation then describes the New Jerusalem, but nothing more is said about a resurrected and transformed earth. So we must leave its details to our imaginations, while being aware that when we speak of the resurrection of the dead we include within that phrase the idea of a resurrected and glorified environment as well. C. S. Lewis vividly portrays a resurrected environment in *The Great Divorce*. Heaven is a state of the body as well as of the soul. In heaven, Lewis implies, the senses are sharper and the environment more poignantly beautiful and more real than at any time on earth.[23] Likewise near-death survivors report a world far more beautiful than earth. This is the main reason they are reluctant to return to their earthly lives.

The resurrection, then, will be the completion and fulfillment of all that is good but transitory and perishing on this earth. Earth is beautiful, but its beauty is transitory and laced with suffering and death. In the resurrected life this will not be so. There we shall experience the fullness of life, of beauty, of glory, of communion and love, both with one another and with God.

The Damned?

But, some might ask, what about the resurrection of the damned? Christian tradition holds that the damned will be resurrected and suffer in their bodies as well as in their souls. In addition to the "pain of loss," that is, the loss of the vision of God, justice requires that they also experience pain in their bodies. And so, traditional Christians thought, the damned would suffer forever from the fire of hell. But to contemporary persons, this seems like cruel and unusual punishment. Certainly it is understandable that those who have chosen to reject God will be deprived of the vision of God. But to add that they will be eternally punished by fire seems to make God into a cruel and vengeful autocrat rather than a God of love. After all, if God is love, then God continues to love even the damned, even though they have cut themselves off from God. Modern treatments of hell typically view the fire as a metaphor for the pain of regret, loss, and despair felt by lost souls. (We will discuss this further in chapter 9.)

Judgment and Salvation

Before proceeding to a chapter on heaven and hell, however, we need to consider how one gets to heaven (or hell). Why are some people saved and others
not? What makes a person just and righteous in the sight of God? In Christian teaching we do not go directly to heaven or hell; we first are judged by
Christ. In the story of the last judgment, Jesus describes how all persons will
be judged at the end of history (Matt. 25:31–46). And Paul writes: "For all of
us must appear before the judgment seat of Christ, so that each may receive
recompense for what has been done in the body, whether good or evil" (2 Cor.
5:10). Are we judged on faith or on what we do or on both? This is the topic
of the next chapter.

8

JUSTIFICATION AND JUDGMENT

Not everyone who says to me "Lord, Lord," will enter the kingdom of heaven, but only the one who does the will of my Father in heaven.

Matthew 7:21

The only thing that counts is faith working through love.

Galatians 5:6

The Problem of Justification and Salvation

How can I be righteous, or justified, before God? This is the problem of justification. If I am judged by God to be righteous, then I will be worthy of God's presence in heaven. But if I am unrighteous, I will be cut off from God and hence be in hell. So there is a lot at stake in the question of justification and salvation.[1]

Martin Luther thought justification was the main theological issue of the Reformation. Luther, like others of his time, feared that many people went to hell because they were not just or righteous before God. The threat of hell was a source of great anxiety for sixteenth-century people, not least for Luther himself. As a monk and a scholar of Scripture, Luther should have had little to fear. But he fretted about even trivial sins; he confessed sometimes twice a day, fasted, prayed, read the Scriptures, mortified his body, and generally wore himself out trying to do "good works" so as to merit heaven. But as hard as he tried, he could not find peace. What if he had forgotten to confess some sin or failed in some requirement? Behind his anxiety was fear of an angry and judgmental God who required strict justice.

The Roman Catholic Church of that day had a series of answers to Luther's concerns. One believed in God, Christ, and the teachings of the Church; faithfully participated in mass, confession, and the other sacraments of the Church; prayed the devotions to Jesus, Mary, and the saints; and performed good works, such as the corporeal works of mercy, fasts, pilgrimages, and works of charity. But Luther thought that the church put too much emphasis on us performing good works and not enough emphasis on Christ's gift of grace. He was particularly troubled by the papal practice of granting indulgences (remission of the penalty for venial sins in purgatory) for monetary donations to the church. Reading Paul's letters, Luther came to realize that we are not saved by good works or by our own righteousness; we are saved by faith in Christ and his righteousness. Because of our faith and trust in Christ as our savior, God imputes or attributes the righteousness of Christ to us. It is through Christ's righteousness, not our own, that we are justified and hence saved. Luther therefore argued that "it is faith alone which, because of the pure mercy of God through Christ and in his Word, worthily and sufficiently justifies the person."[2] Luther's position is known as "imputed justification." Other Protestants, especially Calvinists, followed Luther in this teaching, though the Anabaptists did not.

At the Council of Trent, the Catholic Church rejected this position and argued that faith alone is not enough for justification; the presence of hope and charity in our hearts is also necessary for justification:

> For though no one can be just unless the merits of the passion of our Lord Jesus Christ are communicated to him; nevertheless, in the justification of a sinner this in fact takes place when . . . the love of God is poured out by the agency of the holy Spirit in the hearts of those who are being justified, and abides in them. Consequently, in the process of justification, together with the forgiveness of sins a person receives, through Jesus Christ into whom he is grafted, all these are infused at the same time: faith, hope, and charity. For faith, unless hope is added to it, and charity too, neither unites him perfectly with Christ nor makes him a living member of his body. Hence it is very truly said that faith without works is dead and barren.[3]

Thus justification means, for Tridentine thought, (1) the forgiveness of sins, and (2) the infusion of faith, hope, and love in the heart of the believer. Trent follows Paul, who writes in Romans 5:5 that "God's love has been poured into our hearts through the Holy Spirit that has been given to us." This results in internal justification—the believer really becomes loving and participates in God's love. It is not merely an imputed justification, as in Luther's thought. Trent also taught that there is merit given for good works, such as works of mercy. Our salvation comes to us as a gift, through faith, but also as a reward for good works.[4] This dispute between Luther and the Catholic Church was one of the leading causes in the separation between the Catholic and Protestant churches in the sixteenth century.

Many people find the whole issue of justification and salvation boring and difficult to understand. If they think about it at all, they will probably say that if one is a good person and does one's best, one will go to heaven. But this is precisely what Luther (and Trent) denied; being a good person and doing one's best is not enough. One cannot be saved without faith in God and Christ. This may sound severe today, but it still is the teaching of the major Christian churches that we cannot be saved through our own efforts and that we need the grace of God and Christ for salvation.[5] The New Testament is clear that hell is a real possibility and that becoming worthy of heaven is difficult: "for the gate is wide and the way is easy that leads to destruction, and there are many who take it. For the gate is narrow and the road is hard that leads to life, and there are few who find it" (Matt. 7:13–14). So the problem of justification is serious, and it is relevant to us all. In essence, it concerns the question of how we can become worthy of heaven.

There is not one answer to this question in the New Testament but a range of answers. That is why justification is a theological problem. In the following pages, we will survey the principal New Testament positions and come to a synthesis. This will be followed by a section on judgment.

Matthew: Purity of Heart and Higher Righteousness

In the Sermon on the Mount (Matt. 5–7), Jesus is reported as saying that he has not come to abolish the law and the prophets but to fulfill them (Matt. 5:17). By the "law" he meant the law of Moses (the Torah), including the Ten Commandments. But as Jesus discusses various commandments—do not kill, do not commit adultery, and so on—he insists that they must be applied both to behavior *and* to intentions. It is not enough not to kill, one should not even be angry with one's brother; it is not enough to refrain from adultery, one should not even think lustfully; it is not enough to love one's neighbor and hate one's enemy, one should love even one's enemies and pray for them (Matt. 5:21–48). Good deeds are not enough; we also have to be loving, even to the worst, and pure of heart: "Blessed are the pure in heart, for they will see God" (Matt. 5:8). Forgiveness is also critical: if we forgive others, our Father will forgive us; if we do not forgive others, our Father will not forgive us (Matt. 6:14–15). Jesus, in Matthew's Gospel, calls his disciples to a "higher righteousness." This means following the law not only in one's actions but also in one's intentions—it is the pure in heart who will see God. This higher righteousness culminates in love, as expressed in Jesus's words: "But I say to you, Love your enemies and pray for those who persecute you" (Matt. 5:44).

This is not all Matthew has to say about justification, judgment, and salvation. The most explicit New Testament text on these subjects is found in Jesus's story of the final judgment that appears near the end of Matthew's Gospel (Matt. 25:31–46; this passage has been quoted in full in chap. 2, above). Here, Jesus foresees the end of human history, when he will return as king to judge all the peoples (*panta ta ethnē*). The righteous will go to heaven, but the wicked will go to "the eternal fire prepared for the devil and his angels" (Matt. 25:41). What is the criterion for judgment in this parable? It is acts of mercy to the poor and unfortunate: "I was hungry and you gave me food, I was thirsty and you gave me something to drink, I was a stranger and you welcomed me, I was naked and you gave me clothing, I was sick and you took care of me, I was in prison and you visited me" (Matt. 25:35–36). This is one of the most explicit statements about salvation in the New Testament, but no word is said in the passage about faith or belief. The criterion is what one did.[6] On this accounting, Christians cannot say, "We are saved by faith, not by works, and so will not be judged on our works of charity to others." The law of love is binding for Christians especially, as Jesus made clear in Matthew 5. And the law of love means not just feeling loving; it means acting with loving intentions. In other words, love has to be expressed in deeds if it is genuine love. As Jesus says: "Not everyone who says to me, 'Lord, Lord,' will enter the kingdom of heaven, but only the one who does the will of my Father in heaven" (Matt. 7:21). We will see this also in Luke, Paul, and James.

Luke-Acts: Repentance/Conversion

Repentance is at the core of Jesus's preaching. Mark sums up Jesus's message as follows: "The time is fulfilled, and the kingdom of God has come near; repent [*metanoeite*], and believe in the good news" (Mark 1:15). The verb "repent" in Greek is *metanoein*, which means literally "to change [one's] mind, outlook, attitude." The idea here is not just repenting for a particular sin or action; it is a radical change in attitude that puts God and God's kingdom first and everything else second. It is a change from me-centeredness to God-centeredness. The noun *metanoia* thus means conversion as well as repentance and is a major theme in Luke's Gospel and its sequel, the book of Acts. For example, in Luke 13 Jesus says: "Or those eighteen upon whom the tower in Siloam fell and killed them, do you think that they were worse offenders than all the others who dwelt in Jerusalem? I tell you, No; but unless you repent [*metanoete*] you will all likewise perish" (Luke 13:4–5 RSV).

A number of stories and parables in Luke illustrate what Jesus meant by *metanoia*. The parable of the prodigal son is an example: the son demands his inheritance, wastes it in wild living, and ends up in a foreign country feeding pigs (the deepest humiliation for a Jew). Eventually the son repents and returns to his father, confessing that he has sinned before heaven and before his father (Luke 15:11–32). Another striking parable is that of the lost sheep, which Jesus concludes by saying, "there will be more joy in heaven over one sinner who repents than over ninety-nine righteous persons who need no repentance" (Luke 15:7). Finally, there is the example of the thief on the cross who repents, asking Jesus to remember him when he comes into his kingdom. And Jesus responds, "Truly I tell you, today you will be with me in Paradise" (Luke 23:43). *Metanoia*, therefore, is the key to justification and salvation in Luke's Gospel. True *metanoia*, however, is manifested not only in words but in deeds, as the parable of the prodigal son shows.

Paul: Faith, Love, and the Holy Spirit

The earliest account of the last supper is found in Paul's first letter to the Corinthians:

> For I received from the Lord what I also handed on to you, that the Lord Jesus on the night when he was betrayed took a loaf of bread, and when he had given thanks, he broke it, and said, "This is my body that is for you. Do this in remembrance of me." In the same way he took the cup also, after supper, saying, "This cup is the new covenant in my blood. Do this, as often as you drink it, in remembrance of me." (1 Cor. 11:23–25)

What is the new covenant, and how does it differ from the old covenant? The old covenant, made with the Jews through Moses, was that God revealed the law through Moses. By following this law—encapsulated in the Ten Commandments—the Jews could be justified in God's sight. But because no one could follow the law perfectly, provision had to be made for forgiveness of sins after they occurred. That forgiveness was obtained through the offering of animal sacrifices by the priests. In the new covenant, Jesus himself is the sacrifice; he is the high priest who offers himself in sacrifice (Hebrews), and his sacrifice replaces the sacrifices of animals once and for all. Thus there is a new covenant, or new testament; righteousness is found through the sacrifice of Jesus. All this is spelled out in detail in the Letter to the Hebrews (probably not written by Paul). Paul's own letters also make use of this theology. For Paul, the (Mosaic) law is good: it diagnoses our sin. But, in a very un-Jewish utterance, Paul also claims that no one can be saved by following the law, because no one can live up to the law and because justification comes by faith (Gal. 3:11). If we disobey the law in one particular, it is as if we have disobeyed the whole law (Gal. 3:10). Therefore justification, righteousness, and salvation must be found outside the law. Paul writes:

> But now the righteousness of God has been manifested apart from law, although the law and the prophets bear witness to it, the righteousness of God through faith in Jesus Christ for all who believe. For there is no distinction; since all have sinned and fall short of the glory of God, they are justified by his grace as a gift, through the redemption which is in Christ Jesus, whom God put forward as an expiation by his blood, to be received by faith. (Rom. 3:21–25 RSV)

The righteousness of God manifested outside the law is the righteousness manifested in Jesus, the Righteous one, whose sacrificial death brings salvation to those who have faith in him.[7] We are justified, therefore, by grace through faith: "For by grace you have been saved through faith, and this is not your own doing; it is the gift of God—not the result of works, so that no one may boast" (Eph. 2:8–9). Faith in Christ is not merely verbal profession of belief; it includes the active living out of faith, or what Paul calls "the obedience of faith" (Rom. 16:26). Paul constantly stresses that the life of faith entails living in the gifts and fruits of the Spirit, especially love (1 Cor.13:13), rather than the works of the flesh (Gal. 5:16–26). Paul never uses the expression "faith alone." For Paul, faith includes belief in Jesus as savior, but it also includes living out the faith through the power of the Spirit. This reception of the Spirit makes us sons and daughters of God: "For all who are led by the Spirit of God are children of God" (Rom. 8:14). And the supreme gift and fruit of the Spirit is love: "the only thing that counts is faith working through love" (Gal. 5:6).

Why can't we be justified before God by simply following the law, praying, fasting, giving alms, and doing good works? First, we can never do enough good works to compensate for our sin. Second, according to Paul, no one can entirely avoid sinning: "all men, both Jews and Greeks, are under the power of sin [and] . . . all have sinned and fall short of the glory of God" (Rom. 3:9, 23 RSV). Finally, as Jesus taught, the law extends to intentions also, not just to what we do. Thus when Jesus was asked which commandment is the first and most important, he quoted the Shema: "'Hear, O Israel: the Lord our God, the Lord is one; you shall love the Lord your God with all your heart, and with all your soul, and with all your mind, and with all your strength.' The second is this, 'You shall love your neighbor as yourself.' There is no other commandment greater than these" (Mark 12:29–31). But who can live up to these commandments? How many actually love God and other persons with their whole hearts? Anyone? And so we need a mediator, an intercessor, whose action procures our justification.

Paul uses a striking metaphor for the bondage to sin, namely, the metaphor of slavery. Ancient slaves could never earn enough money to buy their way out of slavery for the simple reason that anything they earned went to their owner. So the only way a slave could be freed was if someone else bought him from his owner and then set him free. This act of "buying back" is what is meant by redemption. For Paul, Jesus's sacrifice paid the price of our slavery and took us out of the slavery to sin, from which we could never escape by ourselves.

Many people typically think that sin is no big deal. And probably in the past, churches harped too much on sin and said too little about love. But sin cuts us off from God and from one another. If you lie or steal or cheat, eventually you will have no friends and no one who trusts you. Sin carries its own reward; it seals us in selfishness and spoils trust and love, so that in the end we are alone, cut off from God and from others.

Paul's answer to the dilemma of sin is that through faith in Jesus we receive forgiveness of our sins and at the same time open ourselves to the grace and love of God. This brings us to Paul's account of the Holy Spirit.

Paul refers to the Holy Spirit both as the Spirit of God and as the Spirit of Christ (Rom. 8). The Spirit brings us gifts and fruits that surpass our natural powers. So, for example, if we are told to love one another as God has loved us, how can we possibly do this? Such love seems to be beyond human power. Love, by the way, is a practical problem in marriage. How are we supposed to love our spouses for a lifetime? Romantic love doesn't last nearly that long: eventually we get old, dumpy, and unattractive. So how are we supposed to continue loving one another? Paul's answer is that long-lasting and self-sacrificing love is a gift of the Holy Spirit, that is, a gift of grace. It is beyond human power but not beyond God's power. Paul speaks of the three great gifts of the Spirit as faith, hope, and love (1 Cor. 13:13), which are virtues needed to become Christlike and worthy of the kingdom of God. These virtues, in fact, perfect us as humans. But we cannot bring them about simply by trying harder. They are gifts of the Spirit, and we have to pray both to receive these gifts and to be made open to receive them. That is Paul's answer to the impossible challenge laid before us by Jesus: to love God with all our hearts and our neighbors as ourselves. The love with which we love God and neighbor is the love given us by the Holy Spirit. Love is the first fruit of the Spirit (Gal. 5:22). As Paul writes in Romans, "God's love has been poured into our hearts through the Holy Spirit that has been given to us" (Rom. 5:5).

For Paul, justification comes not from faith alone, which would be a human work. It comes from faith working through love, which is the gift of the Spirit to those who have faith in Christ: "the only thing that counts is faith working through love. . . . Do not use your freedom as an opportunity for self-indulgence, but through love become slaves to one another. For the whole law is summed up in a single commandment, 'You shall love your neighbor as yourself'" (Gal. 5:6–14).

John and the Johannine Letters

The vocabulary of justification hardly occurs in John's Gospel or in the Johannine Letters. But like Paul, John emphasizes that faith or belief (*pistis*) leads to what Paul calls justification. Through believing and trusting in Jesus, we become children of God: "But to all who received him, and who believed in his name, he gave power to become children of God" (John 1:12). (What is translated as "believe" in English is the Greek verb *pisteuein*, the noun form of which [*pistis*] is translated as "faith.") But in John, as in Paul, belief or faith means much more than verbal profession or simple belief; it means living the life of love: "God is love, and those who abide in love abide in God, and God abides in them. . . . Those who say 'I love God,' and hate their brothers or sisters, are liars; for those who do not love a brother or sister whom they have seen, cannot love God whom they have not seen" (1 John 4:16–20).

The result of faith in God is unity with Jesus Christ and with God. In many places, John speaks of this unity as "abiding" (*menein*) in God and Christ. The best-known instance of this is the image in John 15 of Jesus as the vine and his disciples (past and present) as the branches. There Jesus's command is to love one another: "As the Father has loved me, so I have loved you; abide in my love. If you keep my commandments, you will abide in my love" (John 15:9–10).

Unity with God in this life means living the life of love; in the next life it means eternal life (*zōē*), a life that goes beyond biological life (*bios*) because it is deathless life with God. "For God so loved the world that he gave his only Son, so that everyone who believes in him may not perish but may have eternal life" (John 3:16). This eternal life is the equivalent of salvation in John.

Works and Deeds

As much as Paul stresses that righteousness comes through faith and not through following the law, he also stresses the role of works and deeds, even in Romans, where he insists that the just shall live by faith. Speaking of God's righteous judgment, he writes: "For he will repay according to each one's deeds: to those who by patiently doing good seek for glory . . . he will give eternal life; while for those who are self-seeking . . . there will be wrath and fury" (Rom. 2:6–8). Furthermore, in his second letter to the Corinthians, he writes: "For all of us must appear before the judgment seat of Christ, so that each may receive recompense for what has been done in the body, whether good or evil" (2 Cor. 5:10).

This theme about judgment according to works and deeds is found in many other New Testament texts. In the first letter of Peter we read: "If you invoke as Father the one who judges all people impartially according to their deeds, live in reverent fear during the time of your exile" (1 Pet. 1:17). Judgment according to works is especially prominent in the book of Revelation: "And I saw the dead, great and small, standing before the throne, and books were opened. . . . And the dead were judged according to their works, as recorded in the books. . . . Death and Hades gave up the dead that were in them, and all were judged according to what they had done" (Rev. 20:12–13). Again: "See, I am coming soon; my reward is with me, to repay according to everyone's works. I am the Alpha and Omega, the first and the last, the beginning and the end" (Rev. 22:12–13). Finally, the Letter of James takes up the relation of faith and works explicitly:

> What good is it . . . if you say you have faith but do not have works? Can faith save you? If a brother or sister is naked and lacks daily food, and one of you says to them, "Go in peace; keep warm and eat your fill," and yet you do not supply their bodily needs, what is the good of that? So faith by itself, if it has no works, is dead. . . . Even the demons believe—and shudder. . . . Was not our ancestor Abraham justified by works when he offered his son Isaac on the altar? You see that faith was active along with his works, and faith was brought to completion by the works. . . . You see that a person is justified by works and not by faith alone. (James 2:14–24)

James has often been read as if he were contradicting Paul, who, it is supposed, proclaimed "faith alone" as the basis of salvation. But, as we have seen, "faith" for Paul meant more than just believing; it meant the active living out of one's faith in the power of the Spirit and in a life of love. New Testament scholar Richard Hays notes this forcefully: "Paul, like James, was insistent that faith is manifest in active obedience, and (interestingly) Paul never uses the expression 'justification by faith *alone'(sola fide* is a slogan of the Reformation, not of Paul). The teaching of James is a corrective against a distortion that Paul himself vehemently forswore (Rom. 3:8; 6:1–2)."[8]

On balance, Scripture emphasizes both faith and works. Works by themselves are insufficient for justification: "all have sinned and fall short of the glory of God" (Rom. 3:23). But faith without works is dead. Furthermore, living faith and love are the gifts of God through the Spirit. We cooperate, however, in receiving and exercising the gifts of faith and love, and our cooperation is the expression of faith and love in works of love. Thus the *Joint Declaration on the Doctrine of Justification* of the Lutheran World Federation and the Roman Catholic Church states: "But it is nevertheless the responsibility of the justified not to waste this grace but to live in it. The exhortation to do good works is the exhortation to practice the faith."[9] Another way of putting this is in Johannine language: through faith we "abide" (*menein*) in Christ (see John 15) and seek to do his will, which is love.

Justification

What then is justification? It is forgiveness of sins, through faith in Christ. But it should lead to the inner transformation that comes from the outpouring of God's love in the hearts of believers. This love, *agapē*, is also the gift of the Holy Spirit (see Rom. 5:5). The transformation of our life into the life of love is what is meant by *sanctification*—we are sanctified by the presence of the Holy Spirit in our lives, whose principal fruit is love. Justification, then, is completed by sanctification, and the whole process is salvation. We are saved from a life of selfishness (which ends ultimately in hell), are justified (our sins are forgiven by the grace of Christ), and become sanctified through the presence and gifts of the Holy Spirit, especially the gift of *agapē*, love. This love is the love of God in our lives, in which we participate or "abide." And it is through this love, and only through it, that we will be able to relate to God, Christ, and the community of the blessed in heaven. As the writer of 1 John says: "Beloved, let us love one another, because love is from God; everyone who loves is born of God and knows God. Whoever does not love does not know God, for God is love" (1 John 4:7–8). Love fulfills the two great commandments given by Jesus: to love God and to love neighbor.

Judgment

The whole point of justification is to be found righteous or justified when we have to face God and Christ and render an account of our lives after our deaths. But these days we do not hear much about God's coming judgment. The emphasis now is on self-esteem and feeling good about ourselves. But this is a cultural illusion, and a dangerous one. In the end, all of us will be held accountable by God for our lives, as the biblical texts cited above state. Belief in the judgment of God, however, has been severely distorted by the image of a God of wrath who hurls sinners into hell. Because of this misunderstanding, many people reject the notion of divine judgment. But judgment is not simply appearing before a wrathful God. It is seeing ourselves and our whole lives as we really are; it is coming into the truth and leaving behind our selfish denials and illusions. Put another way, it is seeing ourselves in the context of God's love, which is also truth. For most of us, this will be both joyful and painful, liberating and surprising, because encountering God's love, as expressed in Jesus, will reveal all those occasions in our own lives when we fell short of love, as well as those occasions when we responded with love.

Belief that God exercises judgment on humanity is found throughout both the Hebrew and the Christian Scriptures. God's judgment is a consequence of God's justice; to deny judgment would be tantamount to denying that God is just. We have seen above the importance of righteousness in Scripture. Conversely, it is sin that cuts off humanity from God. Sin in the Old Testament is conceived first of all as disobedience to God's command (as in the Garden of Eden story). Later, it is conceived as failure to observe the commandments of the law of Moses and as breaking the covenant (Deut. 28). Jesus, in the Sermon on the Mount (Matt. 5–7), includes bad intentions as sin; thus it is not enough to avoid adultery, for even to look at another lustfully is to commit adultery in one's heart (Matt. 5:28). His summary of the law as the love of God and of neighbor (Matt. 22:36–40) means that sin is the failure to love. This is also apparent in the story of the sheep and the goats, where failure to help the needy is condemned (Matt. 25:31–46).

In the early books of the Hebrew Scriptures, God's judgment is thought to occur in this life: the virtuous are rewarded and the wicked punished. This belief survived into New Testament times, as reflected in the disciples' question to Jesus about the man born blind: "Rabbi, who sinned, this man or his parents, that he was born blind?" (John 9:2). However, by the time of the Maccabean Wars (167–164 BCE), when many Jews were martyred for their refusal to break the commandments, it had become apparent that the just were not usually rewarded in this life, nor were the wicked always punished. Thus in the last few centuries before Christ, the belief in judgment after death developed in Judaism and was carried on into New Testament times.

Jesus himself refers to the "day of judgment" (for example, Matt. 10:15) and to the threat of hell. Judgment in Jesus's preaching was intrinsic to the coming of the kingdom of God, for the main characteristic of the kingdom was the establishment of God's just reign on earth and the defeat of the power of Satan. And yet the judgment itself was associated with the resurrection of the dead and with the second coming of Jesus, which would take place at the end of history (Matt. 25:31–46).

Who is it that will judge humanity? The Father? Jesus? Each of these answers can be found in the New Testament. In one famous passage, it is Christ who will be the judge when he returns at the second coming (Matt. 25:31–46). Paul also says we all must appear before the judgment seat of Christ (2 Cor. 5:10). But other passages speak of God as the judge. Jesus implies this when he says that if you forgive others, the Father will forgive you (Matt. 6:14). First Peter speaks of invoking as Father "the one who judges all people impartially according to their deeds" (1 Pet. 1:17). Paul speaks of the "judgment of God" (Rom. 2:3), and in John's Gospel Jesus says: "God did not send the Son into the world to condemn the world, but in order that the world might be saved through him" (John 3:17). Further, Jesus says, "I came not to judge the world, but to save the world" (John 12:47). In John's Gospel, it is not Jesus himself who judges the world, but the word that he has spoken that is the judge: "The one who rejects me and does not receive my word has a judge; on the last day the word that I have spoken will serve as judge" (John 12:48). Finally, Paul writes that it is Jesus "who rescues us from the wrath that is coming" (1 Thess. 1:10).

So the New Testament witness is not consistent. The best we can say is that God will judge the world through Jesus. But this could be understood in several ways. If Jesus is the revelation of God's love, it is in comparison to the model and standard set by Jesus—the perfect human being—that we will be judged by God.[10] As Cardinal Ratzinger writes: "Christ inflicts perdition on no one. In himself he is sheer salvation. Anyone who is with him has entered the space of deliverance and salvation. Perdition is not imposed by him, but comes to be wherever a person distances himself from Christ."[11] Wolfhart Pannenberg cites Ratzinger's words with approval and concludes that it is the word of Jesus that will be our judge.[12] My own conclusion is that Jesus himself does not condemn but that we will be judged according to his words and according to the example of obedience and love that he demonstrated in his life. Not that we will be expected to have lived the same life Jesus himself lived, for each of us has a unique vocation. Here it is appropriate to recall a saying of Rabbi Akiba: "God will not ask me, 'Why were you not Moses?' he will ask me 'Why were you not Akiba?'" So will it be with us. Each of us will be judged on how well we fulfilled our own call from God.

Though some biblical images portray a God of wrath who will hurl the wicked into hell (for example, Rev. 20:11–15), this is seriously misleading. We will be judged by a God who is love, not a God who is hate, and in the light of Christ—the perfect human being—a man of love. God does not cast people into hell; people put themselves in hell by cutting themselves off from God. Hell is where they would prefer to be. Sin carries its own reward. If we lie, cheat, and steal, we cut ourselves off from one another and from God and condemn ourselves to a life of loneliness. But love is also its own reward; love brings us into communion with one another and with God. And heaven, as we will see, is nothing other than communion in love with God and with all those who love God. Thus love of self leads to self-isolation and hell, whereas love of God leads to communion with God and heaven.

Another way of conceiving the judgment is that it is simply our entrance into the light of truth; we see ourselves as we truly are, stripped of all our illusions (good or bad). Just as God is love, God is also truth, and whoever would be with God has to be in the truth. There is no room for the selfish illusions we cherish on earth. Here too Ratzinger is right on target:

> The masquerade of living, with its constant retreat behind posturing and fictions, is now over. Man is what he is in Truth. Judgment consists of the removal of the mask in death. The judgment is simply the manifestation of the truth. . . . God is the truth for us as the one who became man, becoming in that moment the measure of man.[13]

We can get an idea of what judgment is like from those times when we have come under judgment in our lives. Sometimes we are vindicated. Often, though, something we have covered up or forgotten is exposed and we feel deeply ashamed.

Christian tradition gradually distinguished between an individual judgment, immediately upon death, and the final or general judgment of all humanity at the end of history. The usual distinction is this: sometime before death, the individual person made a choice for or against God and is no longer able to reverse that choice after death. Those who have decided for God go to heaven; those who have decided against God go to hell. So the individual judgment concerns the relation of each person to God. Later, at the end of time, there will be a general judgment and the resurrection, and all of humanity will be judged. The character of this judgment will differ from the individual judgment. At this judgment will be revealed the long-term effects of all that each person has done. Each of us will see how we fit into the total saga of humanity, which will be complete only at the last judgment.

The idea that each of us goes to heaven or to hell immediately upon death, however, may be too simple. John Polkinghorne, an Anglican priest, notes that most of us are neither wholly bad nor wholly good. Put in terms of the story of the sheep and the goats, each of us is both a sheep and a goat. He therefore suggests, "Perhaps judgment is a process rather than a verdict. Perhaps its fire is the cleansing fire that burns away the dross of our lives. . . . Perhaps judgment builds up the sheep and diminishes the goat in each of us. We are approaching here a concept of Purgatorial judgment."[14] Purgatory, of course, is a Catholic belief, rejected by Luther and the Protestants after him. But a number of Protestant thinkers, such as Polkinghorne, Jerry Walls,[15] and even C. S. Lewis[16] have made strong cases for purgatory for the very reason that Polkinghorne suggests. If Jesus meant what he said ("Be perfect [*teleioi*], therefore, as your heavenly Father is perfect," Matt. 5:48) and we have to be perfect in love to enter into the fullness of God's presence, that is, into heaven, then either most of us will not make it into heaven at all or there must be opportunity for us to complete the process we have begun in this life of dying to self and growing into the love of God. Luther avoided this problem by his idea of imputed justification. But Luther did not really address the related problem of sanctification, that is, how do we become holy, perfect in love, as God is holy so that we can enter into God's presence ("You shall be holy, for I the LORD your God am holy," Lev. 19:2). Polkinghorne's suggestion, with which I agree, is that most people at the end of this life have not totally rejected God (and so do not belong in hell) nor have they become perfect in love of God and neighbor (and so do not merit immediate entrance into the fullness of heaven). Most of us are in between.

Therefore, I argue, those of us whose love of God and neighbor is imperfect will need after death a time of purification or of growing into the full love of God and neighbor. Perhaps God could purify our love instantly so that this state would require no time, but that is not how we grow. We typically need time to receive and absorb the fullness of God's love. How then can we become worthy of heaven if we are not fully worthy when we die? I will take up this problem in the next chapter on heaven, hell, and purgatory.

9

HEAVEN, PURGATORY, AND HELL

What no eye has seen, nor ear heard, nor the human heart
conceived, what God has prepared for those who love him.

1 Corinthians 2:9

It is relatively easy to imagine hell: a state in which the damned are wholly turned in on themselves, cut off from God and one another, and frozen in hate, despair, and selfishness. We know something of this condition from this life on earth. It is much harder to imagine heaven, the exact opposite, where the blessed are open to an infinity of love. Portraying goodness is difficult; portraying infinite goodness impossible. Writers from St. Paul to Dante to modern figures have confessed that heaven surpasses the imaginations of even the greatest artist. This is not because heaven is vague or unreal; it is because it is, so to speak, infinitely real. As our physical eyes are blinded by too much light, the eyes of the mind cannot behold the splendor of heaven unless they are strengthened by supernatural grace. But even then, these visions can barely be expressed in language.

There are at least two ways to think about heaven. One is theocentric, that is, God-centered, and the other anthropocentric, that is, human-centered.[1] The former envisions heaven as the eternal contemplation of God; the latter sees heaven as the fulfillment of human desires. Both perspectives are found in Scripture and in the Christian tradition, and both are important in our attempts to imagine heaven.

In the theocentric view, heaven is where God is; heaven is less a place than a state of being in the full presence of God. As Psalm 16:11 says, "in your presence there is fullness of joy." In John 14:1–4, Jesus explains that he must return to God the Father and prepare a place for his disciples. Eternal life, heavenly life, will be knowing God fully through love. In the vision of the heavenly Jerusalem in Revelation 21, the city has no temple and no sun or moon, for its light is the glory of God. God is fully present in the heavenly city. The theocentric understanding of heaven is predominant in the Western tradition. Thus St. Augustine wrote: "He shall be the end of our desires who shall be seen without end, loved without cloy, praised without weariness."[2] This was also Thomas Aquinas's emphasis: heaven was the eternal beatific vision of God. Dante also, in the final cantos of his *Paradise*, pictures the saints arranged in a celestial white rose, contemplating the eternal love that moves the sun and the other stars.

The anthropocentric vision, by contrast, emphasizes heaven as the fulfillment of human desires: we will be with the communion of saints in a beautiful land of peace and harmony, with all our desires fulfilled. Thus heaven is presented as a garden, the earthly paradise, first imaged in the Genesis descriptions of Eden. In paradise there is no strife; God is present to God's creatures and there is harmony between humans and nature. Heaven is also portrayed as the heavenly city (Rev. 21), that is, the community of those who love God and one another, centered on God and Jesus. Again we must read this symbolically as an imaginative attempt to portray a world in which our desires are satisfied.

Note, however, that not all our desires can be satisfied in heaven. If my desire is to be number one and others have the same desire, those desires cannot all be satisfied in heaven. In general, selfish desires are incompatible with heaven. But our deepest desires—for love, understanding, beauty, freedom, goodness, and holiness—are not diminished by being shared with others; they are increased. Heaven is the state of perfect human fulfillment, which means fulfillment in a community of love.

Let us try to bring together these two approaches to understanding heaven. Try to imagine heaven as the vision of God but also as the fulfillment of our deepest desires. Heaven is the fullness of God's presence; it is full communion with God. But this is abstract; what does this mean concretely? We can open up this idea by thinking of God as infinite love, infinite goodness, infinite beauty, infinite truth, and infinite freedom. These are analogical ways of thinking about God, found throughout the Christian tradition. Analogies differ from metaphors. If we say (as the Psalms do) "God is a rock," that is a metaphor. God is reliable and steadfast, like a rock, but God is not a rock in any literal sense. But if we say, "God is love" (1 John 4:16), this is literally true of God.

We are taking a term from human life (i.e., love) and applying it to God in an unrestricted sense, without its human limitations, because God is infinite. That is an analogy. Let us consider God and heaven, then, under each of these analogies: love, goodness, beauty, truth, freedom.

God as Love

God is the fullness of love. This follows from the Christian conception that the one God is triune—Father, Son, and Spirit—three "persons" or subjects who share one being, one consciousness, one will, bound together in an infinite unity of love.[3] Heaven, then, is participating in the love of the triune God, or, put another way, it is like falling in love with God. Most of us have fallen in love in our lives. But even if we marry our loved one, the bliss of romantic love does not last forever. Mostly this is because the person we love is not perfect. But God is infinite love, and so the love of God will be inexhaustible and endless. Furthermore, God's love also encompasses Jesus and the whole company of the blessed, the communion of saints. To share in this company, we have to be loving as they are loving; this is the main reason we have to change to be a part of heaven. It is not a matter of receiving an extrinsic reward or even of being worthy of heaven. It is a matter of being able to receive and reciprocate the selfless love that is the very being, language, and currency of heaven.

God as Goodness

God is infinite goodness and holiness. Therefore all who would come into the presence of God must themselves be good and holy: "You shall be holy, for I the LORD your God am holy" (Lev. 19:2). Sinfulness, whether of attitude or behavior, cuts one off from the good God and from heaven. But it is not that God gets angry at sin,[4] it is that sin renders us incapable of entering fully into the love that is the language and music of heaven. The essence of sin is selfishness: turning our will from the good of God and others to a self-aggrandizement. But the question is, Can we simply decide not to sin? This was the problem tackled by Augustine and worked out in his *Confessions*. After struggling for years against sexual attachment and the desire for fame, Augustine realized that he could not overcome these vices by himself. It was only with the help of God and God's grace that he could be freed from them. Thus we cannot by ourselves attain the holiness and goodness of God. These come to us as a gift or grace of God; it is God's own holiness, goodness, and love that is shared with us. We are free to open or to close ourselves to God's holiness. It is like tuning in a radio; the radio waves (God's love) are always and everywhere present, but only those whose radios are tuned to the right frequency can receive and participate in the music. This, however, is a metaphor. Theologically, the principle is that we must be like God to participate in God's goodness or love. If we are unlike God, God's love is still present, but we are cut off. Thus our deepest freedom is the freedom to open ourselves to God's grace and cooperate with it or to close ourselves off to it.

God as Beauty

God is infinite beauty, and in heaven the contemplation of God will be the contemplation of infinite and inexhaustible beauty. Beauty requires diversity, not just homogeneity. So another way to understand the beauty of God is to think of God as the source of infinite diversity that is a harmony rather than a cacophony. Aquinas thought that the ideas or forms of existent entities, but also of all that could possibly exist, exist as ideas in the mind of God. Again this is an analogy. We can't really understand the mind of God. But certainly if God is personal and responds to prayer, as the whole biblical and Christian tradition holds, then God must know, and know infinitely, all that exists or could exist. Creation is simply God's bringing into existence some of the infinite range of "ideas" in the mind of God.

So perhaps contemplating the beauty of God would be knowing as God knows all the forms of things. But a more likely image for this is the resurrected creation, which we discussed in a previous chapter. The New Testament, in a few places, envisions the resurrection as embracing the whole of creation, not only humans (see Rom. 8:21; Rev. 21:1). A resurrected creation would restore all the beauties of this creation but in a transfigured and transformed materiality, which does not entail perishing or decay. Furthermore, recent speculations in physics about parallel universes or multiverses open the possibility of a whole range of universes that would be open to our exploration in the transformed state of heaven. In addition, one of the most consistent testimonies of those who survive NDEs, even those who had no previous religious belief, is that they experienced a world of overwhelming love and beauty.

God as Truth and Understanding

God is infinite truth, knowledge, and understanding. What was said above about the ideas in the mind of God applies here. Heaven, understood as the presence of God, will entail the prospect of an adventure in exploration and discovery that will be inexhaustible. This follows from God's infinity: if God is infinite knowledge and truth and if the forms of all possible entities exist in the mind of God, then the fullness of God's presence will mean that this infinite knowledge and truth is open to all who participate in the love of God.

God is infinite understanding. As the great Catholic theologian Bernard Lonergan put it, "God is the unrestricted act of understanding, the eternal rapture glimpsed in every Archimedean cry of Eureka."[5] And being in God's presence means sharing in this understanding, at least so far as we as finite creatures with finite minds can do so. But this means that in heaven we understand the why of everything and how all things ultimately fit together. Heaven is where everything finally makes sense. We will see our life within the whole history of all lives and where we fit into the entire picture. Dante expresses this in a magnificent image near the end of his *Paradise*, the third volume of his *Divine Comedy*. There he writes of the pilgrim's observation in heaven: the Eternal Light "contains within its depths all things bound in a single book by love of which creation is the scattered leaves."[6] For Dante, all the creatures of creation are like the scattered leaves of an immense book, which in heaven will finally be assembled into one coherent volume.

God as Freedom

God is infinite freedom. As finite creatures, we can never experience the full freedom of God—we will always be finite and hence limited. This is true even of the angels. But heaven will certainly entail an enormous expansion of our freedom. On earth, we are limited by space, time, our aging bodies, limited memories, limited abilities, and so on. And to one degree or another, most of us are still not free from the slavery of sin. We have a degree of freedom on earth, but only within a narrow range of choices. All the aspects of heaven considered above, however, will entail an enormous expansion of our freedom—a freedom for infinite love, infinite beauty, infinite knowledge, infinite exploration, and so on. We will still be finite creatures, of course, but we will exist in transformed bodies and a transformed space and time.

God is the source of all the diversity and beauty we behold in the created world, and it does not make sense that in heaven this diversity and beauty would be less than what we experience on earth. All that is good in this life will be not only preserved in heaven but also exalted. Since God is infinite, it would follow that in heaven there will be an infinite diversity and beauty to discover and enjoy, and all of this will reflect God much more perfectly than the created things of this earth. I see heaven as an endless journey into God, whose depths and beauty will be inexhaustible. But this view of heaven raises a number of problems that we will have to consider, such as: Is there time in heaven? Is there matter and space in heaven? Are there animals in heaven? Are only Christians in heaven? Are infants, who have died well before their maturity, in heaven? And so on.

Time, Space, and Eternity in Heaven

Time, space, matter, and energy are all interconnected in modern physics. All apparently came into existence with the Big Bang. Thus we cannot envision space without matter or time, or matter without space and time. Time, space, matter, and energy are intrinsic to human existence in this life and to animal life and the created world. So the question is, Can we imagine a heaven in which there is no time or no space? The traditional picture of heaven, stemming from Boethius, Augustine, and Aquinas, was that there is no time in heaven. Heaven is eternity, but eternity is not endless time; rather, it transcends time so that all moments of time—past, present, and future—are timelessly present in an eternal now. Augustine expresses this in a beautiful passage: "Your [God's] years are one day, and your day does not come daily, but is today, because your today is followed by no tomorrow and comes after no yesterday. Your today is eternity."[7] This is God's "time," and it is the time that the saints in heaven enter into. Thus there is no change in heaven; everything is perfected. Perfect here means changeless, for change indicates either the presence of a lack that must be remedied or the introduction of a lack, both of which result in imperfection. Accordingly, there is no change in God. Aquinas explains this by holding that there is no potency in God; God is pure Act and so cannot change. This does not mean that God is static; far from it: God is pure Act or Activity or Energy (to use a modern metaphor). But this means that God does not change. And since heaven was conceived as the eternal contemplation of God, heaven would not change either. All desires would be perfectly satisfied by the contemplation of God, who is the highest end of human beings, according to Aquinas.[8]

This view of heaven as changeless has been seriously challenged by many contemporary theologians and by science. We know scientifically that the human being cannot exist on earth without change and process; our bodies and brains are never still as long as we are alive; if we stopped all biological processes, we would die. Furthermore, every created thing exists in a dynamic web of relationships and can't be imagined without those relationships. Communication is always occurring among members of the web, and energy is always flowing through the web. This is obvious in the simple physical processes that keep us alive: breathing, eating, drinking, moving around, communicating, and modifying our environment.

Given this, the New Testament passages that envision a renewed and transformed earth make sense. These passages are Revelation 21:1 ("Then I saw a new heaven and a new earth . . .") and Romans 8:19–21: "For the creation waits with eager longing for the revealing of the children of God; for the creation was subjected to futility, not of its own will but by the will of the one who subjected it, in hope that the creation itself will be set free from its bondage to decay and will obtain the freedom of the glory of the children of God." Hope for a renewed creation as part of the resurrection has been constant in the Eastern Orthodox tradition from ancient times and is becoming more common among contemporary Western theologians as well. There would be no point to a resurrected body without a resurrected or transformed environment in which the resurrected body is situated and with which it is interconnected through its senses. It is logical, therefore, that heaven would include such a transfigured environment. Heaven, then, would offer the prospect of an endless adventure and exploration into God—and God's beauty, love, goodness, truth, and freedom.

Of course, we cannot know this for sure. All our knowledge of heaven is but glimpses, and it would be going beyond what we can know for sure to insist that heaven must be an eternal process of development or must be an eternal timeless moment. Indeed, it is conceivable that it is both and that in heaven there are degrees of participation in God so that those who still wish to continue learning can do so and those who wish to rest in contemplation can also do so. It does not fit with what we see of God's creation in this life to insist that heaven must be the same for all its inhabitants. That is certainly not true on earth, where no life, human or animal, is the same as any other. Why should heaven be different?

Purgatory

From very early times, Christians prayed for their dead. We have seen above an early example of this in the story of Perpetua (ca. 200 CE) praying for her brother Dinocrates, who had died years before of a disfiguring cancer (see chap. 3). Augustine approves of prayer for the dead also: "There is no doubt that the dead are helped by the prayers of the holy Church, by the saving sacrifice [that is, the Eucharist], and by the alms given for their souls, in order that God may deal more mercifully with them than their sins have deserved."[9]

This practice has continued in both the Western and Eastern churches up to the present. Luther, however, and with him most Protestants, rejected prayer for the dead. Luther's rejection followed partly from his doctrine of salvation by faith alone. If one is saved only by one's own faith, then the prayers of another cannot be efficacious.

The practice of praying for the dead implies that the dead can be helped by our prayers. This means that they are not already in hell or heaven (as traditionally conceived). By definition, in Christian tradition there is no exit from hell or from heaven. So if the dead are either in hell or in heaven, they cannot be helped by our prayers. Thus prayer for the dead assumes that the dead are in some kind of state where our prayers can help them. It is from this practice of praying for the dead that the doctrine of purgatory developed. Already the idea of a state of purification was present in Augustine's writings, even if he did not use the word *purgatory*. He wrote: "However, not all men who endure temporal punishment after death come into those everlasting punishments which are to follow after that judgment. As I have already said, some will receive forgiveness in the world to come for what is not forgiven in this; and these will not suffer the eternal punishment of the world to come."[10]

This signals the early development of a belief in purgatory, but it also signals the limitations of this idea: it is conceived as a state of punishment. In the Roman Catholic Church, the accent was on purgatory as a place of expiation for the penalty due to sins for which no penance had been done in life. In the Eastern Orthodox church, by contrast, the emphasis was on purgation as a state of growth in holiness.

The story of Luther's rejection of indulgences and purgatory is well known. The practice of selling indulgences had developed in the Catholic church. Indulgences were pardons, authorized by the pope, that could be purchased and applied to the remittance of the punishment of sins in purgatory. This practice was seriously abused in Luther's time. Luther's response was to reject not only the selling of indulgences but the whole belief in purgatory and prayer for the dead. If one is saved by faith and grace alone, there is no need for intercessory prayers. Luther also challenged the doctrine of purgatory because, he alleged, it is not found in Scripture. Therefore it was a fiction.

Roman Catholicism still defends the existence of purgatory, but these days it tends to be presented more as a state of growth and purification of love after death rather than a state of paying penalties for venial (that is, nonmortal) sins.[11] I would defend both senses of purgatory but want to concentrate here on the sense of purgatory as purification of love after death. So I will respond to the objections to purgatory, then I will lay out the reasons why I think that the doctrine of purgatory, rightly understood, is true.

First, many caricatures of purgatory are misleading. There was much medieval debate about the presence of (literal) fire in purgatory, but no one defends this any more. Those in purgatory do not have physical bodies, so physical fire would not affect them, and indeed, could not even exist in a nonmaterial state. Second, purgatory has come to be thought of as a "third state," conceived almost entirely in terms of suffering and paying back the penalties for sin. But this was not entirely true even in the Middle Ages. Dante, who wrote more about purgatory than anyone, in his great poem *The Divine Comedy* pictured purgatory as a state of suffering but also as a state of anticipation and joy. It is not true, however, that purgatory is a "third state" in formal Catholic thinking; rather, it is a part of heaven—heaven's antechamber, as it were. All those in purgatory eventually go to heaven; no one falls back into hell. Purgatory is a state of preparation for the fullness of heaven, which is why it is hopeful and joyful. Those in purgatory want to be there because they are not yet completely ready for heaven.

The objection that purgatory is not found in Scripture is a serious challenge. Certainly the word *purgatory* is not in the New Testament. There are some passages, however, that refer to the forgiveness of sins after death. The clearest is Matthew 12:32: "whoever speaks against the Holy Spirit will not be forgiven, either in this age or in the age to come." A more indirect passage is found in the Sermon on the Mount, when speaking of the danger of hell, Jesus says, "Come to terms quickly with your accuser while you are on your way to court with him, or your accuser may hand you over to the judge, and the judge to the guard, and you will be thrown into prison. Truly I tell you, you will never get out until you have paid the last penny" (Matt. 5:25–26). Why is there no clear mention of purgatory? The reason I think is this. The first generations of Christians clearly thought that the resurrection was a sign that the end times were upon them. Paul himself expected the Lord to return and the general resurrection to occur in his lifetime: "Then we who are alive, who are left, will be caught up in the clouds together with them [the dead who have risen] to meet the Lord in the air" (1 Thess. 4:17). No one expected a prolonged period between death and the resurrection. This is clear in Jesus's saying: "you will not have gone through all the towns of Israel before the Son of Man comes" (Matt. 10:23). At the very least, this indicates that Matthew and his readers expected the return of Jesus within their lifetime. Jesus may have believed the end times were imminent also, but I will leave this as an open question.[12] In any event, there is a lot in the New Testament on the coming judgment but little on any intermediate state, which would have been very brief if the resurrection and judgment were coming soon.

However, it is not the case that everything Christians believe is found explicitly in Scripture. The doctrine of the Trinity is not found explicitly in Scripture; the baptismal formula at the end of Matthew offers the best evidence for this doctrine (Matt. 28:19). But this by itself does not state that the Father, Son, and Spirit are one God. That belief is the result of a long theological development based on what is implied, but not spelled out, in Scripture. Another example is the Christian attitude toward slavery. Several passages in the New Testament appear to explicitly endorse slavery, for example, Ephesians 6:5: "Slaves, obey your earthly masters with fear and trembling, in singleness of heart, as you obey Christ." A similar passage appears in 1 Timothy 6. Yet no Christian theologian today defends slavery. Why not? Because it is seen as incompatible with the general biblical principle that all humans are created in the image of God and all are equally children of God. The prohibition against slavery, then, is not only not found explicitly in the Bible, but it is apparently contradicted by the Bible. The present Christian position on slavery is the result of a long theological development based on what is regarded as foundational biblical teaching, rather than on a conditional concession for a period of time. So the lack of explicit references to purgatory need not be definitive for Christian belief.

But what, then, are the reasons for a belief in purgatory? The main reason is that to come fully into the presence of God, we must be loving as God is loving. If we are not, our love needs to be purified of self-centeredness and recentered on God and others. This is essentially what is meant by sanctification in the Roman Catholic, Orthodox, and Methodist traditions. Though santification begins in this life, very few people at their deaths are perfect in their love of God and neighbor. Even Paul saw himself as still striving toward perfection late in his life ("Not that I . . . am already perfect; but I press on to make it my own, because Christ Jesus has made me his own," Phil. 3:12 RSV). Yet many people who die have a basic faith in God, even though they have not yet reached sanctification. If we say that one does *not* need to be sanctified to come fully into God's presence, then heaven won't be heaven; it will be full of unloving people. But if we say one does have to be sanctified to enter into God's presence, then we have to say either (1) most people don't go to heaven because they aren't sanctified when they die, or (2) people can be sanctified instantaneously at death, or (3) there is a state in which people gradually are purified in their love after death. Not many people today accept (1), and I don't either. Most Protestants accept (2)—people are instantaneously sanctified. But this does not make sense. It is not that it is beyond God's power to change us suddenly. Rather, it is that we need time to accept God's grace and to change under its influence. Everything in our lives indicates that. Even apparently sudden changes, we now know, are preceded by a long period of psychological preparation. So, we need at least a subjective space of time after death in which we can grow into the purification of love (unless we are perfect when we die, with the perfection Jesus requires; see Matt. 5:48).

Seen in this way, purgatory is a profoundly hopeful doctrine. If I did not believe in purgatory, I would have to believe that almost everyone I have ever known didn't make it into heaven. This is because I find the idea of instantaneous perfection to be very difficult to believe. It simply is not the way we grow into God, in this life or in the next. As Jerry Walls writes: "we are essentially temporal beings whose thorough moral and spiritual transformation cannot occur without a significant temporal process."[13] Catholic theologian Karl Rahner suggests that the human personality has many levels, including deeply ingrained attitudes and habits. Therefore, while a decision to turn back to God in conversion might transform the center of one's personality, it still may take time for the grace of conversion to extend to all the levels of one's personality and to transform the ingrained attitudes and habits of a lifetime. This process may continue after death in purgatory.[14]

English theologian John Hick also thinks some notion of purgatory is necessary: "The basic concept of purgatory as that of a period between this life and man's [sic] ultimate state seems unavoidable. The gap between the individual's imperfection at the end of this life and the perfect heavenly state in which he is to participate has to be bridged; and purgatory is simply the name given in roman [sic] theology to this bridge."[15]

Another way to think about purgatory is suggested by Polkinghorne, who imagines it as a long process of judgment (see chap. 8), in which we are purged of all those parts of ourselves that do not love God and others—that is, that are selfish.[16] In this process, we become the persons we were meant to be, the persons—wholly ourselves, yet wholly in love with God and others—that God envisioned when we were first created. This process, of course, will involve suffering, but it will also be joyful because we will be in the process of being restored to our true selves, and we will anticipate the perfect joy of heaven. Indeed, joy in the midst of suffering is the mark of purgatory in Dante's *The Divine Comedy*.

The importance of prayer for the dead can be seen in the case of suicides and other tragic deaths, such as death from drug overdoses, murder, and so on. There was a time when churches would not allow persons who had committed suicide to be buried in Christian cemeteries, because suicide was regarded as a mortal sin, equivalent to murder, that cut off the departed from God (see *Hamlet*, act V, scene 1). Now, however, churches recognize that depression, fear of hardship, suffering, or torture can diminish the responsibility of the one committing suicide.[17] Nevertheless, we should not assume that those who commit suicide leave all their problems behind when they die. As one woman interviewed by Raymond Moody said: "If you leave here a tormented soul, you will be a tormented soul over there too."[18] Moody also cites the case of a man who had shot himself because of the death of his wife and was subsequently resuscitated. The man stated: "I didn't go where my wife was. I went to an awful place. . . . I immediately saw the mistake I had made. . . . I thought, 'I wish I hadn't done it.'"[19] Thus those who commit suicide, more than many others, need a transitional state in which they can work through their problems and come into the full love of God. To argue that they are magically transformed and catapulted into heaven seems to me to be very naive. But to say that they automatically go to hell seems cruel. It therefore seems plausible that many of them continue to exist after death in an intermediate state[20] in which our prayers can help them in their painful transition back to the love of God. And this is true also for all those who die in tragic conditions, whether from drugs, murder, war, and so on.

Hell

Unlike heaven, which is infinitely diverse and almost beyond the descriptions of human language, hell is stark and simple. Indeed, it may be the simplest reality humans can ever experience, for hell is emptiness and isolation from God. Of course God is present in hell, for God is present everywhere. But since those in hell have rejected God, they are closed off to God's presence. They are in hell by their own choice and would not want to be in heaven, because heaven would mean choosing God over themselves or their ego. So hell is a state of being cut off from God. It is also a state of being cut off from other persons. There is no love in hell. If heaven is the fullness of love, hell is the absence of love. Indeed, if there were love in hell, then there would be the possibility of salvation, for "love [agapē] is from God; everyone who loves [agapōn] is born of God and knows God" (1 John 4:7). So those in hell have chosen against love and thus against God. Hell, therefore, is a state of isolation from God and neighbor, the exact opposite of heaven.

We have seen above that Jesus speaks of hell in several ways: in the Sermon on the Mount (Matt. 5–7) he talks about the possibility of Gehenna. Gehenna was the name of a rubbish dump outside Jerusalem, where refuse was constantly burning. By New Testament times, it had become a symbol of hell. In Matthew 25, Jesus speaks of "the eternal fire prepared for the devil and his angels," and of "eternal punishment" (Matt. 25:41, 46). In Mark, Jesus refers to "unquenchable fire" (Mark 9:43). Elsewhere he refers to "outer darkness, where there will be weeping and gnashing of teeth" (Matt. 8:12; cf. 13:50; 22:13; 24:51).

Christian tradition has almost unanimously affirmed the existence of hell down to modern times. This belief has been unquestioned by Catholics, Orthodox, and the Reformed churches. Nonetheless, many people today, including many Christians, doubt hell's existence. It seems like cruel and unusual punishment, something incompatible with a God of love. Even such a traditional theologian as Hans Urs von Balthasar has questioned whether all might not be saved.[21] Not many Christians seem to be worried about the possibility of going to hell. On the one hand, this might be good: too much of medieval and Reformation Christianity was based on the fear of hell. But on the other hand, if there really is a hell, then it is important that people be warned. This seems to be precisely what Jesus himself did, according to the Synoptic Gospels (see, for example, Matt. 25:31–46).

The argument for hell[22] is based first on the justice of God and second on human free choice. If God is just, then the good should be rewarded and the wicked punished, if not in this life then in the next. Jews before and during Jesus's time believed that God would reward the good and punish the wicked in this life, but hardly anyone believes that now. There is too much evidence to the contrary: often the wicked flourish while the good suffer. "Nice guys finish last," as the saying goes. If God is just, therefore, recompense must come after death. This is a powerful argument; it seems outrageous that fiends like Stalin, Hitler, or Pol Pot should get away with their crimes and elude punishment forever. To say they do get away with their crimes unpunished is tantamount to saying there is no God.

There is also the argument from human freedom. Our freedom is a gift from God. But this freedom means we can choose against God and against love; if we could not so choose, we would not have real freedom of choice. Of course our freedom in this life is limited. Someone who grows up in a ghetto, surrounded by crime, will be tempted to follow a life of crime. Presumably God takes such temptations into account in the judgment. That is why only God can judge the state of a person's guilt or innocence. But even if freedom is limited and afflicted with temptations, that does not mean we have no freedom at all. Perhaps we can complain that God has given us too much freedom and too much responsibility. Such a complaint, however, seems childish, as if it would be better to be children or even animals and thus not burdened with the responsibility of freedom. In any case, most of the Christian tradition has affirmed that humans have the freedom to choose for or against God. The exception was Calvin, and possibly Luther. Because Calvin held that God's grace is irresistible, like an implacable force, he also held that humans have no freedom when it comes to their salvation. But this meant that God predestines some to heaven and others to hell. This was upheld for several centuries in the Calvinist churches, but few Christians today defend this doctrine. One can see why. Any God who predestined some to hell could no longer be called "good" but instead would be a capricious tyrant.

In fact the doctrine of hell, like many Christian doctrines, has been badly misunderstood, even to the point of caricature. The caricature is that an angry God hurls sinners into hell, where they burn forever. In fact, the teaching of the Catholic church, and many other churches, is that anyone who is in hell is there because of his or her free choice against love and against God.[23] The choice for ultimate selfishness is finally the choice for hell, because selfishness is the denial of love, which requires self-surrender to another. Hell, therefore, is not due to God's wrath but to human freedom.

Hell is usually pictured in Christian art as a place of fire, demons, and torments, which include thirst, physical tortures, and so on. Dante, in his *Inferno*, pictured hell as afflicting all the senses—fetid smells, fire, sinners in boiling pitch, and Satan, at the lowest pit of hell, frozen forever in ice. But the question still remains, Is hell physical at all? Most of the Christian tradition has held that it is, namely, that the dead will be resurrected, both to heaven and to hell. And Jesus himself , according to Matthew's Gospel, spoke of "the eternal fire prepared for the devil and his angels" (Matt. 25:41). So it could be that the physical features of hell—the fire, tortures, and the like—are due to the resurrection. But there are strong arguments against this position. To modern people, it seems to be cruel and unusual punishment. Wouldn't separation from God and loved ones be punishment enough? Do we have to add eternal fire? For many, probably most people today, the eternal fire of hell raises questions about the love and goodness of God, suggesting a sadistic God of wrath and vengeance. Such a God is not the God of Christianity.

It seems more accurate, and more in keeping with a God of love—who continues, after all, to love even those in hell—that the persons in hell are cut off from God by their own choice, that they do not want to be reconciled with God. The fire of hell is a metaphor for the pangs of regret and disappointment at the loss of their earthly desires. For no matter what those desires were—money, power, fame, lust—they cannot be satisfied in hell. There the earth and its beauties are gone. In the Catholic tradition, this is known as the "pain of loss," which is distinguished from the "pain of sense" (that is, the fire).

An interesting variant on the idea of "pain of loss" is suggested by writing on NDEs. Raymond Moody, author of *Life after Life*, the book that introduced millions to this subject, wrote a sequel, *Reflections on Life after Life*. In that book, he responds to questions he received about judgment. He answers that if what the subjects of his study reported were true, then during their "life review" they saw not only what they had done with their lives but also what the effects of these actions were. They saw countless individual tragedies and deaths caused by their actions, all "vividly portrayed before them," Moody writes. "In my wildest fantasies, I am totally unable to imagine a hell more horrible, more ultimately unbearable than this."[24]

What about the eternity of hell? Jesus speaks not only of the "eternal" (*aiōnos*) fire but also of the damned going off to "eternal" (*aiōnos*) punishment (Matt. 25:46). This has led the Christian tradition to believe that hell and its torments are eternal. "Eternal" can mean two things: everlasting time or the transcendence of time altogether, so that all time is present in one timeless moment. The latter, however, is true of God and those who participate in the life of God. But this is not the case for those in hell. Therefore hell has been pictured as everlasting torment. But again, this raises questions about God's goodness. Yes, some theologians have argued that any sin against God is infinite, since God's goodness is infinite, so such a sin deserves infinite punishment. But many Christians today find such arguments unconvincing. Why would a good God create persons he foreknew would be damned? Why would God continue to hold them in existence? Would it not be more merciful to annihilate them than to allow them to suffer eternal torment? Finally, could not God override their free choice and so bring them to salvation? And it is worth noting that almost no other religion envisions an everlasting hell. In Hinduism and Buddhism, those in hell eventually exhaust their bad karma and are reborn in higher realms; no one stays in hell forever. Islamic theologians speculate that God might shorten hell and simply annihilate those in it, rather than prolong their punishment. Only Christianity (along with Orthodox Judaism and some schools of Islam) envision an everlasting hell.

There are arguments on both sides of this question. On the one hand, Matthew 25:31–46 presents Jesus as speaking of hell and its punishment as eternal. And one could ask, If those in hell are there by their own choice, what would cause them to change their minds? Indeed, could they change their minds? On the other hand, eternal punishment seems unworthy of and even contradictory to God, who is love. Further, an eternal hell would mean that in the end there is an irreconcilable dualism in reality: God, the communion of saints, and the redeemed creation, and the black hole of hell where the damned dwell. Finally there is the tough question, Wouldn't those in heaven still love and miss their loved ones who were in hell? But if so, then their happiness in heaven would not be complete.

One possible answer is universalism, the doctrine that all will eventually be saved. John Hick states this forcefully:

> The faith that God has made us for fellowship with himself, and that he so works in his creative power as to enable us to reach that fulfillment, carries with it the faith that in the end all human life will, in traditional theological language, be "saved." . . . In faith we affirm God's love as both a present and an eternal reality; and as it looks to the future this becomes a faith in the universal triumph of divine love, when God shall be "all in all" and the entire creation shall have become his kingdom.[25]

Universalism posits, therefore, that God somehow saves those who have rejected God. Perhaps God's grace changes their wills even after death (this would seem to be Hick's position). There are a few passages in Scripture that can be used to support this position, mainly 1 Timothy 2:3–4: "God our Savior, who desires everyone to be saved and to come to the knowledge of the truth." Paul also writes, "for as all die in Adam, so all will be made alive in Christ" (1 Cor. 15:22). But Paul also speaks of those made for destruction: "What if God, desiring to show his wrath . . . has endured with much patience the objects of wrath that are made for destruction" (Rom. 9:22), and "the Lord Jesus . . . inflicting vengeance on those who do not know God and on those who do not obey the gospel of our Lord Jesus. These will suffer the punishment of eternal destruction" (2 Thess. 1:7–9). There are many similar passages that speak of hell and punishment as everlasting, such as Jesus's words in Mark 9:48, which speak of hell (*Gehenna*) as a place "where their worm never dies, and the fire is never quenched" (see also Matt. 5:22, 29; 10:28; 13:41–42; 25:31–46; John 3:36). Furthermore, there is little support for universalism in the Christian tradition—Gregory of Nyssa's suggestion that all might in the end be saved was not accepted. So to make a case for universalism, one must have strong arguments that would outweigh the testimony of Scripture and the almost universal consensus of the Christian tradition.

Another possibility is "annihilationism," that is, that God eventually annihilates those in hell. Annihilationism has little or no support in Scripture or tradition. Yet many today favor it because it seems more worthy of a God of love, who would not allow creatures to suffer forever in eternal torment. Jerry Walls proposes the interesting argument (against universalism and annihilationism) that those in hell have chosen their own destiny and would not want to be with God: "a person who had chosen evil decisively would be a person who had consistently wanted evil at all levels of desire."[26] He cites examples from C. S. Lewis's book *The Great Divorce*, in which Lewis introduces the reader to characters who choose hell over heaven because they stubbornly will not give up their self-righteousness (or whatever other sin they are attached to).[27] God gives us our freedom and does not override it. I tend to agree with Walls's line of argument, but there are powerful arguments on both sides. I therefore leave it to the reader to decide.

The official Roman Catholic position is that hell is eternal.[28] This is also the position of many evangelical churches and generally of the Orthodox churches. Nonetheless, some of the fathers of the church, and some contemporary theologians as well, express hope that all might be saved in the end. Orthodox theologian and bishop Timothy Ware writes: "It is heretical to say that all *must* be saved, for this is to deny free will; but it is legitimate to hope that all *may* be saved."[29] Certainly God continues to love even those in hell, more than we do. So while we may hope for the salvation of all, in the end we must leave their ultimate destiny to God, who alone can comprehend the fullness of the mystery of heaven and hell.

The possibility of hell raises in its starkest form the question of dying well. At a minimum, a good death, even if it is terribly painful, is one that leads to heaven or purgatory on the other side. And a bad death, even if it is painless, leads to isolation from God and from blessedness. We will take up the question of dying well in the next chapter.

10

Dying Well

For I am convinced that neither death, nor life, nor angels, nor rulers, nor things present, nor things to come, nor powers, nor height, nor depth, nor anything else in all creation, will be able to separate us from the love of God in Christ Jesus our Lord.

Romans 8:38–39

Death is often a trial, in some cases the supreme trial of our lives. That it is a physical trial is a fact brought home by the deaths of Jesus, the martyrs, and many whom we have known. I remember my mother, near her death, not having the strength to lift her head off the pillow and begging me to do it because she had a pain in her neck. I could not imagine ever being so weak. Death can also be an emotional trial, often afflicting the dying with anger, depression, loneliness, despair, and humiliation. It can also be a spiritual trial, a test of our faith. Do we really trust God to bring us through death to a good afterlife? Or do we give way to despair?

Because they think of death as involving suffering, many people think that the best death is quick and sudden, with no pain, no worry, no long decline. But the Christian tradition holds that quick, sudden deaths are not usually good deaths. In his moving book, *Dying Well*, Ira Byock argues the same thing.

> While sudden deaths are attractive among the healthy, in reality they leave many
> things undone, and they are often the hardest deaths for families to accept. In
> contrast to an abrupt, easy death, dying of a progressive illness offers precious
> opportunities to complete the most important of life's relationships. . . . This
> includes the chance to reconcile strained relationships, perhaps between previous
> spouses or between a parent and an estranged adult child. When the story of
> two people ends well, a warm light is shone on all that has preceded. Even at the
> very end of life, healing a relationship can transform the history of a family.[1]

Sudden deaths are often the worst kind for family and friends to accept, because the dying person has no chance to say good-bye, to forgive and be forgiven, to make reconciliations, or to set his or her affairs in order. Furthermore, he or she usually has had no time to make peace with God. So he or she leaves this life and enters the next unprepared. Death, I tell my students, is like graduation. If you have prepared well, it's a happy farewell to college days and the beginning of a new chapter in your life. But if you have not prepared, it can be a haunting failure. Death is the end of one part of our journey and the beginning of another. As such, it is one of the most critical moments in our lives. This is recognized not only in Christianity but in other religions as well, especially Buddhism, which regards the moment of death as pivotal: If one dies spiritually prepared and with a clear mind, one can reach Enlightenment right after death. If one dies afraid, unprepared, angry, depressed, or despairing, one will be reincarnated, probably in a worse state of life. Thus from the perspective of Christianity, Buddhism, and other religions, one of the worst ways to approach death is not to think about it at all, not to prepare for it, and to maintain an attitude of denial.

The Christian faith gives us at least two important helps for the trial of death. One of them is the love of God and the love of Jesus Christ, which can accompany us through the ordeal of dying. God's love, Paul assures us, will not desert us, even in death. Jesus is a fellow sufferer, who has himself been through death and yet still lives. He can be our comforter, guide, and intercessor as we travel through death. The other great help is the hope and vision of heaven awaiting us on the other side. But to avail ourselves of these helps, we need to have developed a deep relationship with God in prayer. If we have not done this, God will be there with us, but we may be tuned out, unable to hear or receive the comfort of God's love. And if we are not sure of the existence of heaven, or any afterlife, then of course the hope of heaven will not console us as we die. So for both of these helps to be effective in a person's death, that person needs to have prepared by developing a personal relation with God in prayer.

A Good Death

What is a good death? In the last chapter of his book *Dying Well*, Byock tells the remarkable story of a seemingly ordinary woman, Mo Riley, who in her dying "transform[ed] herself from a vibrant, loving mother and person living in the world into an almost lofty being of beauty and spirit." Riley (a pseudonym) had raised a family of six children as a single parent. At sixty-five years of age, she was diagnosed with a fatal cancer at the base of her brain, but her deep faith in God and afterlife allowed her to pass gracefully and beautifully from this life to the next. Byock writes:

> Every now and then . . . I meet a person who while dying seems to flow smoothly out of worldly concerns and relationships and toward an ethereal, spiritual state. Such people may have worked hard earlier in their lives on relationships and aspects of themselves, acquiring in this way the skills to accomplish the taskwork of dying. Their lives were, thus, fairly well in order before the time of dying, freeing them to focus on growth within the realms of spirit and soul. Growing up, growing old, growing on—this was Mo Riley. . . . In her dying, Mo epitomized a blessedness that comes with letting go both of the burdens and delights of daily life—ultimately letting go of life itself and willingly slipping into another realm.[2]

Riley accepted some initial radiation therapy but then decided not to pursue further radiation or chemotherapy. She knew she was dying and that her time had come. "I've said my good-byes, my life is in order, the kids are taken care of. Actually, I've been ready for a while."[3] Certainly, Riley had the usual physical difficulties during dying: weakness, pain, and a catheter, but the pain was controllable with medication and she was tenderly cared for by her family. As her condition deteriorated, she became more detached, "letting go of worldly attachments and focusing on someplace beyond."[4] Her journey was helped by prayer, as Byock notes: "Her faith and religious conviction provided a foundation of confidence for moving toward the unknown without fear, ultimately allowing her to let go even of the pangs of loss."[5] In the end, Riley died the way she had lived. She had lived well through her adult life, building strong relationships with family and friends and deepening her relationship with God. When she died, her life was complete. Her dying process consisted of letting go of attachments to this life, to family, and to friends and completing her journey into the realm of transcendence. Byock concludes: "Mo was as complete a person as I have ever known. In dying, this completeness gave her freedom to let go of herself and grow into pure spirit."[6]

One way to understand a good death is to contrast it with a bad death. What is a bad death? Certainly a death with unrelenting pain is a bad death. So is an isolated death, cut off from friends and family (which may happen in hospitals). So is a death that cuts short the hopes and dreams of our lives. And so is dying in fear, in hopelessness, or in depression. Finally, most of us would think that dying in a state of mental decline or childlike dependency is an unbecoming death. So the converse of a bad death would be a death without pain, surrounded by friends and family, our life's goals achieved, without fear, hopelessness, or depression. Such a death would seem to be a good death.

But some deaths that have been recognized as good by generations of Christians do not fit this pattern. What about the deaths of martyrs? We saw an example of a martyr's death, that of Perpetua, in chapter 3 above. Her death entailed terrible torture and suffering. She died in her early twenties and had to surrender her infant child to be raised by her father. In her death she had the company of a few Christians, but in the Roman amphitheater she was faced with a hostile and bloodthirsty crowd. By any modern criterion, we would have to say she died a terrible death. Yet the Christian tradition, from the third century on, has held up her death as a model of heroic faithfulness and imitation of Christ. She saw her approaching death as a battle with Satan in which she would be victorious.

There are many stories of famous martyrs, such as Stephen, the first Christian martyr. Stephen was stoned to death for preaching to the Jewish council (see Acts 7). Like Perpetua, he died a physically painful and degrading death in front of a hostile crowd. Yet before his death, he had a vision of Jesus standing at the right hand of God, which led directly to his stoning. So even though Stephen died a painful death at the hands of a murderous mob, the church has held up his death as a model of heroic witness in dying.

Finally, of course, there is the death of Jesus himself, as painful, agonizing, shameful, lonely, and terrible a death as we can imagine. Was Jesus's death a good death? It is hard to say "Yes," but it is also hard to say "No." Crucifixion was designed to be as painful and degrading as possible, and it accomplished this intention. It was also a public humiliation of the worst sort. So Jesus died abandoned by most of his disciples. According to almost any criteria of a good death, therefore, we would have to say that Jesus's death was terrible. Yet the early Christians interpreted his death as a victory that reconciled sinful humanity to God and defeated the power of death and Satan. Seen in this way, his death was a triumph, a victory that was much more important than his suffering and humiliation.

The examples of the martyrs and Jesus's own death lead me to conclude that what is essential in a good death, from a Christian point of view, is dying into God. Yes, it is good to die without pain. Yes, it is good to die at a ripe old age with one's hopes fulfilled. Yes, it is important to reconcile with family and loved ones, to repair old rifts, and above all to forgive. Jesus said, "If you do not forgive others, neither will your Father forgive your trespasses" (Matt. 6:15). But as the deaths of the martyrs and of Jesus show, it is essential to die reconciled and at one with God, having fulfilled God's will in one's life, even if one dies at an early age or in pain or among enemies.

Granted, not many people today are called to be martyrs, and perhaps the example of martyrs here will be thought extreme. But the point is, dying at one with God suffices for a good death. Nothing else can ultimately harm us. Paul makes this point beautifully in Romans 8: "For I am convinced that neither death, nor life, nor angels, nor rulers, nor things present, nor things to come, nor powers, nor height, nor depth, nor anything else in all creation, will be able to separate us from the love of God in Christ Jesus our Lord" (Rom. 8:38–39).

Death, then, ought to be the time when we can surrender ourselves completely to God in faith and trust. It may be the supreme trial of our lives, but it is also the supreme opportunity. Entering the shadow of death, we can see more easily what really counts. (This is the message of *Tuesdays with Morrie*.) Money cannot carry us through death, nor can possessions, fame, family, or friends. In the end, what lasts is love: God's love for us, our love for God, and the mutual love beween ourselves and others.

Alternatively, death can be a final refusal of God. Probably the worst death in the Bible is that of Judas Iscariot, a suicide who died abandoned by friends and human comfort, overwhelmed by his sins, and, apparently, cut off from God (though we cannot know this for sure). In death we are faced with the ultimate moment of choice, a moment in which we decide whether to entrust ourselves to God.[7]

Preparing for Death

How, then, do we prepare for death? Robert Bellarmine, in his book *The Art of Dying Well* (1620), states that the first rule for dying well is living well: "He who lives well will die well."[8] By living well, Bellarmine means dying to the world, that is, giving up attachments to worldly things; practicing faith, hope, and charity; praying; fasting; giving generously to the poor; receiving the Eucharist; and so on. Such practices take time, sometimes a lifetime, to develop. It is like training to be a good doctor, musician, athlete, or scholar;

it takes concentration, daily practice, and years of patient endurance to learn deep faith, hope, and love.

But someone might reply that we do not need to do all that. All that is needed is faith in Jesus Christ as our savior; with such faith we are saved and all will be well. I do think we need to put our faith in Christ and in God. But as I have argued above, living faithfully is precisely not just verbal commitment or intellectual belief or even trust. It is putting one's faith into practice day in and day out; anything less than this is a superficial faith. As James writes: "Was not our ancestor Abraham justified by works when he offered his son Isaac on the altar? You see that faith was active along with his works, and faith was brought to completion by the works" (James 2:21–22). The author of 2 Timothy writes: "I have fought the good fight, I have finished the race, I have kept the faith" (2 Tim. 4:7). And Jesus emphasized that each of us has to take up his or her cross each day (Luke 9:23). Faith, then, needs to be completed by love and the works of love. Even Luther—the great apostle of salvation by faith alone—argued that a Christian, though justified by faith alone, will seek to do works of service to his neighbor. "Therefore he should be guided in all his works by this thought . . . that he may serve and benefit others in all that he does, considering nothing but the need and the advantage of his neighbor. . . . This is a truly Christian life. Here faith is active through love (Gal. 5:6), that is, it finds expression in works of freest service, cheerfully and lovingly done."[9]

But what about deathbed conversions? Can't we repent just before death and still be saved? The classic scriptural example of this is the "good thief," who was crucified next to Jesus, repented in his last hours, and asked Jesus to remember him when he comes into his kingdom. Jesus replied: "Truly I tell you, today you will be with me in Paradise" (Luke 23:43). This story is told only in Luke and is almost certainly Luke's own composition. Mark's Gospel simply says, "Those who were crucified with him also taunted him" (Mark 15:32). Nonetheless, this is inspired Scripture, and we must hold that it is possible to repent and be saved in the last hours of one's life. But several points are important here. First, such a transformation is usually preceded by a long preparation, even if it is only semiconscious. Modern psychology supports this; major decisions are preceded by long periods of reflection. Second, genuine deathbed repentances are rare; almost always persons die as they have lived. Third, putting off repentance until one is near death is risky—it ignores the force of habit. Over long periods of time, vices, like virtues, become habitual and cannot be simply shrugged off. And finally, repentance, *metanoia*, in the Gospels means a complete transformation of attitude, from self-centeredness to God-centeredness. Some people "convert" at the end of their lives out of fear, but one has to wonder how deep these "conversions" really are. In sum, certainly we can hope that persons will repent before their death, but it is extremely risky to put off getting one's life in order and preparing for death until the very end.

Can we be sure that after death the person who has died cannot change her mind? The Christian church has traditionally taught that there is no possibility of repentance after death. But I doubt that we can know this for certain. We saw above (chap. 5), in the story of Howard Storm, that he started to pray for the first time in his life as he was near death, in a comatose, out-of-body state. What if he had begun to pray while out-of-his-body, repented, but died without regaining consciousness? To all appearances he would have died an atheist yet would have repented while he was dying. Thus I think we cannot know what happens to persons after they die. The Catholic and Orthodox churches do declare that some persons are saints. But they do not declare that any particular person (even Judas) is in hell.

If death is the all-important time for decision, what about those persons who die suddenly without, apparently, ever having decided definitively for or against God? Again, it seems to me that we cannot know. We can hope that they gain some clarity after passing into the afterlife and that they will at that moment, if not before, choose to grow into God's love and the love of Christ. We can hope that they will realize in the afterlife what they could not see in this life: that it is God who is the giver and sustainer of all that exists and that our goal in life is to come into love of and friendship with God, through Jesus Christ. If this is the case, then they could continue to grow in the love of God even after their deaths.

This same conclusion would apply to infants and children who die before reaching maturity. There is no reason to think they would be rejected by God. In life they did not have the chance to grow into their own maturity. One of the strengths of a belief in an intermediate state in which purification and growth into God is possible after death is precisely that it makes some sense of the salvation of infants and children. We do not need to imagine that they fall into hell (as Augustine did) or that they are instantly perfected and become saints without, apparently, ever having chosen for God. Rather, it seems to me, we can hope that they continue their journey into God through an intermediate state. Thus they may grow in love, as we do in this life, though possibly without all the hardships we experience.

What about suicides? I have discussed this above (chap. 9), and here will only reiterate that I believe persons who commit suicide die as troubled persons who need our prayers.

The Journey through Death

We can compare preparation for dying to preparing for a long journey. We sell our home and property, leave friends and relatives behind, and set out for a far and unknown land. The journey has three parts: departure, the travel itself, and the arrival. Let us consider these in order and ask, What do we need for the journey through death?

To depart, we need to let go of our possessions. One of the biggest impediments to a good death is being too attached to the things of this world. This includes money, possessions, our own selves, and even family and friends. Attachments prevent us from letting go and moving on. There is a story of a young mother in Byock's book who could not let go of her children and family. She fights against her cancer, prolongs her death, and endures terrible pain and suffering but in the end dies. After her death, her husband senses her presence around the house—even after her death she could not let go and move on.[10] Since our whole culture encourages us to accumulate more money and possessions, and these become central to our identity, letting go can be very difficult. Not many people manage this completely in their lifetimes. But it is an essential part of preparing for death. Otherwise we set out on our journey still looking behind.

What do we need to take for the travel? We can't take possessions. As the Buddhists say, we cannot take even a needle and thread through the passage of death. What we can and do take is our soul and mind; our memories, attitudes, faith, hope, charity, and relationship with God and with Jesus. These can survive even death. This is why the attitude of our mind at death is so important. Rather than dying in a state of fear or depression or despair, we should strive to die in an attitude of faith, hope, and charity.

Faith, hope and charity are the so-called theological virtues. They are gifts from God—that is, they are due to God's grace—but they are also virtues we cultivate. How do we cultivate or develop such gifts? Faith means trusting in God, whom we cannot see (Heb. 11). Hope is grounded in God, not in things we can see. Love means our love of God and neighbor. The traditional way of cultivating these gifts is by praying that God would give them to us, by reading and studying the Scriptures, by reading the lives of holy men and women—that is, people who themselves have been persons of faith, hope, and charity—and by associating with people who have these gifts themselves, in other words, with a Christian community. This was common practice for older generations of Christians but is typically not the case now, especially among younger Christians, who can be greatly influenced by the media. We don't develop deep faith, hope, and love overnight. That is why we need to prepare for death for many years.

We can think of the judgment we will face at death as the customs station—will we be allowed to enter the new country? Faith, hope, and love, but especially love, will be our passports. And many Christians, particularly Catholics, believe that our deeds on earth will be part of the judgment we face (Matt. 25:31–46).

For the arrival, we need love, for heaven is the realm of love. As Paul writes, "love never ends" (1 Cor. 13:8). Faith will come to an end, for in heaven we will know God face to face. Hope will come to an end, for in the presence of God our hope will be fulfilled. But love is the currency of heaven and the way we will relate to God and to the blessed who will be our companions. Knowledge also will continue if, as Gregory of Nyssa wrote, heaven is a ceaseless adventure and exploration into the infinity of God. So love and knowledge will remain. But these will also be one. For the knowledge we seek will not be conceptual knowledge but intuitive knowledge, like the knowledge lovers have of each other. And the love will carry with it knowledge of the beloved. Paul writes, "Then I will know fully, even as I have been fully known" (1 Cor. 13:12). Finally, beauty will remain. This especially comes across in the near-death accounts; survivors have glimpsed a realm of greater beauty than they ever could have imagined.

Of course, heaven is a mystery. There is much about it we cannot know but will discover only when we arrive. But it is not true that we know nothing about heaven or about the afterlife. We know we will be with God and the saints in a communion of love. That is and has always been the hope of Christians and of the church, and it is that great hope that allows us to live in the present with joy.

NOTES

Introduction

1. Jim McDermott, "Christ and Secular Sweden: An Interview with Klaus Dietz about the Swedish Church," *America*, December 24–31, 2007, 16.

2. Carl Sagan, *Cosmos* (New York: Ballantine Books, 1985), 1.

3. Einstein also believed in God, whom he called "the old one," but his God did not answer personal prayers.

4. John Hick, *The Fifth Dimension* (1999; Oxford: OneWorld, repr., 2004), 14.

5. I take up this challenge at length in my previous book, *The Sacred Cosmos* (Grand Rapids: Brazos, 2003).

6. Hans Urs von Balthasar, *Dare We Hope That All Men Be Saved?* (San Francisco: Ignatius, 1988).

7. N. T. Wright, *The Resurrection of the Son of God* (Minneapolis: Fortress, 2003).

Chapter 1 Underworld, Soul, and Resurrection in Ancient Judaism

1. For a collection of the intertestamental literature with introduction and commentary, see James Charlesworth, ed., *The Old Testament Pseudepigrapha*, 2 vols. (New York: Doubleday, 1983–85). For a standard introduction to the Old Testament, see Lawrence Boadt, *Reading the Old Testament* (Mahwah, NY: Paulist Press, 1984).

2. The underworld as the abode of the dead is referred to by several terms in the Hebrew Bible. Theodore Lewis writes: "Several terms are used to denote the abode of the dead in the Hebrew Bible, and they often occur in parallelism to one another. The most common is *sheol*. Both *sheol* and *mawet*, 'death,' are often used in Hebrew to refer to the realm of death. . . ." The Hebrew idea of the underworld is paralleled in the literature of Egypt and Mesopotamia: "We have few descriptive details of Sheol in comparison to the elaborate depictions of the underworld found in Egyptian and Mesopotamian literature. . . . One thinks immediately of the Egyptian 'guide books' for the dead in the underworld (*dat/duat*) which lead through various gates, portals, and caverns. The Mesopotamian story about the descent of Ishtar into the netherworld describes the entrants' journey to the 'land of no return' . . . which is a place 'bereft of light where their sustenance is dust and their food is clay.'" See Theodore Lewis, "Dead, Abode of," in *The Anchor Bible Dictionary*, ed. David Noel Friedman, 6 vols. (New York: Doubleday, 1992), 2:101–2.

Just as there were several words denoting the underworld, so is there more than one word for the dead: "In the realm of the dead the *metim* are also called *rephaim*, 'Spirits of the dead, shadows' (e.g., Isa. 26:14, 19; Ps. 88:11 [10]). The expression *kemete olam*, 'like those long dead' (Ps. 143:3; Lam. 3:6) similarly refers to the shadowy existence characterizing the realm of the dead" (Heinz-Josef Fabry, K.-J. Illman, and Helmer Ringgren, "מות *mût*,"in *Theological Dictionary of the Old Testament*, ed. G. Johannes Botterweck et al., 15 vols. [Grand Rapids: Eerdmans, 1974–2006], 8:204–5).

Thus even though there are different words used for "underworld" and "the dead" in different passages in the Hebrew Scriptures, these words are often used in parallelism and hence denote the same or similar conceptions. Furthermore, the parallels in Egyptian, Mesopotamian, and Greek literature also indicate a similar conception of the underworld. For a good presentation of the ancient Israelite conception of the underworld, death, and afterlife, see Helmer Ringgren, *Israelite Religion* (Philadelphia: Fortress, 1966), 239–47.

3. Robert Gundry, *Sōma in Biblical Theology with Emphasis on Pauline Anthropology* (Cambridge: Cambridge University Press, 1976), 121.

4. Hebrew *nephesh*; the New Jerusalem Bible translates this as "soul."

5. Gundry, *Sōma in Biblical Theology*, 121.

6. Bill T. Arnold raises questions about interpreting this passage "dualistically" and suggests Samuel in this passage is more like a resuscitated physical body "perhaps not unlike the resurrection body of Jesus." It cannot be a resuscitation, however, because Samuel was buried at Ramah (1 Sam. 28:3), whereas Saul visited the medium at Endor, some thirty-five miles away. Furthermore, mediums did not resuscitate the dead; they contacted the dead spirits. Finally, the passage itself states that the woman said, "I saw a god [*elohim*] coming up out of the earth" (1 Sam. 28:13 RSV). This would seem to indicate a spirit, not a resuscitated body. Arnold's point, as I understand it, is that the Hebrews thought of the dead holistically, not dualistically like the Greeks, a point with which I agree. See Bill T. Arnold "Soul-Searching Questions about 1 Samuel 28," in *What about the Soul? Neuroscience and Christian Anthropology*, ed. Joel Green (Nashville: Abingdon, 2004), 75–83.

7. Mark S. Smith writes of the *rephaim* as follows: "References to the Rephaim in the book of Proverbs also indicate that they are the dead dwelling in the netherworld. In Prov 2:18 the house of folly leads (or, sinks down) to death and to the Rephaim. The foolish man does not know that the Rephaim (RSV 'dead') are in the underworld, according to Prov 9:18. Prov 21:16 characterizes the Rephaim as a 'congregation' or 'assembly' (*qahal*)." Smith notes that the Israelite conception of the Rephaim was paralleled in Ugaritic texts and Punic-Latin texts. See Mark S. Smith, "Rephaim," in *The Anchor Bible Dictionary*, 5:675.

8. Homer, *The Odyssey* 4, trans. Robert Fitzgerald (Garden City, NY: Doubleday, 1961), 97–212. All quotes from *The Odyssey* are taken from this translation.

9. For a careful analysis of the relevant passages and the anthropology in the Old Testament, see John W. Cooper, *Body, Soul, and Life Everlasting* (1989; Grand Rapids: Eerdmans, repr., 2000), 33–72; also Gundry, *Sōma in Biblical Theology*, 117–34.

10. N. T. Wright, *The Resurrection of the Son of God* (Minneapolis: Fortress, 2003), 99.

11. Ibid., 102.

12. Wright notes that Greek vase paintings from about 500 BCE show the soul as a small human creature hovering over the body of a dead warrior (ibid., 48).

13. Wright, *Resurrection*, 113.

14. Ibid., 125.

15. Ibid., 164.

16. See, for example, Brian Edgar, "Biblical Anthropology and the Intermediate State: Part 1," *Evangelical Quarterly* 74, no. 1 (2002): 27–45; and "Part 2," *Evangelical Quarterly* 74, no. 2 (2002): 109–21. See also Joel Green, *Body, Soul, and Human Life: The Nature of Humanity in the Bible* (Grand Rapids: Baker Academic, 2008), esp. chaps. 1 and 5. With respect to an intermediate state in the Old Testament, Green writes: "Even in those texts that speak of those who dwell in Sheol, we find no suggestion that some essential part of the human being (whether a

soul or a spirit or some other) has survived death. . . . No suggestion is found in any of these texts that the *rephaim* might be regarded as 'alive' or 'living' or otherwise as having some form of 'personal existence'" (pp. 154–56). Given the passages cited above, especially Isa. 14, where the dead *rephaim* in Sheol are portrayed as being roused to greet the incoming king of Babylon, and 1 Sam. 28, which Green ignores in his book, I find this judgment simply does not fit the texts. Furthermore, if Green is right, then the Israelite conception of the dead differed entirely from that of their neighbors—the Egyptians, the Mesopotamians, and the Greeks—all of whom imagined the dead as continuing in the underworld (see above, note 2). It seems more likely that the Israelite conception was similar to that of their neighbors rather than entirely different. John Cooper writes: "There is continuity between the living and the dead . . . dead Samuel is still Samuel, not someone or something else. . . . Samuel is a 'ghost' or 'shade,' not a Platonic soul or Cartesian mind. For Plato and Descartes the soul is immaterial, non-spatial, and imperceptible by the human senses. Samuel, in contrast, puts in a visual appearance, is recognized by his form" (Cooper, *Body, Soul, and Life Everlasting*, 58–59). Helmer Ringgren, in commenting on Isa. 14, writes: "We discover that the dead live as feeble shades, but nevertheless retain something of their earthly dignity" (Ringgren, *Israelite Religion*, 245). Similarly, Walther Eichrodt writes: "Israel fully shared the primitive belief that a shadowy image of the dead person detached itself from him and continued to eke out a bare existence. . . . What survives, therefore, is not a *part* of the living man but a shadowy image of the *whole* man" (Walther Eichrodt, *The Theology of the Old Testament*, vol. 2, trans. J. A. Baker [Philadelphia: Westminster, 1967], 214). My analysis here follows Eichrodt, Cooper, Ringgren, Robert Gundry, and N. T. Wright rather than Green. Based on the texts quoted, the reader can decide for herself who is correct.

17. See Oscar Cullmann, *Immortality of the Soul, or Resurrection of the Dead?* (London: Epworth Press, 1958).

18. Wright, *Resurrection*, 129.

19. James Barr, *The Garden of Eden and the Hope of Immortality* (Minneapolis: Fortress, 1993), 99.

20. Ringgren, *Israelite Religion*, 242.

21. Cooper, *Body, Soul, and Life Everlasting*, 70.

22. The Wisdom of Solomon is not included in the Jewish Bible or in Protestant Bibles. The formation of the canon of the Hebrew Scriptures and the New Testament is complex. Generally speaking, the early Christian church used the Septuagint (the Hebrew Scriptures translated into Greek) as its Bible, and this contained late Jewish writings, some of them written in Greek, such as the Wisdom of Solomon. When the canon of the Jewish Bible was formed, which occurred after the fall of Jerusalem in 70 CE, however, most late writing and writings in Greek were not included. Luther followed the Jewish canon in his Bible, thereby rejecting a number of Old Testament books that were in the Catholic Bible, such as Sirach, 1–2 Maccabees, and the Wisdom of Solomon. For background and commentary on the Wisdom of Solomon, see "Solomon, Wisdom of," in *The Anchor Bible Dictionary*, 6:120–27.

23. See Plato's famous dialogue *Phaedo*, which narrates the death of Socrates. Socrates would have no weeping at his deathbed because he was going to a better place and leaving the prison of the body behind.

24. N. T. Wright, *The New Testament and the People of God* (Minneapolis: Fortress, 1992), 329–31; see also Wright, *Resurrection*, 164–75.

25. For the primary texts, see Charlesworth, *Old Testament Pseudepigrapha*. Some of the most important primary texts are: *1 Enoch, 2 Baruch, 4 Ezra*, and *The Assumption of Moses*. For secondary literature, see J. J. Collins, *The Apocalyptic Imagination* (1984; Grand Rapids: Eerdmans, repr., 1998); Paul Hanson, *Old Testament Apocalyptic* (Nashville: Abingdon, 1987); Christopher Rowland, *The Open Heaven: A Study of Apocalyptic in Judaism and Early Christianity* (New York: Crossroad, 1982); D. S. Russell, *The Message and Method of Jewish Apocalyptic* (Philadelphia: Westminster, 1964). See also "Apocalypses and Apocalypticism," in

The Anchor Bible Dictionary, 1:279–92. For a study of apocalyptic themes in film and popular media, see John Martens, *The End of the World* (Winnipeg: J. Gordon Schillingford, 2003).

26. C. K. Barrett, "New Testament Eschatology," *Scottish Journal of Theology* 6, no. 2 (June 1953): 138, cited in Rowland, *Open Heaven*, 2–3.

27. Rowland, *Open Heaven*, 1–5, 23–29. The *Anchor Bible Dictionary* follows Collins in defining apocalypse as "a genre of revolutionary literature with a narrative framework, in which a revelation is mediated by an otherwordly being to a human recipient, disclosing a transcendental reality which is both temporal, insofar as it envisages eschatological salvation, and spatial, insofar as it involves another, supernatural, world" (J. J. Collins, ed., *Apocalypse: The Morphology of a Genre*, Semeia 14 [Missoula, MT: Scholars Press, 1979], 9, quoted in "Apocalypses and Apocalypticism," 279).

28. D. S. Russell, "Life after Death," chap. 14 in *The Method and Message of Jewish Apocalyptic, 200 BC–AD 100* (Philadelphia: Westminster, 1964).

29. Ibid., 357–60.

30. Ibid., 360.

31. Ibid., 361.

32. Ibid., 360–61.

33. Ibid., 365.

34. Ibid., 377.

35. Ibid., 380.

36. Ibid., 381.

37. Josephus, *The Antiquities of the Jews* 18.1.4, in *Josephus: The Complete Works*, trans. William Whiston, new updated ed. (Peabody, MA: Hendrickson, 1987), 477. See also Acts 23:6–10; Wright, *Resurrection*, 134; John Meier, *A Marginal Jew: Rethinking Historical Jesus*, vol. 3, *Companions and Competitors* (New York: Doubleday, 2001), 389–487.

38. Josephus, *Antiquities* 18.1.3, in Whiston, *Josephus*, 477.

39. Wright, *Resurrection*, 181–89. See also Josephus, *Antiquities* 18.1.5; Josephus, *The Wars of the Jews* 2.7.

40. See Martha's response to Jesus when he said to her, "Your brother will rise again" (John 11:23). Martha said "I know that he will rise again in the resurrection on the last day" (v. 24). This may indicate the common belief among ordinary Jews of this time.

41. Wright, *Resurrection*, 129–30.

42. Ibid., 205.

43. Ibid.

Chapter 2 Death and Afterlife in the New Testament

1. John P. Meier, *A Marginal Jew: Rethinking the Historical Jesus*, vol. 2, *Mentor, Message, and Miracles* (New York: Doubleday, 1994), 331.

2. Ibid.

3. This powerful passage bristles with exegetical problems. It is found only in Matthew's Gospel. Some scholars might argue that it was not said by the earthly Jesus but was an invention of Matthew's community. Regardless of whether the earthly Jesus uttered this parable, it still comes to us as inspired Scripture and therefore on the authority of the Holy Spirit.

4. John Meier argues extensively that the kingdom is both eschatological and present. See Meier, *Marginal Jew*, 2:289–454.

5. The transcendent dimension of the kingdom is prominent in the following saying of Jesus: "I tell you, many will come from east and west and will eat with Abraham and Isaac and Jacob in the kingdom of heaven, while the heirs of the kingdom will be thrown into the outer darkness, where there will be weeping and gnashing of teeth" (Matt. 8:11–12). The fact that those in the kingdom will be eating with the long-dead patriarchs indicates that the kingdom is not simply this worldly but also transcendent and includes the dead.

6. Animal sacrifices ceased in Judaism as well because the temple was destroyed in 70 CE and has never been rebuilt.

7. For a classic survey, see Gustaf Aulen, *Christus Victor* (New York: Macmillan, 1969).

8. N. T. Wright, *The Resurrection of the Son of God* (Minneapolis: Fortress, 2003), 205.

9. Paul's letters were written between ca. 51 and 58 CE. The earliest Gospel account, Mark, dates from 68 to 73 CE. Matthew and Luke are generally dated about 85 CE, and John between 80 and 110 CE.

10. Wright, *Resurrection*, 477–78.

11. See Pheme Perkins, *Resurrection* (Garden City, NY: Doubleday, 1984), 17–22.

12. John 21 is widely regarded as an epilogue added by another author after the original edition of the Gospel.

13. N. T. Wright, *Surprised by Hope* (New York: HarperCollins, 2008), 111, 115.

14. Wright, *Resurrection*, 129–30.

15. For an extended discussion of these and other passages, see John W. Cooper, *Body, Soul, and Life Everlasting* (1989; repr., Grand Rapids: Eerdmans, 2000).

16. Joel Green, *Body, Soul, and Human Life: The Nature of Humanity in the Bible* (Grand Rapids: Baker Academic, 2008), 159–63. Though he raises several questions about this parable, Green's own position is not that clear. He writes near the end of his analysis: "Given the pervasiveness of references to the intermediate state in contemporary Jewish literature, we should not be surprised to discover parallel ideas in a Lukan parable. However, given the diverse ways in which the intermediate state might be represented (in terms of temporality and spatiality, as well as with regard to the nature of human existence in this abode), we would be ill-advised to imagine that Jesus speaks in this account of disembodied existence in a place and time that stands between this life and the next" (p. 163). Later he writes: "Indeed, Luke's texts find their closest parallels in that literature wherein the dead experience neither a period nor a place of waiting, but enter their eternal reward immediately upon death" (p. 165). This would seem to imply that the dead are resurrected immediately after their death, even while their dead bodies remain on earth. I will consider this opinion in chap. 7.

17. Ibid., 166.

18. Ibid., 163.

19. Green states that this passage might refer to an intermediate state but that the more common use of Paradise refers to the end-time dwelling of the righteous with God (see *Body, Soul, and Human Life*, 163–65). John Cooper takes the promise to mean that the dying thief would be with Jesus in Paradise that very day (see *Body, Soul, and Life Everlasting*, 127–29).

20. Robert Gundry writes: "In moving to Jewish literature of the intertestamental and NT period, we confront an anthropological duality so clear and widespread that it can justly be described as the normative view within late Judaism" (*Sōma in Biblical Theology with Emphasis on Pauline Anthropology* [Cambridge: Cambridge University Press, 1976], 87).

21. See Ben Meyer, "Did Paul's View of the Resurrection of the Dead Undergo Development?" in *Critical Realism and the New Testament* (Allison Park, PA: Pickwick, 1989), 99–128, esp. 115.

22. James Barr, *The Garden of Eden and the Hope of Immortality* (Minneapolis: Fortress, 1992), 114.

23. For an extended argument to this effect, see Cooper, *Body, Soul, and Life Everlasting*.

24. N. T. Wright, *Jesus and the Victory of God* (Minneapolis: Fortress, 1996), 345.

25. Meier, *Marginal Jew*, 2:331–32 and elsewhere.

26. For an excellent commentary on the book of Revelation, see Catherine Cory, *The Book of Revelation* (Collegeville, MN: Liturgical Press, 2006).

Chapter 3 Death and Afterlife in the Christian Tradition

1. Gregory of Nyssa, *The Life of Moses* 2.239, trans. Abraham Malherbe and Everett Ferguson, Classics of Western Spirituality (New York: Paulist Press, 1978), 116.

2. For the texts of the fathers in English, see *The Ante-Nicene Fathers*, ed. A. Roberts and James Donaldson (10 vols.; hereafter *ANF*); *The Nicene and Post Nicene Fathers*, first series, ed. Philip Schaff (14 vols.; hereafter *NPNF* 1); and *The Nicene and Post Nicene Fathers*, second series, ed. Philip Schaff and Henry Wace (14 vols.; hereafter *NPNF* 2). This series was originally published by the Christian Literature Publishing Co., 1885–90, and has been republished by Hendrickson (Peabody, MA, 1995) in 38 volumes.

3. See *The Passion of SS. Perpetua and Felicity, MM*, trans. W. H. Sherwing (London: Sheed and Ward, 1931; repr., San Francisco: Ignatius Press, 2002).

4. See *The Martyrdom of Polycarp* 14.2, in Cyril Richardson, *Early Christian Fathers* (1970; repr., New York: Macmillan, 1979), 154.

5. Eusebius, *History of the Church* 6.42, trans. G. A. Williamson, rev. ed. (London: Penguin Books, 1989), 214. I owe this reference to my colleague Dr. Michael Hollerich. All references to *History of the Church* are to this translation.

6. In this section and those following, I am relying on the interpretations of Fr. Brian E. Daley, whose handbook *The Hope of the Early Church* (New York: Cambridge University Press, 1991; repr., Peabody, MA: Hendrickson, 2003) I have found to be the best guide to patristic eschatology. I want to acknowledge the assistance of Dr. Michael Hollerich, who reviewed this chapter and made helpful contributions.

7. Justin Martyr, *2 Apology* 12; *ANF* 1:192.

8. Justin Martyr, *Dialogue with Trypho* 4; *ANF* 1:197.

9. Ibid. 5; *ANF* 1:197.

10. Justin Martyr, *1 Apology* 19; *ANF* 1:169.

11. Eusebius, *History of the Church* 6.37. I am indebted to Dr. Michael Hollerich for this reference.

12. Tertullian, *A Treatise on the Soul*, esp. chaps. 55–58; *ANF* 3:231–35.

13. Tertullian, *On the Resurrection of the Flesh*; *ANF* 3:545–94.

14. Tertullian, *Against Marcion* 3.24; cited in Daley, *Hope*, 36.

15. This is the title of the best single book on his thought. See Henri Crouzel, *Origen: The Life and Thought of the First Great Theologian*, trans. A. S. Worrall (San Francisco: Harper & Row, 1989).

16. See esp. Crouzel, *Origen*, 169–79.

17. Origen, *On First Principles* 1.pref.5.

18. On Origen's three ways of illustrating continuity and change, see Crouzel, *Origen*, 253–55, and on the resurrected body in general, 248–57.

19. Daley, *Hope*, 60.

20. Ibid., 55.

21. "Seems" because so many of his writings have been lost, and others have had to be reconstructed from citations from other authors, that at times his thought is not clear to us.

22. See Origen, Fragment on Psalm 1:5, in Methodius, *De Resurrectione* 1.22–23; cited in Caroline Walker Bynum, *The Resurrection of the Body in Western Christianity, 200–1336* (New York: Columbia University Press, 1995), 64.

23. Origen, Fragment on Psalms, trans. in Jon F. Dechow, *Dogma and Mysticism in Early Christianity: Epiphanius of Syria and the Legacy of Origen* (Macon, GA: Mercer University Press, 1988), 374–75; cited in Bynum, *Resurrection of the Body*, 65.

24. See Daley, *Hope*, 61–64 .

25. One contemporary philosopher who defends matter as the principle of the body's continuity is Peter van Inwagen. He argues that God, at the moment of death, removes the corpse to a holding area, where it remains a corpse that God will eventually revive at the resurrection. At the same time God creates another corpse to replace the one that has been removed. On this, see Peter van Inwagen, "The Possibility of Resurrection," in *Immortality*, ed. Paul Edwards (New York: Macmillan, 1992), 242–46. Kevin Corcoran defends a different but related position: at

the moment of death, all the "simples" (i.e., molecules, or whatever are the simplest parts) of a body fission so that two bodies are produced, one that is the corpse and the other that survives in an intermediate state or in the resurrection. On this position, see Kevin Corcoran, "Physical Persons and Postmortem Survival without Temporal Gaps," in *Soul, Body, and Survival: Essays on the Metaphysics of Human Persons*, ed. Kevin Corcoran (Ithaca, NY: Cornell University Press, 2001), 201–17.

26. Polkinghorne writes: "My understanding of the soul is that it is the almost infinitely complex, dynamic, information-bearing pattern, carried at any instant by the matter of my animated body and continuously developing throughout all the constituent changes of my bodily make-up during the course of my earthly life. That psychosomatic unity is dissolved at death by the decay of my body, but I believe it is a perfectly coherent hope that the pattern that is me will be remembered by God and its instantiation will be recreated by him when he reconstitutes me in a new environment of his choosing. That will be his eschatological act of resurrection" (John Polkinghorne, *The Faith of a Physicist* [Princeton, NJ: Princeton University Press, 1994], 163).

27. Bynum, *Resurrection of the Body*, 66.

28. Gregory of Nyssa, *On the Soul and Resurrection*; NPNF 2 5:438.

29. Gregory of Nyssa, *The Life of Moses* 2.239, p. 116.

30. Daley, *Hope*, 87–88.

31. Gregory of Nyssa, *On the Soul and Resurrection*; NPNF 2 5:453.

32. Augustine, *Enchiridion* 48; English translation in *Basic Writings of Augustine*, ed. Whitney J. Oates, 2 vols. (New York: Random House, 1948), 1:686.

33. Augustine, *City of God* 8.2; trans. R. W. Dyson, *Augustine: The City of God against the Pagans* (New York: Cambridge University Press, 1998), 541.

34. Augustine, *City of God* 13.8; Dyson, *Augustine*, 549.

35. Augustine, *City of God* 21.13; Dyson, *Augustine*, 1072.

36. Augustine, *Sermo* 172.2; cited in Daley, *Hope*, 138. See also Augustine, *Enchiridion* 110; in Whitney, *Basic Writings*, 1:723.

37. Augustine, *Enchiridion* 89; in Whitney, *Basic Writings*, 1:710.

38. Augustine, *City of God* 22.21; Dyson, *Augustine*, 1152.

39. Augustine, *City of God* 22.21; Dyson, *Augustine*, 1153.

40. Augustine, *City of God* 20.14; Dyson, *Augustine*, 999.

41. Augustine, *City of God* 20.16; Dyson, *Augustine*, 1002.

42. For an introduction to Aquinas's thought, see Etienne Gilson, *The Christian Philosophy of St. Thomas* (New York: Random House, 1956); or Brian Davies, *The Thought of Thomas Aquinas* (Oxford: Clarendon, 1992).

43. Gilson, *St. Thomas*, 187.

44. Cyril Vollert, SJ, trans., *Light of Faith: The Compendium of Theology by Saint Thomas Aquinas* (1947; repr., Manchester, NH: Sophia Institute, 1993), 180.

45. There are different opinions on exactly what Aquinas meant by "form," especially as it applies to the soul. Eleonore Stump argues: "In general, then, a substantial material form is the configurational state of a material object that makes that object a member of the kind or species to which it belongs and gives it the causal powers characteristic of things of that kind" (*Aquinas* [New York: Routledge, 2003], 197). The soul, however, has the power to configure matter: "Aquinas tends to call the soul the act of the body; the soul configures matter in such a way that the matter is actually a living human body" (ibid., 202). Exactly how the soul configures matter is not clear, at least to me. For a criticism of Stump's position, see William Hasker, *The Emergent Self* (Ithaca, NY: Cornell University Press, 1999), 167–70. See also Davies, *Thought of Thomas Aquinas*, 46–49, 126–28, 218–19.

46. Vollert, *Light of Faith*, 74.

47. *Intellectus* for Aquinas includes what we now call intuition, that is, the faculty of direct perception. *Intellectus* differs from *ratio*, which is the faculty of discursive reasoning.

48. Thomas Aquinas, *Summa Contra Gentiles* 4.91.10; trans. the English Dominican Fathers (London: Burns, Oates, and Washbourne, 1929), 310; cited in Bynum, *Resurrection of the Body*, 267.

49. For a historical study of the origins of the belief in purgatory, see Jacques Le Goff, *The Birth of Purgatory* (Chicago: University of Chicago Press, 1984).

50. Ibid., 180.

51. Vollert, *Light of Faith*, 188–89.

52. Cited in Bynum, *Resurrection of the Body*, 268.

53. See Bynum's discussion, ibid., 266–71.

54. Vollert, *Light of Faith*, 190–91.

55. See Bynum, *Resurrection of the Body*, 271–78.

56. The Smalcald Articles, article 1, in *The Book of Concord: The Confessions of the Evangelical Lutheran Church*, trans. and ed. Theodore Tappert (Philadelphia: Fortress, 1959), 292.

57. *The Small Catechism*, article 2 (The Creed), third article; in *Book of Concord*, 345.

58. See Martin Luther, *On Christian Liberty* (Minneapolis: Fortress, 2003), 34–50.

59. The Smalcald Articles, article 2, in *Book of Concord*, 295.

60. *The Small Catechism*, article 3, in *Book of Concord*, 345.

61. Paul Althaus, *The Theology of Martin Luther*, trans. Robert Schultz (Philadelphia: Fortress, 1966), 414.

62. Ibid., 417.

63. John Calvin, *Institutes of the Christian Religion* 3.9.1–2; trans. Henry Beveridge, 2 vols. (1845; repr., Grand Rapids: Eerdmans, 1989), 2:28–29.

64. Calvin, *Institutes*, 2:267.

65. See Terence Nichols, *The Sacred Cosmos* (Grand Rapids: Brazos, 2003), 23–48.

Chapter 4 Scientific Challenges to Afterlife

1. James S. Nairne, *Psychology: The Adaptive Mind*, 2nd ed. (Belmont, CA: Wadsworth, 2000), 4.

2. See Malcolm Jeeves, "Brain, Mind, and Behavior," in *Whatever Happened to the Soul?* ed. Warren Brown, Nancey Murphy, and H. Newton Malony (Minneapolis: Fortress, 1998), 73–98.

3. For a nonmaterialist view within neuroscience, see Mario Beauregard and Denyse O'Leary, *The Spiritual Brain* (New York: HarperCollins, 2007); also, Jeffrey Schwartz, MD, and Sharon Begley, *The Mind and the Brain: Neuroplasticity and the Power of Mental Force* (New York: HarperCollins, 2002). For a materialist view, see Francis Crick, *The Astonishing Hypothesis: The Scientific Search for the Soul* (New York: Charles Scribner's Sons, 1994). For a Christian physicalist view, see Malcolm Jeeves, ed., *From Cells to Souls—and Beyond: Changing Portraits of Human Nature* (Grand Rapids: Eerdmans, 2004).

4. Michio Kaku, *Parallel Worlds: A Journey through Creation, Higher Dimensions, and the Future of the Cosmos* (New York: Doubleday, 2005).

5. John Polkinghorne argues this in numerous writings. See, for example, Polkinghorne's *The God of Hope and the End of the World* (New Haven: Yale University Press, 2002), 117–23. See also Gregory Ganssle, ed., *God and Time: Four Views* (Downers Grove, IL: InterVarsity, 2001); and Alan Padgett, *God, Eternity, and the Nature of Time* (New York: St. Martin's Press, 1992).

6. See George Francis Rayner Ellis, ed., *The Far-Future Universe: Eschatology from a Cosmic Perspective* (Philadelphia: Templeton Foundation Press), 2002.

7. Ian Barbour writes: "Cosmologists expect the universe to expand indefinitely and become too cold to support life. Alternatively, the expansion may slow down and reverse itself, becoming too hot to support life as it collapses. Either prospect ('freeze or fry') seems to make life on earth transient and meaningless. In any case, our sun will burn itself out in a few tens

of billions of years" (Foreword to *Cosmology: From Alpha to Omega*, by Robert John Russell [Minneapolis: Fortress, 2008], v).

8. See James Moore, "Geologists and the Interpreters of Genesis in the Nineteenth Century," in *God and Nature: Historical Essays on the Encounter between Christianity and Science*, ed. David Lindberg and Ronald Numbers (Berkeley: University of California Press, 1986), 334–35.

9. Rudolph Bultmann, *Jesus Christ and Mythology* (New York: Charles Scribner's Sons, 1958).

10. Ibid., 12.

11. Ibid., 14–16.

12. Ibid., 37–38.

13. Ibid., 31–32.

14. See, for example, Francis Collins, *The Language of God* (New York: Free Press, 2006). Collins was the head of the Human Genome Project, which mapped the human genome, but is also an evangelical Christian who argues for a theistic interpretation of evolution. See also Joan Roughgarden, *Evolution and Christian Faith* (Washington, DC: Island Press, 2006).

15. Charles Darwin, *The Origin of Species*, chap. 15 in *Darwin*, ed. R. M. Hutchins, Great Books of the Western World 49 (Chicago: Encyclopedia Britannica, Inc., 1952), 237.

16. See Andrew Wilton and Tim Barringer, *American Sublime: Landscape Painting in the United States, 1820–1880* (Princeton, NJ: Princeton University Press, 2002).

17. The first lines are taken from Wordsworth, "Lines Written a Few Miles above Tintern Abbey," first published in *Lyrical Ballads*, 1798; "survival of the fittest" was coined by Herbert Spencer in his *Principles of Biology*, 1864, 1:444. Finally, the image of nature as "red in tooth and claw" comes from Tennyson, *In Memoriam*, 1850.

18. Plato, *Symposium* 211–12; trans. Benjamin Jowett, *The Dialogues of Plato*, 2 vols. (1892; repr., New York: Random House, 1937), 1:334–45.

19. Augustine, *Confessions*, trans. Rex Warner (New York: New American Library, 1963), 154; italics in the original.

20. See the discussion of the "knowledge born of love" in Bernard Lonergan, *Method in Theology* (New York: Herder and Herder, 1972), 115–18.

21. Nairne, *Psychology*, 4.

22. Ibid., 11–12.

23. Jeffrey Schwartz, MD, and Sharon Begley, *The Mind and the Brain: Neuroplasticity and the Power of Mental Force* (New York: HarperCollins, 2002), 8.

Chapter 5 Near Death Experiences

1. From the BBC DVD *The Day I Died*, a DVD produced by BBC Learning, part of their Films for the Humanities and Sciences series. The video is available from The International Association of Near Death Studies (IANDS) at IANDS.org.

2. There is an enormous amount of material on this topic. An annotated bibliography of the literature down to 1990 has been published by Terry Basford under the title *Near Death Experiences: An Annotated Bibliography* (New York: Garland, 1990). See also the survey of the literature in Gary Habermas and J. P. Moreland, *Beyond Death: Exploring the Evidence for Immortality* (Wheaton, IL: Crossway Books, 1998), as well as authors and titles cited in the notes to this chapter.

3. Raymond Moody, *Life after Life* (New York: Bantam, 1976), 61.

4. See *The Day I Died*.

5. There is a detailed medical account of the surgery, along with Pam Reynold's near death experience, provided in Dr. Michael Sabom, *Light and Death* (Grand Rapids: Zondervan, 1998), 37–47. The DVD *The Day I Died* also has extensive testimony by Pam Reynolds, Dr. Sabom, and the neurosurgeon Dr. Spetzler, who explains the operation in detail.

6. Sabom, *Light and Death*, 41–46.

7. From the DVD *The Day I Died*.

8. See Sabom, *Light and Death*, 13.

9. Michael Sabom, *Recollections of Death* (New York: Harper & Row, 1982), 81–115.

10. The period of time varied "between hospitals from 4 months to nearly 4 years (1988–92). The research period varied because of the requirement that all consecutive patients who had undergone successful cardiopulmonary resuscitation (CPR) were included. If this standard was not met, we ended research in that hospital." Dr. Pirn van Lommel, MD, Ruud van Wees, PhD, Vincent Meyers, PhD, Ingrid Elfferich, PhD, "Near Death Experience in Survivors of Cardiac Arrest: A Prospective Study in the Netherlands," *The Lancet* 358, no. 9298, December 15, 2001, 2039–45. Accessed on 5/7/2007 through Science Direct, at www.sciencedirect.com/science?_ob=ArticleURL&_udi=B6T1B-44PT371-F&_user.

11. Ibid.

12. Ibid.

13. P. M. H. Atwater, *The New Children and Near-Death Experiences* (Rochester, VT: Bear & Co., 2003), 72–76.

14. Elizabeth Kubler-Ross, *On Death and Dying* (New York: Macmillan, 1969).

15. Elizabeth Kubler-Ross, *On Children and Death* (New York: Macmillan, 1983), 207–11.

16. Van Lommel, "Near Death Experience," 6.

17. Greyson explains this on the BBC DVD *The Day I Died*.

18. Howard Storm, *My Descent into Death* (New York: Doubleday, 2005), 22.

19. Ibid., 22.

20. Ibid., 10–12.

21. Ibid., 2.

22. Ibid., 17.

23. Ibid., 18.

24. Ibid., 25.

25. Ibid., 95.

26. See Carol Zaleski, *Otherworld Journeys* (Oxford: Oxford University Press, 1987).

27. N. K. Sandars, trans., *The Epic of Gilgamesh* (1960; repr., Baltimore: Penguin Books, 1965).

28. Zaleski, *Otherworld Journeys*, 24.

29. One of the most famous is Plato's story of the soldier Er in book 10 of the *Republic*.

30. See Bede's *Ecclesiastical History* 5.12, ed. Bertram Colgrave and R. A. B. Mynors (Oxford: Clarendon, 1969), 489.

31. Carol Zaleski, *The Life of the World to Come* (Oxford: Oxford University Press, 1996), 32.

32. Ibid., 33.

33. See Raymond A. Moody, *Reflections on Life after Life* (New York: Bantam Books, 1977), 29–40.

34. See Karlis Osis and Erlendur Haraldsson, *At the Hour of Our Death* (1977; repr., Norwalk, CT: Norwalk House, 1997).

35. Sogyal Rinpoche, "The Near Death Experience: A Staircase to Heaven?" in *The Near Death Experience: A Reader*, ed. Lee W. Bailey (New York: Routledge, 1996), 172.

36. Michael Sabom, in his book *Recollections of Death*, responds to many medical and scientific concerns. So does Dr. Pirn van Lommel in "Near Death Experience." A lengthy consideration of scientific and theological concerns about NDEs can be found in Habermas and Moreland, *Beyond Death*.

37. Moody, *Life after Life*, 137.

38. Sabom's initial reaction upon hearing about Moody's book in a church discussion group was, "I don't believe it." Though a cardiologist, he had never heard stories like this from his patients, nor had his colleagues. It was not until he actually began to talk to his patients about their experiences—which he was reluctant to do—that he heard their stories. Their stories fit

with the pattern described in *Life after Life* and provoked Sabom to pursue his own research in this area. See Sabom, *Light and Death*, 11–17.

39. Melvin Morse, *Closer to the Light* (New York: Ivy Books, 1990), 6.

40. Cf. Kubler-Ross's account, above. See also Kenneth Ring and Sharon Cooper, *Mindsight: Near Death and Out-of-Body Experiences in the Blind* (Palo Alto, CA: William James Center for Consciousness Studies, 1999).

41. Moody, *Life After Life*, 156–62.

42. Morse, *Closer to the Light*, 48.

43. Van Lommel, "Near Death Experience," 2

44. Sabom, *Recollections of Death*, 171–73, citing T. Oyama, T. Ji, and R. Yamaya, "Profound Analgesic Effects of B-Endorphin in Man," *The Lancet* 8160, January 19, 1980, 122–24.

45. Sabom, *Recollections of Death*, 172.

46. See Susan Blackmore, "Near Death Experiences: In or Out of the Body?" in Bailey, *Near Death Experience*, 283–97. Blackmore is also interviewed in the BBC video *The Day I Died*.

47. Sabom's *Recollections of Death* remains the best scientific study, to my knowledge. But scientific studies of NDEs are becoming more common. An example is van Lommel's article "Near Death Experience" in *The Lancet*.

48. Maurice Rawlings, *Beyond Death's Door* (New York: Bantam Books, 1978), 1–8; 85–103; Margot Grey, *Return from Death* (London: Arkana, 1985), 56–72.

49. George Ritchie, *Return from Tomorrow* (Old Tappan, NJ: Revell, 1978), 58–67.

50. Habermas and Moreland, *Beyond Death*.

51. Rawlings, *Beyond Death's Door*.

52. Ritchie, *Return from Tomorrow*.

53. Sabom, for example, thinks that this being might be Satan, an idea that I find unbiblical. In the Bible, Satan is said to be able to deceive, but there is absolutely no indication that he can counterfeit love. No one who has actually encountered the Being of Light comes away thinking it is Satan; it is the incarnation of perfect love—just as Jesus was. Love is the most important gift and fruit of the Holy Spirit, according to Paul (1 Cor. 13:13; Gal. 5:22).

54. See, for example, Janis Amatuzio, *Forever Ours* (Novato, CA: New World Library, 2004), 47.

Chapter 6 On the Soul

1. "Person," in addition to its ordinary meaning, is a technical term in philosophy and theology. In Christianity, the members of the Trinity are "persons," as are angels and human beings. In my usage, a human being is a person at all stages of life: during this life as soon as the soul is formed, in the intermediate state when the soul is separated from the body, and in the resurrected state. I do not want to argue that, in this life, only the soul is a person; it is the embodied soul that is a person. But since the separated soul is the carrier of personal identity in the intermediate state, it makes sense to speak of it as a person also, even though it lacks a body (this position differs from Aquinas, who held that the separated soul was not a person because it lacked a body). For a fine theological study of the meaning of "person," see Philip Rolnick, *Person, Grace, and God* (Grand Rapids: Eerdmans, 2007).

2. Taken from *The Book of Concord*, ed. Theodore G. Tappert (Philadelphia: Fortress, 1959), 20.

3. Westminster Assembly, *The Westminster Confession of Faith* (repr., Forgotten Books, 2007), 62. This confession of faith is fundamental for many Reformed and Presbyterian churches.

4. *Catechism of the Catholic Church* (Mission Hills, CA: Benzinger, 1994), # 366, p. 93.

5. See the table of contents of the *Stanford Encyclopedia of Philosophy*, online at http://plato.stanford.edu/contents.html.

6. Recent books arguing for the existence of the soul include: Joseph Ratzinger, *Eschatology: Death and Eternal Life*, trans. Michael Waldstein (Washington, DC: Catholic University of

America Press, 1988); John Hick, *Death and Eternal Life* (1976; repr., Louisville: Westminster John Knox, 1994); J. P. Moreland and Scott B. Rae, *Body and Soul: Human Nature and the Crisis in Ethics* (Downers Grove, IL: InterVarsity, 2000); John W. Cooper, *Body, Soul, and Life Everlasting* (1989; repr., Grand Rapids: Eerdmans, 2000); Ric Machuga, *In Defense of the Soul* (Grand Rapids: Brazos, 2002); Keith Ward *Defending the Soul* (Oxford: One World, 1992); Gary Habermas and J. P. Moreland, *Beyond Death: Exploring the Evidence for Immortality* (Wheaton: Crossway Books, 1998). Recent books arguing against the existence of the soul include: Owen Flanagan, *The Problem of the Soul* (New York: Basic Books, 2002); Warren Brown, Nancey Murphy, and H. Newton Malony, *Whatever Happened to the Soul?* (Minneapolis: Fortress, 1998). See also Joel B. Green and Stuart L. Palmer, *In Search of the Soul: Four Views of the Mind-Body Problem* (Downers Grove, IL: InterVarsity, 2005); Joel Green, ed., *What about the Soul? Neuroscience and Christian Anthropology* (Nashville: Abingdon, 2004); Kevin Corcoran, ed., *Soul, Body, and Survival* (Ithaca, NY: Cornell University Press, 2001); Michael Horace Barnes, "Science and the Soul: Keeping the Essentials," in *New Horizons in Theology*, ed. Terence Tilley, Annual Volume of the College Theology Society 50 (Maryknoll, NY: Orbis Books, 2004), 96–116.

7. Joel Green, *Body, Soul, and Human Life: The Nature of Humanity in the Bible* (Grand Rapids: Baker Academic, 2008), 166.

8. Robert Gundry gives many more passages from the Pauline literature. See his *Sōma in Biblical Theology with Emphasis on Pauline Anthropology* (Cambridge: Cambridge University Press, 1976), 135–56.

9. See ibid., 87–110 for more evidence of anthropological duality in the Judaism of New Testament times.

10. Bart D. Ehrman, *After the New Testament: A Reader in Early Christianity* (New York: Oxford University Press, 1999), 74.

11. See the writers in Brown, Murphy, and Malony, *Whatever Happened to the Soul?*

12. Michael Arbib, "Towards a Neuroscience of the Person," in *Neuroscience and the Person*, ed. Robert John Russell, Nancey Murphy, Theo C. Meyering, and Michael A. Arbib (Vatican City State: Vatican Observatory Publications; Berkeley: Center for Theology and the Natural Sciences, 1999), 81.

13. Daniel Dennett, *Freedom Evolves* (New York: Viking, 2003), 1.

14. Flanagan, *Problem of the Soul*, 3.

15. Nancey Murphy, *Bodies, Souls, or Spirited Bodies? Human Nature at the Intersection* (Cambridge: Cambridge University Press, 2006), 57.

16. "Materialism" is usually avoided by philosophers today because of its historical association, and "physicalism" is used instead. But this creates the problem that some Christian writers claim to be "nonreductive physicalists" (see next category). So instead of "physicalism" as a title of this category, I am using "materialism" and "reductive physicalism." But these are also problematic: materialism has awkward historical associations, and there are many types of reductionism—metaphysical, causal, theory-reductionism—not all of which are accepted by all reductive physicalists. See the entry by Daniel Stoljar on "Physicalism" in the *Stanford Encyclopedia of Philosophy* at http://plato.stanford.edu/entries/physicalism.

17. Francis Crick, *The Astonishing Hypothesis: The Scientific Search for the Soul* (New York: Charles Scribner's Sons, 1994), 3.

18. Jeffrey Schwartz, MD, and Sharon Begley, *The Mind and the Brain: Neuroplasticity and the Power of Mental Force* (New York: HarperCollins, 2002), 323–64.

19. Flanagan, *Problem of the Soul*, 128.

20. For examples, see John Polkinghorne, *The Faith of a Physicist* (Princeton, NJ: Princeton University Press, 1994); John Haught, *Is Nature Enough?* (Cambridge: Cambridge University Press, 2006); Terence Nichols, *The Sacred Cosmos* (Grand Rapids: Brazos, 2003).

21. See Daniel Stoljar on "Physicalism" in the *Stanford Encyclopedia of Philosophy*, cited above. Stoljar considers nonreductive physicalism to be an atheistic position and leaves no place in his article for the position of Christian nonreductive physicalists.

22. Nancey Murphy, "Human Nature: Historical, Scientific, and Religious Issues," in Brown, Murphy, and Malony, *Whatever Happened to the Soul?* 25. This volume of essays is probably the best introduction to Christian nonreductive physicalism.

23. Ibid., 27.

24. Philip Clayton, "Neuroscience, the Person, and God," in Russell, Murphy, Meyering, and Arbib, *Neuroscience and the Person*, 181–214.

25. Ibid., 196.

26. Ian Barbour, *Nature, Human Nature, and God* (Minneapolis: Fortress, 2002), 94.

27. Ibid., 99.

28. See the chapters by Brown and Jeeves in Brown, Murphy, and Maloney, *Whatever Happened to the Soul?*; see also Malcolm Jeeves, *From Cells to Souls—and Beyond: Changing Portraits of Human Nature* (Grand Rapids: Eerdmans, 2004).

29. Murphy addresses these in several of her writings. See Nancey Murphy, "Nonreductive Physicalism," in Green and Palmer, *In Search of the Soul*, esp. 131–38; and Nancey Murphy, *Bodies, Souls, or Spirited Bodies?* 111–47. See also the criticisms of her position by William Hasker, "On Behalf of Emergent Dualism," in Green and Palmer, *In Search of the Soul*, 143–46. Jaegwon Kim has criticized nonreductive physicalism in general as an unstable position, which in the end reduces to materialism and (reductive) physicalism. Kim writes: "So all roads branching out of physicalism may in the end seem to converge at the same point, the irreality of the mental" (Jaegwon Kim, *Mind in a Physical World* [Cambridge, MA: MIT Press, 2001], 119).

30. A similar problem arises in the case of consciousness. Philosopher John Searle, for example, distinguishes between two types of emergentism: emergent1, which is an emergent property such as liquidity or transparency and is unproblematic; and a more "adventurous conception" of emergence, emergent2, which has causal powers that cannot be explained by the neuron networks of the brain. In other words, the causal powers of emergent2 properties—such as consciousness and free choice—go beyond the physical. As Searle explains: "If consciousness were emergent2, then consciousness could cause things that could not be explained by the causal behavior of the neurons. The naïve idea here is that consciousness gets squirted out by the behavior of the neurons in the brain, but once it has squirted out, it then has a life of its own. It should be obvious . . . that on my view consciousness is emergent1, but not emergent2, In fact, I cannot think of anything that is emergent2" (John Searle, *The Rediscovery of the Mind* [Cambridge, MA: MIT Press, 1992], 112).

31. Murphy, "Nonreductive Physicalism," 132.

32. For example, Aquinas held that in the beatific vision, the blessed in heaven behold the essence of God directly. See Thomas Aquinas, *Summa Theologica* IaIIae, question 3, article 8 (New York: Benzinger, 1947), 1:601–2.

33. René Descartes, Sixth Meditation, in *Discourse Method and Meditations*, trans. Laurence Lafleur (Indianapolis: Bobbs-Merrill, 1960), 134.

34. See Richard Swinburne, *The Evolution of the Soul*, rev. ed. (Oxford: Clarendon, 1997). For other statements of substance dualism, see Stewart Goetz, "Substance Dualism," in Green and Palmer, *In Search of the Soul*, 33–74; John Foster, "A Brief Defense of the Cartesian View," in Corcoran, *Soul, Body, and Survival*, 15–29; Moreland and Rae, *Body and Soul*.

35. See Wilder Penfield, *The Mystery of the Mind* (Princeton, NJ: Princeton University Press, 1975); Karl R. Popper and John C. Eccles, *The Self and Its Brain* (London: Routledge, 1990).

36. See William Hasker, *The Emergent Self* (Ithaca, NY: Cornell University Press, 1999), 147–61, for a good review of the objections to substance dualism.

37. See also Charles Taliaferro, *Consciousness and the Mind of God* (Cambridge: Cambridge University Press, 1994).

38. Cooper, *Body, Soul, and Life Everlasting*, 204–31.

39. Thomas Aquinas, *Summa Theologica*, part 1, question 75, article 4, response (New York: Benzinger, 1947), 1:366. Generally, Aquinas's treatment on the soul is found in the *Summa Theologica* (or *Summa Theoloigae*), part 1, questions 75–90; see also Thomas Aquinas, *Questions on the Soul*, trans. James H. Robb (Milwaukee: Marquette University Press, 1984). For a recent commentary, see Eleonore Stump, *Aquinas* (London and New York: Routledge, 2003), esp. chap. 6, pp. 191–216.

40. Stump, *Aquinas*, 194.

41. Ibid., 200.

42. See Terence Nichols, "Aquinas's Concept of Substantial Form and Modern Science," *International Philosophical Quarterly* 36, no. 3 (1996): 303–18.

43. Polkinghorne, *Faith of a Physicist*, 163. See also Polkinghorne's *The God of Hope and the End of the World* (New Haven, CT: Yale University Press, 2002), 103–7.

44. See Hasker, *Emergent Self*; see also William Hasker, "Persons as Emergent Substances," in Corcoran, *Soul, Body, and Survival*, 107–19; and Hasker, "On Behalf of Emergent Dualism," 75–113.

45. Hasker, "Persons as Emergent Substances," 115.

46. Ibid., 116.

47. Ward, *Defending the Soul*, 145; see also Ward, *Religion and Human Nature* (New York: Oxford University Press, 1998), 145–47.

48. See Karl Rahner, *Hominisation* (New York: Herder and Herder, 1965); see also Barnes, "Science and the Soul," 96–116.

49. For a concise explanation of Hinduism, including reincarnation, see Anantanand Rambachan, *The Hindu Vision* (Delhi: Motilal Banarsidass, 1992), esp. pp. 26–32. For a Tibetan Buddhist view of reincarnation, see Sogyal Rinpoche, *The Tibetan Book of Living and Dying* (San Francisco: HarperSanFrancisco, 1992). For a survey of theories of reincarnation, see Hick, *Death and Eternal Life*, 297–396. I wish to thank my colleague Peter Feldmeier for assistance with this paragraph on Hinduism and the following paragraph on Buddhism.

50. See Hick, *Death and Eternal Life*, 332–62.

51. In two classical texts, the Buddha describes the relationship between his teaching and ultimate reality. In *Majjhima Nikāya* 63, he describes how discussion of philosophical questions hampers spiritual progress and that his teaching was only for the purpose of attaining Nirvana. In *Majjhima Nikāya* 22, he provides two images of holding on to the teaching. Here the dharma is like a poisonous snake that needs to be lightly grasped and like a raft that needs to be dropped once one was on the other side of the river (Nirvana). In an additional text (*MN* 72), he teaches that any reference (philosophical or otherwise) to him after his death did not apply. Ultimate truths for Buddhists are inaccessible to thought (*atakkāvacara*) and beyond conceptual range (*avisayasmi*), even for the Buddha himself.

52. See the article on "Metempsychosis" in *The Oxford Dictionary of the Christian Church*, ed. F. L. Cross, 3rd ed. (Oxford: Oxford University Press, 1997), 1077.

53. Karl Rahner, *Foundations of Christian Faith* (New York: Crossroad, 1982), 442.

54. See the article by J. E. Royce on "Metempsychosis," in *The New Catholic Encyclopedia*, 2nd ed., 15 vols. (Detroit/New York: Thomson/Gale, 2003), 9:556.

55. W. Norris Clarke has written that "to be is to be substance-in-relation." My idea of the soul as subject-in-relation draws from his insights. Clarke argues that ancient and medieval philosophers focused on substance but neglected relationality. Modern philosophers, conversely, have focused on relationality. But every existent being is both a substance and exists in a network of relations with other beings in the universe. See W. Norris Clarke, "To Be Is to Be Substance-in-Relation," in *Explorations in Metaphysics* (Notre Dame: University of Notre Dame Press, 1994), 102–22.

56. I do not think the mind and the soul are identical; the soul not only includes the mind but also entails other capacities—such as being the organizational principle of the body and being a bridge between spirit and matter—that we would not attribute to the mind.

57. See Hasker's chapter "Why the Physical Isn't Closed," in *Emergent Self*, 58–80.

58. I do not want to take an explicit position on the time of ensoulment—that is, when the soul comes into being—namely, whether it occurs at the moment of conception or somewhat later. My theory allows for both possibilities. There are some problems with insisting that the soul comes into being immediately at conception. First, fertilized ova can split into identical twins, or occasionally two fertilized ova will fuse, up to about fourteen days after conception. This obviously creates problems if we insist that the soul has formed at conception. Second, one-third or more of fertilized ova are spontaneously aborted. Most of these "are caused by chromosome problems that make it impossible for the baby to develop" (Medline Plus, www .nlm.nih.gov/medlineplus/ency/article/001488.htm; thanks to Jeffery Wittung for this reference). I doubt we would want to insist that they all have souls. On the other hand, the Roman Catholic Congregation for the Doctrine of the Faith, without taking an explicit position on the time of ensoulment, does insist that "the human being is to be respected and treated as a person from the moment of conception" (see "Instruction *Dignitas Personae* on Certain Bioethical Questions," section 4, June 20, 2008, www.vatican.va/roman_curia/congregations/cfaith/documents/ rc_con_cfaith_doc_20). I agree with the CDF on this point. For an argument that ensoulment is delayed, see Joseph Donceel, SJ, "Immediate Animation and Delayed Hominization," *Theological Studies* 31, no. 1 (1970): 76–105. For arguments that at conception the embryo is a person, see Rose Koch-Hershenov, "Totipotency, Twinning, and Ensoulment at Fertilization," *Journal of Medicine and Philosophy* 31 (2006): 139–64; see also Mark Johnson, "Delayed Hominization: Reflections on Some Catholic Claims for Delayed Hominization," *Theological Studies* 56, no. 4 (1995): 743–63.

59. Aquinas argues that the soul is naturally immortal. By this he means that the soul has an immortal nature given to it by God. It is not naturally immortal according to the powers of physical nature as nature is understood by scientists today. So the question is, What does one mean by *nature*.

60. Polkinghorne, *God of Hope*, 107.

61. Polkinghorne once told me he prays for his parents every day and that "survival in the mind of God is not a purely passive filing system." Thus I think that my idea and his are not far apart. Note the following passage from his pen, which indicates he believes souls can undergo purification while awaiting resurrection: "We may expect that God's love will be at work, through the respectful but powerful operation of divine grace, purifying and transforming the souls awaiting resurrection in ways that preserve their integrity" (*God of Hope*, 111).

62. He writes: "In a Thomistic philosophy it is quite possible to say that finite spirit is conceived as a limitation of exactly the same reality which confers on matter what is positive in it, namely, 'being,' and that what is material is nothing but a limited and as it were 'solidified' spirit, being, act" (Rahner, *Hominisation*, 57).

63. In the Christian mystical tradition, there are many affirmations that the highest contemplative knowledge/love of God is not mediated by images, thoughts, or feelings. For example, Gregory of Nyssa writes: "The contemplation of God is not effected by sight and hearing, nor is it comprehended by any customary perceptions of the mind" (*The Life of Moses* [New York: Paulist Press, 1978], 93). St. John of the Cross writes: "It [the soul] must be like to a blind man, leaning upon none of these things that he understands, experiences, feels, and imagines. For all these are darkness which will cause him to stray . . . a soul may lean upon any knowledge of its own, or any feeling or experience of God, yet, however great this may be, it is very little and far different from what God is; and in going along this road, a soul is easily led astray" (*Ascent of Mount Carmel* 2.4.2; in E. Allison Peers, *The Complete Works of Saint John of the Cross*, 3 vols. [Westminster, MD: Newman Bookshop, 1946], 1:74–75).

64. See Ian Barbour, "Neuroscience, Artificial Intelligence, and Human Nature: Theological and Philosophical Reflections," in Russell, Murphy, Meyering, and Arbib, *Neuroscience and the Person*, 278–79.

Chapter 7 Resurrection

1. The literature on the resurrection of Jesus is immense. For an overview of recent writings, see Gerald O'Collins, SJ, "The Resurrection: The State of the Question," in *The Resurrection*, ed. by Stephen Davis, Daniel Kendall, SJ, and Gerald O'Collins, SJ (Oxford: Oxford University Press, 1997). See also Ted Peters, Robert John Russell, and Michael Welker, eds., *Resurrection: Theological and Scientific Assessments* (Grand Rapids: Eerdmans, 2002); N. T. Wright, *The Resurrection of the Son of God* (Minneapolis: Fortress, 2003); N. T. Wright and John Dominic Crossan, *The Resurrection of Jesus: John Dominic Crossan and N. T. Wright in Dialogue* (Minneapolis: Fortress, 2006); Richard Swinburne, *The Resurrection of God Incarnate* (Oxford: Clarendon Press, 2003); Stephen Davis, *Risen Indeed: Making Sense of the Resurrection* (Grand Rapids: Eerdmans, 1993); Gerald O'Collins, SJ, *The Resurrection of Jesus Christ: Some Contemporary Issues* (Milwaukee: Marquette University Press, 1993); Carolyn Walker Bynum, *The Resurrection of the Body in Western Christianity, 200–1336* (New York: Columbia University Press, 1995). Still valuable is Raymond Brown, *The Virginal Conception and Bodily Resurrection of Jesus* (New York: Paulist Press, 1973).

2. For example, John Dominic Crossan interprets Jesus's resurrection as "the continuing presence in a continuing community of the past Jesus in a radically new and transcendental mode of present and future existence" (*The Historical Jesus* [New York: HarperCollins, 1992], 404).

3. See Walter Alvarez, *T Rex and the Crater of Doom* (New York: Vintage Books, 1997, 1998).

4. See, for example, Michio Kaku, *Parallel Worlds: A Journey through Creation, Higher Dimensions, and the Future Cosmos* (New York: Doubleday, 2005).

5. Lisa Randall, *Warped Passages* (New York: HarperCollins, 2005).

6. Terence Nichols, *The Sacred Cosmos* (Grand Rapids: Brazos, 2003), 183–98, first published as "Miracles in Science and Theology," *Zygon* 37, no. 3 (2002): 703–15.

7. See Nichols, *Sacred Cosmos*, 188.

8. See John D. Barrow, "The Far, Far Future," in *The Far Future Universe: Eschatology from a Cosmic Perspective*, ed. George Ellis (Philadelphia and London: Templeton Foundation Press, 2002), 23–40.

9. John Polkinghorne, *The God of Hope and the End of the World* (New Haven: Yale University Press, 2002), 9.

10. Russell writes, "eschatology entails a transfiguration of the entire cosmos based on the bodily resurrection of Jesus such that all of nature is taken up into God and made into the New Creation" (Robert John Russell, *Cosmology: From Alpha to Omega* [Minneapolis: Fortress, 2008], 293).

11. See N. T. Wright, *Simply Christian* (New York: HarperCollins, 2006), 217–37.

12. Nichols, *Sacred Cosmos*, 183–98.

13. It is true that Paul does not mention this, but, as N. T. Wright argues, that is because it is implicit in the idea of being buried and then raised from the dead.

14. Polkinghorne, *God of Hope*, 121.

15. Brian Daley, "A Hope for Worms: Early Christian Hope," in Peters, Russell, and Welker, *Resurrection*, 136.

16. Origen, Fragment on Psalms; trans. in Jon F. Dechow, *Dogma and Mysticism in Early Christianity: Epiphanius of Syria and the Legacy of Origen* (Macon, GA: Mercer University Press, 1988), 374–75, cited in Bynum, *Resurrection of the Body*, 65.

17. Augustine, *City of God* 20.21; as cited in Daley, "Hope for Worms," 150.

18. John Polkinghorne, *Science and Theology: An Introduction* (Minneapolis: Fortress, 1998), 115–16. Polkinghorne thinks that what survives is the molecular pattern of the whole human being. This "form" or "soul" survives bodily death in the memory of God and will be reconstituted as an embodied person in the resurrection, albeit in a different kind of matter and environment that is imperishable.

19. Cyril Vollert, SJ, trans., *Light of Faith: The Compendium of Theology by Saint Thomas Aquinas* (1947; repr., Manchester, NH: Sophia Institute, 1993), 189.

20. Karl Rahner, "The Intermediate State," in *Theological Investigations*, vol. 17 (New York: Crossroads, 1981), 115.

21. Wright, *Resurrection*, 205.

22. The International Theological Commission [of the Roman Catholic Church] writes: "the whole Christian tradition, without any important exceptions, has, up to our own day, conceived of the object of eschatological hope as embracing two phases. Between the death of people and the consummation of the world, it believes that a conscious element of people subsists which it calls by the name of 'soul' (*psyche*). . . . At the parousia of the Lord, which will take place at the end of history, there is to be expected the blessed resurrection of those 'who are Christ's' (1 Cor. 15:23)" ("Some Current Questions in Eschatology," *Irish Theological Quarterly* 58, no. 3 [1992]: 220–21).

23. See C. S. Lewis, *The Great Divorce* (1946; repr., New York: HarperCollins, 2001).

Chapter 8 Justification and Judgment

1. I will follow theological usage and mean by *justification* the event of being justified or made righteous before God. Following ecumenical usage, I will also distinguish *sanctification* from justification. Sanctification means being sanctified or made holy by the indwelling of the Holy Spirit. Justification does not necessarily imply sanctification. One can be justified before God if one's sins are forgiven because of his/her faith in Christ. Sanctification through the presence of the Spirit and the Spirit's gift of love in one's heart (Rom. 5:5) is a further stage after justification. Luther tended to focus only on justification; Catholics, Orthodox, Methodists, and Holiness churches focus on both justification and sanctification but think of them as different moments or events in the whole process of salvation. *Salvation*, then, I will take to refer to the whole process by which one is freed from ignorance and slavery to sin and brought into fellowship with God. Salvation encompasses more than justification—because in coming into fellowship with God, sanctification is also necessary—"You shall be holy, for I the LORD your God am holy" (Lev. 19:2).

2. Martin Luther, *On Christian Liberty* (Minneapolis: Fortress, 2003), 41. This short book by Luther is a very good expression of his doctrine of justification.

3. Council of Trent, session 6, chap. 7, trans. Norman P. Tanner, *Decrees of the Ecumenical Councils*, vol. 2, *Trent to Vatican II* (Washington, DC: Georgetown University Press, 1990), 673–74.

4. Council of Trent, chap. 16, trans. Tanner, *Decrees of the Ecumenical Councils*, 2:677–78.

5. *Lumen Gentium*, the *Document on the Church* issued by Vatican Council II, modified this claim and said that those who are not Christians and even those without explicit belief in God can be saved under certain conditions. See *Lumen Gentium* 16.

6. There is an interpretative problem with this passage. The first question is, Did Jesus really say this? The passage is found only in Matthew. If it was so central to Jesus's teaching, why is it not also in Mark and Luke, and for that matter, in John? Maybe the historical Jesus did not say this. However, if one believes (as almost all Christians profess) that the New Testament is inspired by the Holy Spirit, then even if these words were not spoken by the historical Jesus, it comes to us on the authority of the Spirit. Second, what is meant by *panta ta ethnē*, "all the peoples"? Does this comprise everyone, including Christians, or just the Gentiles (i.e., non-Christians)? Opinions can be found on both sides. I tend to think that here Jesus meant everyone, including Christians.

7. See Richard B. Hays, "Justification," in *The Anchor Bible Dictionary*, 6 vols. (New York: Doubleday, 1992), 3:1129–33.

8. Ibid., 3:1132.

9. "Annex to the Official Common Statement," § D, in *Joint Declaration on the Doctrine of Justification* (Grand Rapids: Eerdmans, 2000), 45.

10. Compare this to the "judgment" experienced by persons in NDEs, where they see their whole life replayed in the presence of the "being of light," a being of perfect love. Often people see all they have done, and the short-term effects of what they have done, but in the light of a being of total love. Typically they return ashamed and determined to do better (see Raymond Moody, *Life after Life* [New York: Bantam Books, 1976], 64–73). How does this peculiar element of NDEs relate to the individual or the last judgment? Certainly it is not the last or final judgment, in which we see our lives in the context of all of human history. Rather, it seems to be a foretaste or a preview of the individual judgment—it is a judgment by one's own conscience, after all—but in the light of a loving being. As noted above, we are not judged only once at the end of our lives but periodically during the course of our lives as well. Whenever we are justly convicted of wrongdoing, either by an external judge or by our own consciences, we are experiencing an aspect of individual judgment. And, presumably, those who experience a life review during an NDE will also experience an individual judgment at the end of their lives.

11. Joseph Ratzinger, *Eschatology: Death and Eternal Life* (Washington, DC: Catholic University of America Press, 1988), 205.

12. Wolfhart Pannenberg, *Systematic Theology*, 3 vols. (Grand Rapids: Eerdmans; Edinburgh, T&T Clark, 1998), 3:614.

13. Ratzinger, *Eschatology*, 206.

14. John Polkinghorne, *The God of Hope and the End of the World* (New Haven: Yale University Press, 2002), 130.

15. See Jerry Walls, *Heaven: The Logic of Eternal Joy* (New York: Oxford University Press, 2002).

16. C. S. Lewis, *The Great Divorce* (1946; repr. New York: Harper Collins, 2001).

Chapter 9 Heaven, Purgatory, and Hell

1. See Jerry Walls, *Heaven: The Logic of Eternal Joy* (New York: Oxford University Press, 2002), 7; Colleen McDannell and Bernhard Lang, *Heaven: A History* (New Haven, CT: Yale University Press, 1988).

2. Augustine, *The City of God* 22.30; cited in Walls, *Heaven*, 37.

3. The Trinity is the deepest of Christian mysteries. For an introduction, read M. John Farrelly, *The Trinity* (Lanham, MD: Rowman and Littlefield, 2005).

4. God's wrath or anger is a common theme in the Old Testament, especially in the psalms and prophets. For example, "Serve the LORD with fear, / with trembling kiss his feet, / or he will be angry, and you will perish in the way; / for his wrath is quickly kindled" (Ps. 2:11–12). God's wrath is less often referred to in the New Testament, except in Paul's letters and in the book of Revelation. Here the distinction between analogy and metaphor is apposite: God's wrath is a metaphor, not an analogy. What God's wrath expresses is the alienation from God caused by sin and the destructive effects of that alienation. But we would not say God is essentially wrathful in the same way we would say God is essentially love: the members of the Trinity relate through love, but certainly not through wrath. When Paul discusses the wrath of God (Rom. 1:18–32), he describes it as God giving sinners up to the effects of their sinfulness—"God gave them up to a debased mind and to things that should not be done" (Rom. 1:28). Sin, therefore, is its own reward. This is also true in the passages on God's wrath in Revelation. Stephen Travis writes: "Evil is self-destructive, and God's wrath is his allowing the worshippers of the beast to be involved in that self-destructive process" ("Wrath of God [NT]," in *The Anchor Bible Dictionary*, ed. David Noel Freedman, 6 vols. [New York: Doubleday, 1992], 6:998).

5. Bernard J. F. Lonergan, *Insight: A Study of Human Understanding* (New York: Harper & Row, 1978), 684. Here Lonergan argues that acts of insight or understanding lead to further acts of insight or understanding, which ultimately lead to God. This argument has been a prominent theme in the work of John Polkinghorne, who was influenced by Lonergan's *Insight*. Polkinghorne writes: "I believe that Christian belief is possible in a scientific age precisely because it is the search for truth, and science is one, but only one component, and in many ways quite a humble component, in that search for truth" (John Polkinghorne, *Serious Talk* [Valley Forge, PA: Trinity Press International, 1995], 16).

6. Dante, *The Divine Comedy*, vol. 3, *Paradise*, canto 33, lines 85–87, trans. Mark Musa (New York: Penguin Books, 1986), 392.

7. Augustine, *Confessions* 11.13, trans. Rex Warner (New York: New American Library, 1963), 267.

8. Aquinas argues, for example, that no created good can satisfy the human desire for happiness; only God can, since God is the end of all human life (*Summa Theologiae* 1.2, Q.2, a.8).

9. Augustine, *Sermo* 172.2; cited in Brian E. Daley, *The Hope of the Early Church* (New York: Cambridge University Press, 1991; repr., Peabody, MA: Hendrickson, 2003), 138. See also Augustine, *Enchiridion* 110.

10. Augustine, *The City of God against the Pagans*, ed. and trans. R. W. Dyson (Cambridge: Cambridge University Press, 2002), 1072.

11. The *Catechism of the Catholic Church* §1030, concerning "The Final Purification, or Purgatory," states: "All who die in God's grace and fellowship, but still imperfectly purified, are indeed assured of their eternal salvation; but after death they undergo purification, so as to achieve the holiness necessary to enter the joy of heaven" (*Catechism of the Catholic Church*, [Mission Hills, CA: Benziger, 1994], 268). Elsewhere the *Catechism* associates holiness with the perfection of love: "All Christians in any state or walk of life are called to the fullness of Christian life and to the perfection of charity. All are called to holiness" (*Catechism* §2013, p. 488). But §1031 on purgatory does cite Gregory the Great, who speaks of the remission of lesser faults in the age to come (see *Catechism*, 269).

12. How one answers this question depends on whether one thinks the historical Jesus really said the words of Matt. 10:23 or whether these words were placed on his lips by the writers of the early church.

13. Walls, *Heaven*, 54.

14. See Peter Phan, *Eternity in Time: A Study of Karl Rahner's Eschatology* (Selinsgrove, PA: Susquehana University Press, 1988), 124–25.

15. John Hick, *Death and Eternal Life* (Louisville: Westminster John Knox, 1994), 202.

16. See John Polkinghorne, *The God of Hope and the End of the World* (New Haven, CT: Yale University Press, 2002), 130–32.

17. See the *Catechism of the Catholic Church* §2282.

18. Raymond Moody, *Life after Life* (New York: Bantam, 1975), 143.

19. Ibid.

20. Purgatory, of course, exists in the intermediate state, that is, the state between death and bodily resurrection at the end of human history. But the intermediate state would also include those in heaven—the saints—unless we imagine them as already resurrected (a position known as "immediate resurrection"). And it would include those in hell, if they are in fact to be resurrected also at the end of history. Presumably, those who see dead relatives and other discarnate beings in NDEs are seeing beings in the intermediate state. A difficult problem is what becomes of those who have died in infancy or childhood before they could have made a choice for or against God. Traditionally, those infants who were baptized were saved, even though they had not made a full choice for God. But what of unbaptized infants? We cannot imagine them as being in hell (though Augustine did teach this), because one goes to hell only by deliberate choice (see the next section). But unbaptized infants also have not chosen God or

heaven. So what is their state? Catholic theology used to assign them to limbo, a kind of state of natural happiness, not heaven, not hell. But this teaching, which never had official support of the Catholic magisterium, has since been dropped. The *Catechism of the Catholic Church* says: "As regards *children who have died without Baptism*, the Church can only entrust them to the mercy of God, as she does in her funeral rites for them" (*Catechism of the Catholic Church* §1261, p. 321; italics in original).

21. Hans Urs von Balthasar, *Dare We Hope That All Men Be Saved?* (San Francisco: Ignatius, 1988).

22. The best philosophical argument for hell I know of is Jerry L. Walls, *Hell: The Logic of Damnation* (Notre Dame: University of Notre Dame Press, 1992).

23. *The Catechism of the Catholic Church* speaks of hell as "self-exclusion from communion with God" (§1033, p. 269) and states that "God predestines no one to go to hell; for this, a willful turning away from God (a mortal sin) is necessary, and persistence in it until the end" (§1037, p. 270).

24. Raymond Moody, *Reflections on Life after Life* (New York: Bantam, 1977), 38–39.

25. Hick, *Death and Eternal Life*, 259.

26. Walls, *Hell*, 121.

27. See C. S. Lewis, *The Great Divorce* (1946; repr., New York: Harper Collins, 2001).

28. *Catechism of the Catholic Church* §1035, p. 270.

29. Timothy Ware, *The Orthodox Church* (New York: Penguin Books, 1963), 267.

Chapter 10 Dying Well

1. Ira Byock, *Dying Well* (New York: Riverhead Books, 1997), 53.

2. Ibid., 218, 217.

3. Ibid., 224.

4. Ibid., 233.

5. Ibid., 235.

6. Ibid., 239.

7. Concerning this final choice, see Karl Rahner, "On Christian Dying," in *Theological Investigations*, vol. 7 (New York: Seabury, 1977), 285–93.

8. Robert Bellarmine, *The Art of Dying Well* (originally published in Latin in 1620; repr., Manchester, NH: Sophia Institute, 2005).

9. Martin Luther, *The Freedom of a Christian*, in *Three Treatises* (Philadelphia: Fortress, 1982), 302; text is from the American edition of Luther's Works, vol. 44 (Philadelphia: Fortress).

10. Byock, *Dying Well*, 193–216.

Index